Communication and Identity in the Classroom

Critical Communication Pedagogy

Series Editors: Ahmet Atay, The College of Wooster and
Deanna L. Fassett, San José State University

Critical pedagogy, as Cooks (2010), Freire (1970), and Lovaas, Baroudi and Collins (2002) argue, aims to empower and liberate individuals to achieve social change and transform oppressive and unequal social structures. This book series aims to contribute to the discourse of critical communication pedagogy by featuring works that utilize different dimensions of critical communication pedagogy to foster dialogue, to encourage self-reflexivity, and to promote social justice by allowing marginalized voices to be heard. Even though projects that focus on dynamics between teachers and students and their issues within classroom settings are crucial, this series aims to focus on works that utilize critical and cultural theories to interrogate the role of larger structures as they influence these relationships in higher education. Hence, in this proposed series we will feature works that are built on critical communication pedagogy—works that function within a critical/cultural studies framework, and works that interrogate the notion of power, agency, dialogue, and "voice" within the context of higher education and beyond. We argue that the work of educators and their educational philosophies are not limited to the classroom; hence, critical communication scholars are interested in connecting classroom pedagogy with its real-life applications. Therefore, this series is interested in publishing work that captures these facets.

Titles in the Series

Communication and Identity in the Classroom: Intersectional Perspectives of Critical Pedagogy Edited by Daniel S. Strasser

Advocating Heightened Education: Seeing and Inventing Academic Possibilities by Kathleen F. McConnell

Grading Justice: Teacher-Scholar-Activist Approaches to Assessment Edited by Kristen C. Blinne

Mediated Critical Communication Pedagogy by Ahmet Atay and Deanna L. Fassett

Critical Administration: Negotiating Political Commitment and Managerial Practice in Contemporary Higher Education by Jay Brower and W. Benjamin Myers

Communication and Identity in the Classroom

Intersectional Perspectives of Critical Pedagogy

Edited by
Daniel S. Strasser

LEXINGTON BOOKS
Lanham • Boulder • New York • London

Published by Lexington Books
An imprint of The Rowman & Littlefield Publishing Group, Inc.
4501 Forbes Boulevard, Suite 200, Lanham, Maryland 20706
www.rowman.com

6 Tinworth Street, London SE11 5AL, United Kingdom

British Library Cataloguing in Publication Information Available

Library of Congress Control Number: 2020947633

ISBN 978-1-7936-1805-4 (cloth)
ISBN 978-1-7936-1807-8 (pbk)
ISBN 978-1-7936-1806-1 (electronic)

Contents

Preface

Bernadette Marie Calafell

More than ever, identities matters.
For some of us they have *always* mattered.
But now, it seems struggles and fights around identity or
what some call "identity politics" are everywhere.

Whether it manifests as attacks against historically marginalized communities everyday through events like Charlottesville, the continuous killing of African Americans by police, or the increasing rise of white supremacist movements, it's clear that identity has become significant for all of us. Other identities, those of historically marginalized groups, have been the frequent target of the unethical, dangerous, and irresponsible political regime known as the Trump administration, all the while failing to outwardly acknowledge its own investment in white nationalist and supremacist movements. *Black folks are killed every day doing mundane things that the majority of us take for granted. Trans women of color continue to be killed simply for existing. Where is the outrage and outcry?*

Within the halls of academia, attacks and backlash against identity and intersectionality continue (Lethabo King 2015; May 2015). *I know these attacks quite well.* Simply speaking, empowering Others and speaking truth to power has never been so important. Thus, more than ever we need careful unpacking of power and identity, such as those included in this volume. We must move beyond simplistic constructions of "identity politics"; which itself has become a site of contest meaning and in some cases "fighting words." The analytic or lens through which these complex identities and "identity politics" are explored is through critical pedagogy.

More often than not, studies in pedagogy, and even in critical approaches, still center the experiences of a white, able-bodied, cisgender, heterosexual male instructor who comes into a classroom of mostly white, able-bodied, cisgender, and heterosexual students. Furthermore, difference is framed as something the instructor must negotiate or "deal with." This mythical normative instructor is also seen as value neutral, when we all know that no one walks into the classroom ideologically free. It just doesn't work that way. *This has been my ongoing frustration as a former student and as a faculty member. When will the field catch up to shifting demographics? When will "difference" not be constructed as a problem?* As I have asked in my own work, "When will we all matter?" (Calafell 2010), meaning when will we move beyond superficial engagements with difference and the assumption that as instructors we share the same experiences or identities in the classroom? It is hard to find space or investment in a field when you fail to see yourself represented in it. Those of us who are Others are always mindful of our difference, not simply because of our own self-awareness, but because other students, staff, other faculty, and administrators will make sure we know we are out of place in a university system that was never made for us in the first place.

This volume is a step toward a vision of an intersectional approach to critical pedagogy as it offers layered and thick intersectional critical autoethnographies that attest to the experiences of varied intersectional Others in the classroom. They use their personal narratives to stand against or reverberate alongside the larger cultural, political, economic, and social landscape. The chapters included in this book provide us with vulnerable and embodied experiences from instructors who literally put their bodies and identities on the line every time they enter the classroom, especially in an environment that has become increasingly antagonist toward difference and higher education in general. During this anti-science and anti-humanities moment (or should I say movement), we need to listen to these voices as they disrupt master narratives of one-dimensional identity and simplistic framings of higher education. *They call us not only to listen, but to act and be accountable through co-performative witnessing. Will you accept this challenge? Will you accept their call for response-ability?*

REFERENCES

Calafell, Bernadette Marie. 2010. "When Will We All Matter?: Exploring Race, Pedagogy, and Sustained Hope For the Academy." In *The Sage Handbook of Communication and Instruction*, edited by Deanna L. Fassett and John T. Warren, 343–359. Thousand Oaks, CA: Sage.

Lethabo King, Tiffany. 2015. "Post-Indentitarian and Post-Intersectional Anxiety in the Neoliberal Corporate University." *Feminist Formations*, 27, no. 3: 114–138. doi:10.1353/ff.2016.0002.

May, Vivian M. 2015. *Pursuing Intersectionality, Unsetting Dominant Imageries.* New York: Routledge.

Introduction

Daniel S. Strasser

BOOK BEGINNINGS

The genesis of this project stemmed from conversations with my friends and colleagues at the 2017 Eastern Communication Association (ECA) conference in Boston. Our ECA group came together from a diverse background of life and education. Each of us brought to the conference and academia a passion for critical scholarship, research, and pedagogy grounded in radical love, social justice, and the will to make a difference in our communities' and students' lives. We encouraged, empathized, supported, and really saw each other.

At this time in 2017 we were reeling from the election of Donald Trump. We shared stories of how we were trying to navigate the social, cultural, and political atmosphere while teaching. Each of us had horror stories of how our identities, our bodies political, were thrust into the center of conversations surrounding identity. From there, as often happens at conferences, the phrase "We need to create a panel about this" occurred. The seeds were firmly planted. The conversations became imperative conference paper/panel conversations three years running. Again and again panel papers led to conversations about intersectionality, identities, and critical pedagogy.

In 2018 during the ECA conference in Pittsburgh, I was approached and encouraged by an acquisition editor to create a project that would embody those conversations, and more importantly, to highlight the experiences of critical communication pedagogues in the midst of the challenges and resiliencies within the university pedagogical space. Over the next two years as we continued our panels (2020 cancelled by COVID), I decided that the time for the book was right. Over the past year and a half I have had the distinct pleasure to read the wisdom of some of the finest critical communication scholars. Channeling the feelings of the initial conversations that sparked this project, each of the contributors highlights the imperative work of educators and mentors in our world today. In my role as editor, I have been privileged to be the catalyst and the conduit for the voices of these incredibly brave and vulnerable scholars.

MY STORY

I am a nontraditional academic. Raised in a white, working-class poor family in the Midwest, my destination of occupation did not, in any probability, land me here. Roofer, yes. Bartender, yes. Musician, yes. Associate Professor of Communication Studies? Absolutely not. Through a series of choices, including dropping/failing out of college, six years of bartending, through ten years of construction, I am here. My introduction to Communication Pedagogy began in the first year of my master's program at Northern Kentucky University. In a new program under Dr. Cady Short Thompson, Dr. Jacqueline McNally, Dr. Jimmie Manning, and my advisor, Dr. Andrea Lambert South, I learned about teaching communication. Being a nontraditional student, my professors were my age. And I, fresh from the roof, bar, and stage, had an incredible amount to learn about who I was, how I was perceived, and what I had to do as a cisgender, white man to engage more equitably in a world than privileges me.

My pedagogical journey continued as I was fortunate to continue my education at the University of Denver. There I began the intense task and indoctrination into the culture of critical work and community. Taking courses with Dr. Roy Wood, a Levinasian ethicist, I was introduced to writing as inquiry, confusion as pedagogy, and seeing myself in the face of the Other. He taught me to be present in the moment and to write authentically what I know from a critical perspective. With him, as another white male scholar, I learned to be silent and to listen. At this, he was a master and I was a dedicated student. I was also fortunate to take classes from Dr. Bernadette Marie Calafell. Dr. Calafell embodied critical work through critical, radical love. She taught me to be silent, to listen. She taught me to read and learn—everything—from BIPOC and queer scholars. She taught me to decolonize everything. She taught me to mind my body; to realize that my white, cisgender, male body read toxic and unsafe to certain communities. She did this with care, curiosity, and confidence. At this, Dr. Calafell was a fierce master and I was a dedicated student.

In each of their embodied pedagogical spaces and in their classroom, each emboldened me to do more with the privileges that I embodied. I learned to use my privileged voice to offer voice to others; to stand in front of, next to, or behind the voiceless. My avenue for this became teaching and mentoring.

With the knowledge gleaned from Drs. Wood and Calafell, and in continuous work and play within the queer community in Denver with my queer family, Dr. Richard G. Jones, Jr., Dr. Kathryn Hobson, Dr. Amy Zsohar, Dr. Cassidy Higgins, and Dr. Andy Kai-chun Chaung (to name a few), I became immersed in the world and culture of critical communication.

After completing my PhD in gender and family communication, I continue the work that was imparted to me by these amazing scholars now as an Associate Professor at Rowan University in South Jersey. In my classes on Critical Perspective in Human Communication, Communicating Gender, Masculinities and Communication, Family Communication, and Communication Theory, my work, my students' work is grounded in critical communication pedagogy, critical theory (e.g., Intersectionality, CRT), and critical methods. We work to deconstruct and dismantle patriarchal systems of oppression. We talk and listen to each other as we share our vulnerabilities, our embodied experiences, our stories. We hold each other up, breathe together, see each other, and do the work of critical scholars for ourselves and each other.

Twelve years since I first walked into a classroom as an educator, I now find Critical Communication Pedagogy more important than ever. As we head into Spring semester 2021 amidst the uncertainty and fear of COVID-19, the poignancy, potency, and power of the Black Lives Matter movement, and the looming implications of the most important election in our history, I am reinvigorated to walk into the classroom with mask and (face)shield ready once again to stand behind, next to, or in front of my students as we continue the fight for voice and social justice.

THE COLLECTION

As a nation we are divided; as individuals we are isolated; every day we are inundated with constant tragedies and travesties. Often our divisions and our feelings of isolation and helplessness linger into the classroom. Our students experience divisive issues and events in their personal lives. As teachers, we allow our curriculum to flex with our pedagogical choices about how to incorporate these public traumas in the classroom. Inevitably, these choices are made in and through our own identities.

As educators, many of us were taught to leave ourselves out of the classroom—the space only meant for offering information. This stance reinforces teacher as "other," divorced from personal identity. Students, left only to guess after who we are, project images upon us that may be far from true. However, our knowledge as teachers comes through our minds and bodies. We are living texts. Our bodies are visible and political. Thus, our work is to embody our critical identities, not only through the ideas we teach but through our embodied practices. Through our own experiences and interactions, we have the capacity to break down barriers of education in order to reach—not just teach—students.

In this collection, we demonstrate instances in teaching that allowed us to draw upon our identities to better understand, to more fully reach, to mentor, to challenge, and to critically engage students in learning experiences surrounding intersectional identities. In the moments when we are able to break the barriers of student/teacher and move to a more inclusive, vulnerable space where we all are learners, sharing ourselves and our identities broadens how we as educators see our jobs, our selves, and our students. To offer a glimpse into the experiences of critical communication pedagogues, the collection offers autoethnographic and personal narratives of pedagogical experiences that highlight how intersectional identities can be crafted, altered, utilized, challenged, and reified within the classroom space. Within these experiences as educators this collection asks the questions:

- How do we negotiate challenging cultural and individual events to initiate collaborative learning?
- How do we navigate the (dis)ability to address privilege in the classroom based on the bodies and varying intersectional identities in the classroom?
- How do teachers utilize their identities in the classroom in order to offer a space where critical thinking, learning, listening, and pedagogy take place?
- How do we as critical communication pedagogues enact radical love in times that are trying to both us and our students?

Each contributor to this text comes to the classroom with varying experiences in negotiating their own bodies, identities, and the privileges—or lack thereof—that emerge or are suppressed in those spaces. Stemming from intersectional identities covering race, ethnicity, neuro-diversity, physical ability, religion, sexual orientation, gender performance, class, and age, the autoethnographic and narrative accounts within this text give a personal, experiential perspective on how these intersectional identities influence critical perspectives taken by educators in differing classroom and mentoring spaces. Through these narratives the contributors offer insight to those who may hold similar identities and reach toward those who may hold radically different identities.

As such, this text works to mend the broken bridges of communication through positive pedagogical practices; to make connections between situational pedagogical practices and the insights that can be offered in and through those autoethnographic and narrative experiences. Although the contributors come from and explore varying intersections and areas of scholarship, each brings unique challenges that often thwart or enhance our efforts to effectively teach. Equally, if not most important, are the skills of resiliency that we have acquired through our collective years of teaching. Through these challenges and resiliencies, the contributors offer narratives in order to promote reforming, reconstructing, and engagement through nuanced new perspectives on critical communication pedagogy. Through this exploration, the contributors explore and discover opportunities for growth, acknowledgment, and the emergence of a new approach to teaching and mentoring.

This collection promotes conversation about our experiences across intersections, and not only gives us a free space to explore narratives that help us better understand privilege, oppression and identity, but additionally constructs intersectional discourses and perspectives that will continue to build new communicative bridges as we prepare to face the next interaction, student, class, and event that draws on our challenges and resiliencies.

CRITICAL PEDAGOGY AND RADICAL LOVE

When I imagined the creation of a text on critical pedagogy and intersectional identities, I was reminded of Bryant Keith Alexander and John T. Warren, my first exposure to critical autoethnography. Alexander and Warren (2002) addressed their understanding of pedagogy and the university pedagogical space and asked educators to "reflect upon their own experiences within the educational context and how issues of race, culture, ethnicity, sex, and gender rubbed against the always and already fragile construction of their own identities" (330). They referenced the struggle of finding and fighting for voice and identity in the university space:

> [I]n our positionality, or the political space that we claim as teachers, we are implicated in that struggle and committed to opening a dialogue on how these issues situate themselves on the material nature of bodies. Bodies marked not only by race, sex, and gender, but more importantly bodies that are affected by and through cultural practice. Thus the notion of materiality is not limited to the texture of skin but the intertextuality of experience. (330)

Through this understanding, educators are called to be critical of their bodies, of their politics, of their intersecting identities, and acknowledge in words and actions as educators that our bodies *are* political. Our performance of being human is read as text both by the institutions in which we teach and by the students who share our classroom space.

Throughout this collection the contributors expand upon theories and methods of critical communication scholarship, radical love, and intersectionality using their embodied pedagogical experiences to ground the scholarship. The

overarching reach of this collection draws from the foundational work of
Paulo Freire (1972), bell hooks (1994), and Fassett and Warren (2006).

In *Pedagogy of the Oppressed*, Freire offers pedagogy as a space of collective emancipation; a space in which the teacher and the student learn and are
vulnerable together in their work to push back against structural inequities.
In this foundational text, Freire not only works to show the injustices in the
systems outside of the classroom, but he also interrogates and deconstructs
the macro and micro interactions in the classroom. Here, Freire recognized
that emboldening teachers to be purveyors of all knowledge is dangerous
and oppressive instead of reframing how the classroom space is situated so
that students become credible sources of knowledge, and where teacher and
student learn with and from each other in vulnerability. Freire pushed to
restructure and reimagine what education could be, how is it accomplished,
and where it can be used to enact social change and justice.

In close conversation with Freire, hooks (1994) furthers the theoretical and
practical methods and assumptions of critical pedagogy. The fire in hooks is
kindled in her ability to compile an inquiry that exposes systems of oppression in contemporary education while blazing ground for transformational
teaching and learning practices. In the critique and analysis of teaching
institutions, hooks, like Freire, calls for a drastic reimagining of who holds
knowledge, and what and whose knowledge is important. Far from the
assumption that teachers are the sole holders of knowledge, hooks, through
her call to liberate and enliven, redirects our attention to a pedagogy of hope,
love, inclusion, vulnerability, and change.

Fassett and Warren build from Freire and hooks teaching us that critical
pedagogy embraces profound ideological differences and socioeconomic
contexts as constitutive of what happens in schools and classrooms (2006,
26). They call on educators to situate their inquiry in relation to larger, macro
sociocultural, socioeconomic structures, "to explore ways in which racism,
sexism, classism, homophobia, and other forms of oppression permeate classrooms and research on classrooms, teachers, and students" (27). Fassett and
Warren (2006) offer ten commitments in critical communication pedagogy
that can be used to craft classrooms and constitute educators who reify the
imperative critical nature of contemporary education institutions.

1. In critical communication pedagogy, identity is constituted in
   communication.
2. Critical communication educators understand power as fluid and complex.
3. Culture is central to critical communication pedagogy, not additive.
4. Critical communication educators embrace a focus on concrete, mundane communication practices as constitutive of larger social structural
   systems.

5. Critical communication educators embrace social, structural critique as it places concrete, mundane communication practices in a meaningful context.
6. Language (and analysis of language as constitutive of social phenomena) is central to critical communication pedagogy.
7. Reflexivity is an essential condition for critical communication pedagogy.
8. Critical communication educators embrace pedagogy and research as praxis.
9. Critical communication educators embrace—in their classrooms and in their writing, within their communicates, and with their students, research participants, and co-investigators—a nuanced understanding of human subjectivity and agency.
10. Critical communication educators engage in dialogue as both metaphor and methods for our relationships with others.

From the foundation of critical communication pedagogy to this collection, one of the most important lessons of a critical pedagogue is that the work is never finished and does not have a finite space. Critical pedagogy occurs within liminal spaces of identity, offices, classrooms, and community. In this collection through autoethnography and personal narrative, the contributors embody and explore those liminal spaces.

With this in mind, variations of methodological exploration abound. Each contributor offers a unique perspective in autoethnography and/or personal reflections of pedagogy. Thus, this collection affirms:

> We all exist between the lines of our narrated lives, the stories we tell and the stories that are told about us. We all exist between the lines, the unsaid thoughts in the other's description. We also read between the lines, adding our hopes the unspoken dream and the dailiness of our shared experience . . . as a way of reading between the lines of [our] own lived experience and the experiences of cultural familiars—to come to a critical understanding of self and other and those places where we intersect and overlap. (Alexander 1999, 310)

Additionally, the contributors offer varied perspectives that may not speak specifically to intersectionality as a theoretical, methodological, and practical framework, but as embodied harbingers and sojourners of the power of intersectional bodies in pedagogical space.

Hill Collins (2015) explains, "The term intersectionality references the critical insight that race, class, gender, sexuality, ethnicity, nation, ability, and age operate not as unitary, mutually exclusive entities, but as reciprocally constructing phenomena that in turn shape complex social inequalities" (2). Hill-Collins (2015) suggests that "definitions emerge from more iterative, grassroots processes that enable intellectual and political consensus to emerge through everyday practices such as organizing sessions, developing syllabi, or choosing citations" (3). The essence of Hill-Collins and Crenshaw's (1991) work on intersectionality is alive in this collection.

Finally, as we enter into the collection, Calafell (2007) reminds us that the more complex and reciprocal the relationships between educators/ mentors can be with students, particularly within marginalized communities, the more radical love can enter to create and maintain communities of resistance, home places, and life rafts. These homeplaces "are central to both our well beings" (Calafell 2007, 427), and central to fighting against exhaustion, invisibility, and being cultural collateral. Calafell encourages us as critical scholars and pedagogues to connect with students in an affiliative, loving performance, "to challenge these assumptions that make us avoid performances of affiliation by thinking of mentoring as the homeplace driven by an ethics of love" (437).

From these foundations, this collection and the contributors who offer themselves, continue the constructive work of building a relationally based, authentic pedagogical paradigm for a more loving and inclusive community.

THE STRUCTURE OF THE BOOK

This collection is divided into two sections. In the first section, "Autoethnographic Accounts of Critical, Intersectional Pedagogy," the authors took a specific methodological choice to utilize autoethnography, and in certain instances, critical autoethnography to explore their pedagogical experiences. In the second section, "Personal Narratives and Reflections on Critical, Intersectional Pedagogy," the contributors present personal narrative reflections as they navigate and narrate their individual pedagogical experiences inside and outside of the classroom.

In chapter 1, "Finding Space and Place within the Ivory Tower: Conversations on Intersectionality, Voice, and Silence," Tomeka M. Robinson and Jahnasia Booker explore their mentor–mentee relationship over the course of several years. Through multiple transitions in their careers and relationship, they utilize journal entries, critical race theory, and intersectionality to interrogate their place and space within academia and why their voices and silences are necessary.

In chapter 2, "You Are *Not* My Child, I Am *Not* Your Parent: A Case Against the Infantilization of Students," Meggie Mapes and Benny LeMaster ask the following question: "How does infantilizing students (re)inscribe power dynamics, constrain the student-instructor relationship, and center White constructs of civility?" Through autoethnography they theorize the critical implications of student infantilization as they emerge in relation to the authors' identities as a white queer non-childbearing feminist and a mixed-race Asian/white queer non-childbearing trans scholar.

In chapter 3, "Empath(olog)ic Pedagogy: An Autoethnography of Health, Class, and the Classroom," Brandi Lawless explores pedagogical possibilities for communicating with students about health as it relates to class. Beginning with a critique of the medical-industrial complex, Lawless' autoethnography articulates theories of embodiment as they relate to health, knowledge, pedagogy, epistemological incongruence, and describes the reflexive process educators must undergo in order to develop more empathetic pedagogies.

In chapter 4, "'Bad Hombre' in the Classroom: Pedagogical Politics of Performing 'Brown Man' in a Conservative Time," Antonio De La Garza and Andrew Spieldenner share their experiences of Brownness as they interrogate the toxic whiteness that alienates and abuses Brown bodies in university systems. The chapter describes their subject position as bad hombres and explores the pathologizing and stigmatizing discourses that produce feelings of precarity and racial fatigue. Closing their work, De La Garza and Spieldenner offer counternarratives to subvert white supremacist discourse and find power and healing in owning our identity as bad hombres.

In chapter 5, "What Difference Does it Make? Navigating the Privileged Halls of Academia as a Queer Black Woman Professor," Elizabeth Whittington highlights narratives of teaching in the walls of academia as a Black queer woman. Through moments of challenge and triumph, Whittington examines times in which she encourages students to awaken the desire to be change agents and to critically think about how they can contribute to a more robust and diverse society while staying true to herself and her Black, Revolutionary Feminist Pedagogical perspective.

In chapter 6, "Teaching While Vulnerable: Connection through Shared Vulnerability as a Pedagogical Stepping Stone To Queer Consciousness," Richard G. Jones, Jr. navigates a pivotal pedagogical and personal moment that altered his perspective as a scholar and practitioner of critical communication pedagogy. In this autoethnography, Jones infuses intersectional, critical reflexivity and a pedagogy of vulnerability to explore how these moments connect through shared vulnerability and develop queer consciousness.

In chapter 7, "Queer-Femme-Pedagogy: Telling Our Tales // Confessing Our Truths," Bri Ozalas and Kathryn Hobson explore the concept of "the confessional" as it relates to gendered and sexual identities while problematizing the external and internal struggles of what it means to come out and stay out in the classroom. In this autoethnography, they reference their experiences to take a closer look at the intersections of queer femme identity, disclosure, and confession, ultimately questioning the ways in which heteronormative institutions create and perpetuate this predicament in the first place.

In chapter 8, "Pedagogy, Passing, Privilege," Rachel Silverman, as a tenured, associate professor of communication at a private, southern, white, and male-dominated STEM institution, explores multiple aspects of her identity. As a self-identified queer, Jewess, Silverman offers her experiences of teaching and the difficulties felt in sharing her identities with her classes while calling on herself and other scholars to not only be inclusive in their understanding of critical scholarship but to be open to a fearless sharing of their identities in university spaces.

In chapter 9, "Sawubona—We See, Value and Respect You: A Critical Pedagogical Invitation to Communicate," Eddah M. Mutua reflects on the ways that her African cultural upbringing and experiences as a foreign-born faculty member in the United States inform the conceptualization of intersectional and transnational communication praxis. This interrogation elucidates the differences between a teacher's experiences and those of their students and what is needed to create shared meaning in the classroom. Mutua discusses lived experiences in Kenya and in the United States that shape her understanding of the concept of *Sawubona* as an acknowledgment of the presence of *self* and the *other* and a decolonizing practice in the classroom.

In chapter 10, "Family Stories, Pedagogy, Inclusive Practices and Autohistoria," Sergio Juárez utilizes Anzalduá's *Autohistoria-teoria* as a methodology to interrogate the pedagogical choice of telling of family story. Through a lens of Aztec mythos, Juárez explores the process of self-discovery and disseminating through personal story to lead to social-discovery and new social knowledge in the pursuit of creating a home space for both himself and his students.

In chapter 11, "Unmasking the Hegemony of English: Exploring English Neo-Imperialism and the Internationalization of Whiteness," Sachiko Tankei-Aminian illustrates as a border-crossing educator/scholar a deeper understanding of the hegemony of English, Anglo-Americanization. Additionally, Tankei-Aminian problematizes English linguistic imperialism in the Western academic community and its relation to pedagogical ideologies while addressing and analyzing experiences of teaching. Tankei-Aminian, from a transnational framework, also offers a perspective of how English neo-imperialism mediates the expansion of whiteness on a global scale.

In chapter 12, "Managing Mental Health in the Classroom: A Narrative Reflection on Pedagogy," Andrea L. Meluch explores how her identity as an academic who struggles with anxiety influences her pedagogy. Furthermore, through research and narrative, Meluch offers a variety of means to help students managing mental health issues. Through being open to sharing our own identities and learning about student experiences, she encourages educators in ways of supporting students on their own academic journey while resisting structures that stigmatize mental health issues.

In chapter 13, "Navigating Intercultural Identities at A Crossroads of Mindfulness and Instruction," Aayushi Hingle offers a narrative reflection on her experiences as a cultural nomad navigating the world as a Communication Studies instructor. In these reflected interactions, Hingle illustrates the importance of understanding identity in the classroom, building community, establishing credibility, navigating intersectional identities, and learning to trust herself and her students as she teachers without fear and hate.

In chapter 14, "Going the Extra Mile: Mentoring Black Undergraduate Students," Lance Kyle Bennett offers his unique experience of not only being mentored as a young, Black student, but what that experience meant/means and how he became a mentor for other traditionally marginalized students. Through his narrative exploration, Bennett suggests different strategies for mentorship while expressing the imperative nature of mentoring as inseparable and integral to critical pedagogical practices.

MOVING FORWARD

Together, the contributors in the collection offered themselves and their narratives in order to better understand their unique perspectives of embodied identities in academia. The work that they put forth highlights the often unseen and certainly thankless toil that goes into being a teacher, scholar, researcher, mentor, advisor, and so on. Their work also elucidates the passion and fervor they have for critical communication and pedagogy, for making a difference in the lives of their students. As their editor, I thank them for their kindness, patience, efforts, and energy in producing a collection that I am, and I hope they are, proud to be a part of.

To conclude, although this collection offers a wide representation of identities and the challenges of navigating patriarchal systems of oppression with those identities, like the initial conversations had at ECA in 2017, this is just a beginning. I hope that this collection can provide the beginnings of more conversations and spaces in which other identities can be voiced, seen, cited, and celebrated.

REFERENCES

Alexander, Bryant Keith. 1999. "Performing Culture in the Classroom: An Instructional (Auto)Ethnography." *Text and Performance Quarterly*, 19, no. 4: 307–331. http://www.tandfonline.com/doi/abs/10.1080/10462939909366272.

Alexander, Bryant Keith, and John T. Warren. 2002. "The Materiality of Bodies: Critical Reflections on Pedagogy, Politics and Positionality." *Communication*

Quarterly: Identity Negotiation: An Exploration of Racial, Cultural and Gendered Identities, 50, no. 3–4: 328–343. http://www.tandfonline.com/doi/abs/10.1080/01 463370209385667.

Calafell, Bernadette Marie. 2007. "Mentoring and Love: An Open Letter." *Cultural Studies Critical Methodologies*, 7, no. 4: 425–441.

Collins, Patricia Hill. 2015. "Intersectionality's Definitional Dilemmas." *Annual Review of Sociology*, 41, no. 1: 1–20.

Crenshaw, Kimberly. 1991. "Mapping the Margins: Intersectionality, Identity Politics, and Violence Against Women of Color." *Stanford Law Review*, 43, no. 6: 1241–1299.

Fassett, Deanna L., and John T. Warren. 2006. *Critical Communication Pedagogy*. Thousand Oaks, CA: Sage.

Freire, Paolo. 1972. *The Pedagogy of the Oppressed*. New York: Herder and Herder.

Part I

AUTOETHNOGRAPHIC ACCOUNTS OF CRITICAL, INTERSECTIONAL PEDAGOGY

Chapter 1

Finding Space and Place within the Ivory Tower

Conversations on Intersectionality, Voice, and Silence

Tomeka M. Robinson and Jahnasia Booker

Our relationship began during fall 2015 during my Intercultural Communication course. Following a particularly challenging class where I asked students to critically reflect on their identity, one of my students came into my office with tears in her eyes, "Miss Tomeka, I don't want to be a Black girl." Puzzled, I asked her, "What do you mean?" Her response, "I am tired of carrying the burdens of being a Black woman with me everywhere I go—all the time. It is exhausting." I understood exactly what she meant and responded, "Sweetie, the sooner you accept that you are a strong Black woman, the sooner you can recognize the power that this brings."

Being one of the few women of color within our predominantly white campus, I could recognize her struggle. There are days when walking into the classroom—and even a building—can really take a toll on your soul. I am called upon to serve as a teacher, mentor, and beacon of hope for my students of color while simultaneously figuring out ways to enact my identity without alienating my white students and colleagues. For this young woman, she has to battle asserting her identity and perspective without being perceived as speaking too loudly, creating tension, or simply being too Black as she finds her place within the academy. Within every interaction, there is a complex enactment of gender, race, class, power, and privilege. Scholars have stated: "[we] live in a territory between voice and silence . . . if [we] continue to speak from [our] experience [we] may find that [our] voice is out of relationship, too loud, off key. If [we] remain silent [we] are in immediate danger of disappearing" (Taylor et al. 1995, 202).

As scholars that employ intersectionality and Critical Race Theory (CRT) as theoretical frameworks in our work, throughout this chapter, the dimensions of oppression and marginalization within academic spaces will be utilized. Intersectionality was founded in Black Feminism as a way to account for the various facets of identity in concrete, material, and positional ways (Crenshaw 1991). Intersectionality includes but is not limited to race, class, gender, and sexuality to interrogate the ways that people have access to power and privilege, as well as how this access informs perceptions and beliefs. Intersectionality is not a static feature, but rather is fluid and can be used to explore norms and power in relation to a wide range of identities.

Critical race theory (CRT) specifically address how power is enacted through the lens of race. The CRT model consists of five elements: (a) the centrality of race and racism and their intersectionality with other forms of subordination, (b) the challenge to dominant ideology, (c) the commitment to social justice, (d) the centrality of experiential knowledge, and (e) the transdisciplinary perspective (Solorzano 1997; Solorzano and Yasso 2000). Critical Race Theory also uniquely relies on narratives to substantiate claims. An essential tenant of Critical Race Theory is counter storytelling (DeCLuir and Dixson 2004) which emphasizes the role of individual narratives to the sense-making process, as we understand context through narrative. Therefore, in this chapter, we will focus on our mentor–mentee relationship over the course of several years, and identity as she (the mentee) transitioned from an undergraduate to a graduate student to now an instructor. Specifically, we will refer to our individual journal entries throughout this time using the tenants of CRT and the concept of intersectionality as our foundation, as well as we will document conversations we have had about and our place and space within academia and why both our voices and silences are necessary.

NOTES FROM THE JOURNAL:
BEFORE WE MET—JAHNASIA

In high school, I was an A/B student surrounded by children who looked like me and shared similar life stories. We all had a "hustler's" mentality where we were going to "make it" by any means necessary. We all worked hard to either put food on our tables, clothes on our backs, help our moms "get out" the 'hood, or get into college, so we could in turn help put more food on the table, have more clothes for our backs, and insure our mothers never had to return to the 'hood. For me, school was a hustle. I figured if I worked hard, it would pay off, so I made sure to get accepted into multiple colleges. I think this might be a common experience for other POC students, but specifically for WOC. We are taught early that we have to be twice as good, in order to receive half the credit.

When I decided to pursue higher learning, like many of my peers, I grappled with the financial aspect of affording higher education. "How am I going to afford this?" "Will I receive financial aid?" "I didn't play a sport—I was working! Will they accept me?!" I was the first in my family to attend college and I was the representative for not only my family but my community.

Let me back up a bit. I am from Syracuse, New York. No, not the beautiful Syracuse University campus it is known for, but the "hyper-segregated" city featuring among the worst racial income gap and racially segregated public schools in the nation (McMahon 2016). I lived in the inner city, rode the city Centro buses, and attended the aforementioned racially segregated schools. College was my escape from this environment, so when I received the call from Hofstra University's New Opportunities at Hofstra (NOAH) program offering an impressive scholarship, I immediately accepted.

On my first day of classes, I was swallowed by a sea of white faces with only speckles of Black and Brown people. Classes were a complete juxtaposition to high school where, this time, I was the minority. I felt out of place as I was surrounded by privilege I had only seen in movies. While some of my peers had Louis Vuitton purses, Chanel glasses, and drove Mercedes Benzs or BMWs, I, on the other hand, could not even afford a book for Biology class, much less look at a Benz. By this time, I was mentally exhausted. Thus, when I saw the swarthy skin of fellow NOAH students or just other melinated students in general, I exhaled deeply. The way the program was constructed with a month of interaction with only each other, our professors, and the counselors, we were able to create a sense of community. This was something I desperately needed. However, I noticed how we performed our distinct ideas of Blackness when in the comfort of swarthy skin in contrast to when we were surrounded by masses of whiteness. I did not feel like I belonged—this Black girl with the "Black name" and the "ghetto girl" tendencies. I did not feel smart enough—white enough. No matter how much I studied; no matter how much I changed the pitch of my voice to sound less of a Black woman; no matter how much I straightened my hair; or wore beautifully sculpted outfits, or buffed up my lexicon, I was still a Black woman—and it infuriated me. Finding my place in the space of whiteness was a rather daunting task because I severely suffered from imposter syndrome. Imposter syndrome is an "internal experience of intellectual phoniness in people who believe that they are not intelligent, capable or creative despite evidence of high achievement" (Clance and Imes 1978). For me, there was a constant internal battle. In some classes, I had to deal with professors that at best thought that I should be representative of all of Black people, and at worst, thought that I didn't belong. I often didn't feel like I was good enough and that I was failing everyone that believed in me. On one hand, I rejected anything I associated with Blackness. On the other hand, I reasoned that this was a form of internalized self-hatred. Thus, to combat such socialization, I reluctantly leaned in to "fighting the good fight" from time to time.

Not having many mentors of color (at the time) to turn to for advice, I spoke to one of the few Black *men* in the administration, about my struggles. Although sharing similar feelings, he ascribed them to "just being the 'Black experience.'" He also advised that I learn to wear different hats at different times. Despite research clarifying that men also experience impostor syndrome, acculturation to academia coupled with sexist messages encourage men to externalize their failures and internalize successes while encouraging women to do the opposite (Clance and Imes 1978). However, intersectionality theory acknowledges that traditional "single axis" analysis—either gendered *or* racialized—of exposed groups misses the mark and neglects to consider how racism and sexism interrelate to create a nuanced and exacerbated form of oppression.

As the weeks continued, I felt more and more emotionally taxed because I was consumed with whether I belonged, if I made people uncomfortable, or if people perceived me as intelligent. For instance, I was hyper-conscious about my delivery of messages, changing the tone, pitch, and dialect when around certain groups of people. In other words, code-switching. Code-switching is the process of shifting from one dialect to another (depending on the setting) and is deeply practiced (and ingrained) in American society (Morrison 1992). While code-switching seldomly refers to switching swiftly between languages, it generally refers to conforming to the dominant culture by changing one's dialect. For Black people, it is a relentless shift between African American Vernacular English (AAVE) and white standard English, but it can also be the difference between succeeding and failing in white-dominated spaces. Social psychologists and socio-linguists found "lower-class" minority speech styles to be attractive or possess integrity; however, speakers are typically "less competent," "less intelligent," and "less ambitious" (Edwards 1999). While I relentlessly forced myself to learn code-switching (and enact it), I also suffered with feeling like a sell-out.

NOTES FROM THE JOURNAL: OUR
MEETING—TOMEKA

Today, a student came to my office after completing an assignment called, *Growing Up Culturally*, where I ask the students to critically reflect on the messages they learned from childhood about who they are. This semester, I decided to focus specifically on ethnicity. I am used to students struggling a little on this exercise. I struggled with this when I went through the training from the Anti-Defamation League, which is where I adapted this exercise. Today, however, one of my students, Jahnasia, came to my office after we completed the in-class portion of the assignment with tears in her eyes. She told me "Miss Tomeka, I don't want to be a Black girl." Puzzled, I asked her, "What do you mean?" Her response, "I am tired of carrying the burdens of being a Black woman with me everywhere I go—all the time. It is exhausting." I don't even know where to begin to unpack that. Part of me understands exactly where she is coming from with this statement, but the other part of me also understands the part of her journey that she shared in class about not ever feeling Black enough in certain spaces. As a mixed-raced person, I have often had to prove my Blackness when among other Black individuals, women in particular. It is a double-edged sword and within academic spaces, it can be even harder because you already don't feel like you belong. There is no community. There is no one that quite gets what you are grappling with. But this is not about me right now. I need to be there for this student. I want to give her the mentorship that I wished that I would have had and part of our relationship also has to drop all pretense of code-switching. It has to be authentic. During our conversations, we will speak in ways that we feel comfortable and not adapt to the ways in which white audiences expect us to speak because just like Jahnasia is tired of always having to hide herself, so am I.

NOTES FROM THE JOURNAL: OUR MEETING—JAHNASIA

During my Junior Year of my undergraduate studies, my assessment of Blackness transmuted due to encountering my first Black-woman-full-time-professor, Tomeka Robinson. For me, meeting Tomeka was equivalent to meeting Michelle Obama. Granted, I have encountered successful Black women previously, but they were inaccessible. They were the CEO's of companies that were unapproachable and intimidating; however, Tomeka was there every Tuesday and Thursday eager and willing to assist students in the best way she knew how. Furthermore, Tomeka's career did not seem far-fetched compared to the CEOs I have met. "I could attain this," I thought. "I could be successful like her." Moreover, I was even more inspired when I enrolled in her Intercultural Communication class because we were encouraged to critically think—and discuss—race and culture. One particular assignment about cultural identity, I wrote and performed a heartfelt poem about my journey accepting my Blackness. I explained how I associated anything—and everything—negative in my life with Blackness. Then, I ended the poem with "My name is Jahnasia. And yes, I am a Black girl." The last line was pertinent not because I was declaring acceptance of Blackness to the class, but I was declaring it to myself. Afterward, I joined Tomeka in her office with a tear-stained face expressing how I grappled with accepting Blackness entirely. Accepting my Blackness meant that I must take all the nuances, challenges, implications, trauma, and imperfections that came with it. Because this was something I did not want to do, thankfully, I found a way to work through such feelings: speech and debate.

Tomeka introduced me to speech and debate at the perfect time because it allowed me to glare whiteness in the face and say, "Trauma is what you caused, but I will rise above it." The poetry program was poignant as it was about being an "Angry Black Woman." At the beginning of the season, performing this program avowed my anger as a Black woman. Yet, it was apologetic, passive-aggressive, and a plea for white people to be my ally. When performing the program, I carried the burden of explaining Black women's experiences. Contrarily, by the end of the season, the program changed into an assertive decree—an ode to Black women everywhere. Instead of "Blacksplainin," this variant placed the burden on white audiences. The personal moments I included allowed me to purge built-up negativity. In sum, speech and debate helped me find my voice.

NOTES FROM THE JOURNAL: THE UTILITY OF SHARING IDENTITY IN THE CLASSROOM—TOMEKA

One of the ways that I have found to relate to my students is to share components of my identity at the very beginning. As others have written, I find autobiography to be a powerful tool for both myself and students when connecting textbook concepts to the real world (Greefield 2006; Powers 1998). I seek to build in my students an understanding of how our biases and the intersection of our various privileges can at times imped on our communication with others. Therefore, one of the very first assignments I do in my intercultural communication course is to put identity categories on the board and have my students guess about me. I encourage them throughout that there are no dumb guesses. Part of the purpose of the assignment is to get them to see that some things like race, ethnicity, class, gender, sex, and sexual orientation people often think that they can guess, but it can become more complicated. So I allow them to guess and at the end of the exercise, I reveal the answers to the questions. The race and ethnicity questions are typically the ones where students feel the most comfortable guessing; though their guesses are always completely wrong. This is partially because of my complicated mixture of Creole (Spanish, French, African, and American Indian) and Mexican American, which I have to explain what Creole is often. But others like class, sex, gender, and sexual orientation, students often feel uncomfortable guessing. When I reveal, that I am a cis-heterosexual upper-middle-class female, they are not surprised. The other reason for the assignment is to illustrate vulnerability and openness for my students. If I am going to ask them to reveal portions of their identity and have authentic engagement, I have to be willing to do the same.

I do not expect students to take any risks that I would not take . . . It is often helpful if professors take the first risk, linking confessional narratives to academic discussions so as to show how experience can illuminate and enhance our understanding of academic material (hooks 1994). After the students finish guessing, I reveal the correct answers to each of the categories. By allowing students to locate their own perspectives and experiences within academic frames, I create a classroom environment where students feel less anxiety about creating rigid boundaries (Friedman and Rosenberg 2007).

As a young woman of color faculty member at a predominately white institution, I find that being as forthcoming as possible allows me to better craft the narrative that I wish to expose. I may be the first and only professor that they have and will ever encounter that looks like me. Students come in with different assumptions about the course in general and even more about my ability to teach the course materials, so it is important for me to share not only my identity, but also personal experiences both within and outside of the academy about various topics to complement the scholarly readings. For instance, when discussing microaggressions, I share my experience with the chief of the Campus Police Department at my previous institution telling me that he would have me arrested while I was dropping off students after a debate trip late one evening. I also share some of the comments that students have made on course evaluations like about only appreciating my choice of shoes. An intersectional framework argues that explicit attempts to explain and share personal experiences that integrate identity markers can help students understand marginality on a more nuanced level (Collins 1986; Crenshaw 1989). Moreover, I have found that allowing students the opportunity to see themselves intersectionally and really interrogate their positionality in the various social systems of privilege and oppression, that they learn how to mend these connections and understand at a deeper level what it truly means to communicate across difference. I choose connection inside and outside of the classroom and have found that students actually appreciate this approach. Students often note this within conversations with me as well as in their course evaluations.

LET'S TALK ABOUT GRADUATE SCHOOL

Tomeka: Okay, let's have the conversation that I know you have been avoiding. What's next for you?

Jahnasia: I don't know. I don't know what to do. Actually, I am pretty lost without school.

Tomeka: Have you considered graduate school?

Jahnasia: School has always been the most consistent thing in my life, but I have enough debt from undergraduate student loans. Going to graduate school would mean more debt. I want to go, but I don't want to keep putting myself in debt to obtain higher education.

Tomeka: There are assistantships especially through Forensics. Let's look at a few programs that have assistantship opportunities, but also with people that I know and trust.

Jahnasia: Ugh, I don't know about this, Miss Tomeka.

Tomeka: Will you just trust me in this?

NOTES FROM THE JOURNAL:
GRADUATE SCHOOL—JAHNASIA

On the first day of graduate classes, Intro to Graduate Study, I had the most debilitating experience. My white, male professor had assigned readings that I found quite difficult to digest except for one. The majority of the readings were vapid and written at a level of scholarly writing I had not yet encountered. However, the article I found interesting was written performatively causing me to digest the information faster while also enjoying it. When asked for critiques of the reading assignments, I shared this in class. His response to my revelation (compared to his response to everyone else) was cutting and condescending. Embarrassingly, he suggested my inability to comprehend graduate-level writing was due to ineptitude, *and* the reason I could understand performative written article was because it was for an undergraduate. Also, he obliquely stated I did not belong in graduate school. I was ostracized and used as a scapegoat, bullied in ways other students were not. Thus, snidely, I responded, "I never said I could not comprehend the material. I said the material was difficult to digest because it was boring." Back in my Hofstra-days, I would have ignored his passive-aggressive comment in fear of being perceived as the "confrontational Black woman"; however, I worked too hard to build my confidence in my Blackness to the point that I was not willing to be this professor's verbal punching bag. While at the moment, I was strong, the remainder of the semester, I felt intimidated by him.

I diligently fought feelings of inferiority, but could not help feeling like an imposter. Thus, I spoke less in class and only commented on topics that I thoroughly examined to prove to him that I was competent and that I, in fact, did belong in graduate school. I was also vigilant in my writing, constantly writing and rewriting papers to appear less Black and more white because for me speaking "white' equated to academic voice.

It was not until the second semester of my graduate career that I felt less of an imposter. This was due to a white professor encouraging me to write my thesis on Black diasporic hair. I was extremely surprised by his support of this topic; his support bolstered my esteem. I began to speak more in classes and felt less inclined to whitewash my writing. I even began writing performatively. And when racial topics arose—I being the only POC in the room—was obliged to being the "Black representative." This was fair in the beginning because it created dialogue for understanding. Nevertheless, there were times I did not want to be consulted for questions about grape soda, watermelon, and fried chicken stereotypes. I just wanted to exist the same as other students.

NOTES FROM THE JOURNAL: GRADUATE SCHOOL—TOMEKA

I checked in with Jahnasia today about how graduate school was going. She shared her struggles with one particular professor suggesting that she did not belong in a graduate program. I offered her what advice and encouragement I could. But I remember having a professor like hers when I was in graduate school in Texas. I was the only master's level student in this doctoral seminar and while, no, I did not have the same background as the other students in the class, I was keeping up. This was not enough for this particular professor (white woman), who I was told later mentioned in a meeting that she did not think I could write. Another professor challenged her on this and said you do realize that you have said this about every Black and Hispanic student that has come through this program. Her response, "well maybe they all should learn how to write better." Her ignorance bolstered my desire to complete my studies and to even become a professor. While I switched programs for my doctoral work, I knew that ultimately, I wanted to go back into a Communication program and that I would be even better just to prove her wrong.

Within the field, there have been increased conversations about the pervasiveness of white masculinity and the necessity to decolonize the communication discipline (Caruth and Caruth 2013; Chakravartty et al. 2018; Gunning 2000). However, there are still some that reject decolonization and try to shift the conversation to issues of meritocracy. I reject this ideology and my classroom is a decolonized space though I often find myself having to have lively debates with colleagues about how we should approach our curriculum. This is imperative because colonization maintains its position by constructing, perpetuating, and disseminating a certain mode of thought, a set of acceptable narratives, mythologies, traditions, and even modes of research practice. Decolonization demands developing counter-mythologies that admit the fallacies in the myths by which we have constructed our discipline because just as myths are constructed mechanisms, they can and should be consciously deconstructed.

GRADUATING FROM GRADUATE SCHOOL

Jahnasia: Miss Tomeka, okay, I have this degree. What do I do now?

Tomeka: What do you want to do with it? Want to go into a doctoral program or work?

Jahnasia: After that experience, I do not want to look at another paper, read another book, or attend another class. Grad school tired me out, okay? I am done. Done! If I decide to go back for a doctoral degree, that will be later, but right now, I just want to work. Yeah, let's talk about work.

Tomeka: Okay, do you want a professor job or do you want to work in another field for a while?

Jahnasia: Hmmm. I wanted to go into Public Relations, but I was offered me a position working with a team in Tennessee, what do you think about that?

Tomeka: I think that is a great way for you to discover whether you actually want to be a professor and this is at an HBCU, which you have always wanted to experience. I say give it a try and if it works out, great, you have some direction. If it doesn't, then we can figure out what the next step will be.

NOTES FROM THE JOURNAL: ENTERING AN HBCU—JAHNASIA

Transitioning within academia from a student to being a member of faculty was intimidating because of where and *how* I began my career. I was far from my northeastern melting pot of a home that I learned to appreciate. Now in Tennessee, a conservative state right in the middle of the "Bible Belt," I jumped head-first into academia after finishing my master's degree serving as a Full-Time Instructor and Assistant Director of Speech and Debate at a HBCU. I also picked up a few additional classes as an Adjunct Professor at two community colleges, one of which had a dual enrollment program designed specifically for high school students. Every semester, I taught five to six classes, some in person and some online.

At the HBCU, I was delighted to begin working; however, my excitement was short-lived because of the low standards set for students, lack of support provided by my department, and the colorism and sexism I faced. For instance, I received backlash from the department chair because a few students disapproved of how I conducted my courses. For instance, I took a different approach to how I taught language in Public Speaking classes. I didn't reject AAVE as being legitimate in a formal speaking environment and instead taught how it was just different. Rather than informing the students on the proper way to navigate this, the chair allowed them to completely ignore protocol, removed power from me (as the professor) and gave all the power to the students. Concerned, I reached out to fellow faculty and staff only to be advised it is our duty to "ease the burden" on Black students since "Out in the world, they will struggle to survive and we don't want them to feel they have to struggle here too." Such notions served to be counterproductive. It is my firm belief that students were not held accountable for their actions and that there was an abundance of blurring the lines between professor and student.

CHECKING IN AT THE HBCU

Tomeka: So, how is it going?

Jahnasia: I hate it here.

Tomeka: Can you explain what is going on specifically besides just saying you hate it there?

Jahnasia: It's a little bit of everything . . . the students, the administration, living here . . . it's everything. I never thought I would face as much adversity in a Black space as I have here. It is not like a PWI that is for sure lol.

Tomeka: Mmmm . . . there is a lot there. I know that I have chosen to only apply to and work for PWIs, but that is because of my own struggles in exclusively Black spaces. I was hoping that that would be different for you.

Jahnasia: It's not. I never thought I would face colorism, racism, and sexism amongst my own people, but I have in ways that I never imagined. Can we talk about doctoral programs now?

Tomeka: What exactly happened first?

Jahnasia: It is a lot of things from being told I am not "down for the cause" because of my light skin to being completely dismissed in meetings because "how dare this little girl speak." Like I said, can we talk about doctoral programs?

Tomeka: Wow! I would like to say that I am surprised, but unfortunately, I am not. I have my own experiences of this and not just from colleagues of color. But I am glad that you haven't lost your desire to be a professor. Sounds like it will be back at a PWI though, which again present their own unique challenges as you know. But let's look at doctoral programs that might fit you a little better and have financial aid.

NOTES FROM THE JOURNAL: LEAVING THE HBCU
TO FULL-TIME ADJUNCT LIFE—JAHNASIA

I left the HBCU. I couldn't take it anymore and decided that I would just continue working at the community colleges as an Adjunct Professor, while I apply to doctoral programs. Returning to a PWI involved a surfeit of conflicting emotions. While I felt confident in my Blackness, I simultaneously grappled with whether it would make others uncomfortable. I taught at two community colleges. At one college, I taught conventional courses and at the other, I taught one conventional course and three dual enrollment college-level courses that were created for high school students. While the community colleges were burdened with less economic complications, the standard of education and lack of motivation amongst students was eerily similar to the HBCU.

At the first community college, a student twice my size physically threatened me. When I reached out to fellow faculty and the administration for assistance, other faculty expressed they shared similar experiences. Unfortunately, the administration disregarded our pleas to teach in a safe environment. The student in question read at an eighth-grade reading level and threatened every professor that would not allow her to dictate her grades. While this was the only threat of violence from a student, I, unfortunately, learned that plenty of students read on similar levels which caused them to be incapable of comprehending course readings or indulging in classroom discussions.

At the second community college, I was told that I needed to dampen my Blackness. One administrator told me my presence made her uncomfortable, specifically, she deemed the way that I dressed and spoke as being unprofessional. Later in the semester, my credentials were questioned by the same administration and my classes were "secretly" investigated. I didn't understand the cause for this and when I expressed concerns to higher administration, they were diminished and I was advised: "this type of behavior is to be expected." At this point my mental health was in jeopardy and did not know how long I could withstand much more nor did I feel I belonged there anyway.

NOTES FROM THE JOURNAL: SPACE AND PLACE
FOR SCHOLARS OF COLOR—TOMEKA

Numerous studies have outlined some of the factors that contribute to faculty of color leaving academia. From micro and macro aggressions committed at various levels of the institution to issues like lack of support for teaching and scholarship (Arnold et al. 2016; Jones 2019; Pettit 2019; Stewart 2019). And while I get the reasons outlined for checking out of the academy, I refuse to give in. Students of color need to see someone that looks like them in their spaces of learning. All students need to be exposed to people that debunk the stereotypes of how a professor should look, sound, and act.

As outlined by CRT, counter storytelling is essential to challenging the dominant ideologies of the academy. My colleagues and students need to hear my narrative and the narratives of other marginalized individuals. But hearing is not enough, there has to be a commitment to social justice and a willingness to make whatever changes are necessary to make our spaces truly inclusive. This means that colleges and universities as a whole must interrogate to what extent do our scholarly practices legitimize the hegemony of whiteness, masculinity, hetero and cis-normativity, and ablebodiedness. We need to critically evaluate what kinds of knowledge has been and continues to be privileged in our texts and theories. We also need to challenge the misrepresentations of others that legitimize the contemporary global power structures in Western discourses. I refuse to walk away and will continue to challenge the structures on my own campus as well as within the discipline itself, so we stop losing brilliant colleagues and minds. So while that means that I am often overworked, I serve on multiple committees, give lectures on our campus and at regional and national meetings, and even have started to facilitate difficult dialogue sessions with students in an attempt to get them to brainstorm policies and procedures they would like to see implemented to make the campus a more inclusive and safe space. But I feel like it is my duty because if I don't, who will?

CONCLUSION

My [Jahnasia] journey in academia has been exciting and fulfilling, yet simultaneously, spiritually and emotionally grueling. The exhaustion from micro and macro aggressions from (some) students, faculty, and administration, coupled with relentless pressure to be double-conscious, has caused me to become my own aggressor, constantly questioning exhibiting negative internal dialogue. Prolonged feelings of isolation and stress can lead to more serious illnesses such as depression and anxiety. Thus, it is best for me to take proactive steps to rebuild positive internal dialogue, physical and mental health, *and* that means taking a step back from the academy.

While I will miss building relationships with students, my aspirations for teaching have faltered. Contrarily, I have not given up on "fighting the good fight." I still aspire to serve as a beacon of hope for Black women in academia through conducting research laying at the intersection of Blackness, womanism, and mindfulness. I recognize that my experiences are not reflections of all Black women in the academy; however, having a conversation about the mentally strenuous fee one pays when teaching while Black and woman can be a form of activism, creating a safe space for students to also discuss their experiences in academe.

Hearing of Jahnasia's experience at the new community college, I [Tomeka] am not surprised by her decision to not teach anymore. While I believe that she has so much to offer in the classroom space, I also understand how taxing it can be. I experience microaggressions all the time. While I have used those to bolster my career and to strive to be better than those that surround me, it is hard.

In essence, there are days when walking into the classroom—and even a building—can really take a toll on your soul, but as women of color, we are beacons of hope for other young women of color. In this chapter, we discussed what it means to assert our identity and perspective as we continue to navigate the academy using CRT and intersectionality as our theoretical foundation. Frank and open conversations about race, class, and gender discomfit everyone—mentor and mentee alike—as our bodies and experiences take place in these utterances. Teaching while Black and a woman within the framework of communication pedagogy allows for candid conversations, presenting moments where our most censored thoughts become central and foundational to the conversation. But it is always a question of who is listening.

REFERENCES

Arnold, Nicole, Emily Crawford, and Muhammad Khalifa. 2016. "Psychological Heuristics and Faculty of Color: Racial Battle Fatigue and Tenure/Promotion." *Journal of Higher Education*, 87, no. 6: 890–919.

Caruth, Gail, and Donlad Caruth. 2013. "Adjunct Faculty: Who Are These Unsung Heros of Academe?" *Current Issues in Education*, 16, no. 3: 1–10.

Chakravartty, Paula, Rachel Kuo, Victoria Grubbs, and Charlton McIlwain. 2018. "#CommunicationSoWhite." *Journal of Communication*, 68, no. 2: 254–266.

Clance, Pauline Rose, and Suzanne Imes. 1978. "The Imposter Phenomenom in High Achieving Women: Dynamics and Therapeutic Intervention." *Psychotheraphy: Theory, Research, & Practice*, 15, no. 3: 241–247.

Collins, Patricia Hill. 1986. "Learning From the Outsider Within: The Sociological Significance of Black Feminist Thought." *Social Problems*, 33, no. 6: S14–S32.

Crenshaw, Kimberly. 1989. "Demarginalizing the Intersection of Race and Sex: A Black Feminist Critique of Antidiscrimination Doctrine, Feminist Theory, and Antiracist Politics." *University of Chicao Legal*, 8: 139–167.

Crenshaw, Kimberly. 1991. "Mapping the Margins: Intersectionality, Identity Politics, and Violence Against Women of Color." *Stanford Law Review*, 43, no. 6: 1241–1299.

DeCuir, Jessica T., and Adreinne DeniseDixson. 2004. "So When It Comes Out, They Aren't That Surprised That It Is There: Using Critical Race Theory of Analysis of Race and Racism in Education." *Educational Researcher*, 33, no. 5: 26–31.

Edwards, John. 1999. "Refining Our Understanding of Language Attitudes." *Journal of Language and Social Psychology*, 18, no. 1: 101–110.

Freidman, Kathie, and Karen Rosenberg. 2007. "Performing Identities in the Classroom: Teaching Jewish Women's Studies." *Teaching Sociology*, 35: 315–333.

Greenfield, Derek. 2006. "Understanding the Social Structure Through Personal Experience: The Creative Use of Status and Role as Explanatory Factors." *Teaching Sociology*, 34, no. 4: 404–411.

Gunning, Sandra. 2000. "Now That They Have Us, What's the Point?" In *Power, Race, and Gender in Academe: Strangers in the Tower?*, edited by S. G. Lim, M. Herrera-Sobek, and G. M. Padila, 171–182. New York: Modern Language Association of America.

hooks, bell. 1994. *Teaching to Transgress: Education as the Practice of Freedom.* New York: Routledge.

Jones, LaMont. 2019. "Endless Exodus: Faculty of Color Leave the Academy in Search of Fulfillment." *Diverse Issues in Higher Educaiton*, 36, no. 11: 46–49.

McMahon, J. "Syracuse." *Syracuse* (Syracuse, NY). August 26, 2016.

Morrison, T. 1992. *Playing in the Dark: Whiteness and the Literary Imagination.* New York: Random House.

Petitit, E. 2019. "The Cards Are Stacked Against Faculty of Color: Here's a Way to Help." *The Chronical of Higher Educaiton*, 66, no. 9: A8–A10.

Powers, R. 1998. "Using Critical Autobiography to Teach the Sociology of Education." *Teaching Sociology*, 26, no. 3: 198–206.

Solorzano, D. 1997. "Images and Words That Wound: Critical Race Theory, Racial Stereotyping, and Teacher Education." *Teacher Education Quarterly*, 24: 5–19.

Chapter 2

You Are *Not* My Child, I
Am *Not* Your Parent

A Case Against the
Infantilization of Students

Meggie Mapes and Benny LeMaster

I'm sweating, uncomfortable, sitting in a conference room. I'm forced to watch another *institutional training video alleging my capacity to respond in the event of an active shooter. The video ends and I notice my colleagues are equally unnerved. "This is awful," one colleague expresses dissatisfaction. Another adds, "Yeah, I can't imagine growing up like this. Our poor kids must be so scared."* What about us, *I think to myself,* I'm terrified to come to work and there is no compensation for the emotional labor inherent in this sort of work environment or for supporting students navigating these violent gun-laden environments. *A colleague offers, "These trainings empower me to protect my kids better." A number of colleagues' nod in compulsory agreement. Frustrated, I respond: "I don't have kids, I don't want kids, and I have no one to protect but myself in the event of an active shooter." My colleagues stare as I punctuate the point: "They are not my children. I am not their parent. And not all parents are protective nor safe."*

***

Children are, colloquially speaking, "seen and not heard." Or, at least that's what we're told *as* children; what we tell *to* children, particularly through White-familial relationality. Children are, in a Western context, fragile creatures. Indeed, stupid creatures inept at self-sufficiency; dependent.

Conversely, teachers are resilient, parental, strong, capable, and sufficient; safe and, well, adult, and thus, human.

***

I'm sweating, uncomfortable, sitting in a conference room for a panel presentation. I listen intently to a panel meant to discuss feminist pedagogy—the energy is palpable as five women began sharing their experiences as teacher-scholars. I quickly realize the repetition of a distinct reality: many of these participants emphasize feeling individually responsible to handle students' insecurities, personal problems, or other roles deemed outside the bounds of a traditional teacher-role, framing their experiences as somehow parental. "The students become my kids. I can do the mom-things that I want without having biological kids" one participant shares. I cringe. "I do not want kids," I scribble repeatedly on my small white notebook. "I am not their parent."

***

We love pedagogy-talk, believing that talking about teaching makes you a stronger pedagogue; being open to dialogue facilitates reflexive considerations—a circular motion of moving backward to understand how your pedagogy could progress; a continual return to teaching moments. In this chapter, we ask, how does the naming of students in infantilizing terms (e.g., "my kids") (re)inscribe power dynamics and thus constrain the student-instructor relationship within paternalistic terms that center White constructs of civility? Drawing on the rich tradition of autoethnographic methods, we perform a critical interrogation of the mundane communicative constitution of students in infantilizing terms: as students, as pedagogues, and as colleagues. In turn, we theorize the critical implications of student infantilization as they emerge in relation to our identities as a white queer non-childbearing feminist and a mixed-race Asian/white queer non-childbearing trans scholar. We begin by outlining two implications of infantilizing students before turning to two anchors to guide performative refusals of infantilization.

IMPLICATING INFANTILIZATION

"My kids didn't complete the assignment," she said, searching for advice on whether to grant an extension for students' late submissions. "In class today, my kids really stepped up," they mentioned. The mundane oscillation between students/kids regularly occurs in our institutional halls and offices—sites of pedagogical slippage that mark meaningful moments of communicative analysis. Foucault reminds that schooling practices are enactments of power, power that is "impressed on the bodies of subjects to produce a particular type of subject" (Hillier 2012, 52). And creating subjects requires categorizing subjects (Hillier 2012, 63). It is meaningful, in our read, to more deeply explore the infantilizing categorization of students as "kids" and/or in more possessive terms "my kids"—moments of differentiation between instructor and student where we wonder, what kind of communicative implications emerge when students are animated through rhetorics of infantilization? As critical communication pedagogues, we view identity as constituted in and through communication making pedagogy-talk a meaningful area of analysis (Fassett and Warren 2006). In this section, we explore implications of infantilizing students: the re-inscription of power dynamics and the resulting constraining of student-instructor relationships within paternalistic terms that center White constructs of civility.

(RE)INSCRIBING POWER DYNAMICS

Historically, pedagogy and infantilization have long been intertwined, whereby education was/is used as a method of normative socialization through disciplinary power. Koops (2012) defines infantilization as the process that increases the "duration of the childhood stage, which is necessarily accompanied by the increasing distance between the worlds of children and adults" (12). Children—seen as distinct from adults—needed education to "bridge the distance to adulthood" by reducing uncivilized behaviors through teaching the "proper way of behaving" (Koops 2012, 13–15; 57).

The historical push toward infantilization violently emerged alongside coloniality and racism. A key colonialist aim was, for example, eradicating Indigenous values and, instead, educational systems were imposed that socialized children toward European knowledge, culture, and embodiment (Pratt et al. 2018). Such colonial aims, reliant upon an infantilization lens, framed Ingenious ways of life as immature, backwards, and uncivilized. In turn, education—often infused with Judeo-Christian ethos—taught that modern and Western ways of life were virtuous, moral, and civilized (Eshet 2015). In addition to colonialist logics, infantilizing rhetoric is embedded in racialized White supremacy. For example, used to infantilize and belittle Black adult men, "boy" was used as a linguistic "Jim Crow ritual" by which "white people weaponized language to remind black folks of their place" (Demby 2018, n.p.). In light of this history, "boy" functions as a "racialized technolog[y] of the flesh" (Báez and Ore 2018, 331) that rhetorically infantilizes Black men through a logic of civility and in relation to their dialectic power opposite: White adult men, the patriarchs. To infantilize is to categorically situate a subject as less-than or not-yet adult—a categorical decision demarcated by behavioral choices that performatively reify normative values of civility and whiteness. Said differently, infantilizing discourse undergirds and animates civility, a historical racist project. Kristiana L. Báez and Ersula Ore (2018) clarify the point as they turn to their own racialized bodies: "For these bodies—that is, for black and nonblack racialized bodies such as ours—civility is always already an unattainable goal but an expectation nonetheless" (332). Infantilization is dehumanization.

Education is a project of infantilization. Hillier (2012) concurs, arguing that institutionalized education is the "process of discipline through training the body to become docile through various non-physical acts of power; creating docile subjects appropriate for production within our societies" (51). Pedagogy becomes the means to change or alter child-like behavior toward normative, allegedly "adult," pathways. From a communication perspective, rhetoric becomes a pervasive mechanism that defines normative performance and enacts disciplinary responses when normativity isn't reached. LeMaster (2018) assists in defining normativity, reminding:

> A norm is a common cultural pattern. When a norm has a dominant cultural value attached to it, it can be said to be normative. The effect includes a discursively constituted subjectivity rooted in questions of cultural value such that those who hold institutional/normative power are understood as valuable while those who do not are framed as valueless. In this way, normativity is a performatively constituted regime of regulatory power wherein temporally and spatially contextual cultural norms are rendered remarkable and used as a measure of value. (81)

Infantilization, thus, becomes a processual declaration toward normative adulthood: this is what you must learn to become the type of adult deemed institutionally valuable. Put differently, to infantilize—particularly college-age students who, by other definitions, are adults—is to restructure power through disciplinary rhetoric: you are not normative enough when compared to my positionality as "the" adult.

The history of infantilization is significant in that it demonstrates the intersectional significance between disciplinary educational practices, power, and normativity. Rhetorically infantilizing students re-centers institutional power to hierarchically differentiate students from instructors. Writing about the history of infantilization, Koops (2012) narrates that infantilizing pedagogy functions by controlling affective and performative bodily displays that might threaten the stability of the family (13). To become an adult was/is to contribute toward the stability of familial life, and uncivil children held impulses that needed correction. Infantilization, thus, doesn't simply occur by supporting

socialization to *any* performative and behavioral outcomes; instead, normative centers, including traditionalistic concepts of family and white constructs
of civility, mark the desired outcomes. With normative outcomes in mind,
pedagogy creates conditions for producing docile bodies by, for example,
placing student/kids on the correct, normative path.

Consider the phrase that we have often heard: "Wow! My kids really performed well in class today. They were attentive and active." At first glance,
such a sentence appears to be a positive enactment of pedagogy that praises
student performance. However, the language situates students/kids as positive
insofar as their performance is read as the correct socialized behavior, that
is, they were attentive and active based on the adult instructor's assessment.
Conversely yet connected, the negatively veiled statement that "my kids performed really horribly today" quickly disciplines students for their inability to
demonstrate perceived outputs of normative adult identity. In either example,
"kids" becomes the framework in which students are read as valuable or
invaluable based on the presumed performance of normative adulthood.

PATERNAL CIVILITY AND THE
PERFORMANCE OF WHITENESS

As the previous section has shown, infantilization attempts to re-inscribe
power dynamics which, as we'll argue here, similarly co-constitutes instructors, implicitly placing teachers within parental or paternalistic parameters.
When "kid" becomes synonymous with student, "kid" ascribes and prioritizes
a particular identity category over others, implicitly prescribing that identity as pedagogically a priori, erasing student difference and constraining
instructors to act in and through paternal constructs. If students are children,
pedagogy becomes defined and reliant on notions of good parenting, so good
pedagogy becomes operationalized through instructors properly raising and
rearing their students/kids.

Instructors as parents become a damaging and dangerous institutional
expectation for two reasons. First, it re-affirms banking models of education.
Renowned critical pedagogy Paulo Freire is best known for his discussion on
the banking model, writing that this pedagogical approach emerges by subtly
re-centering the student as vessel in need of (parental) guidance and direction
(Freire 1970). Child-like students, through a banking model, require depos-
its of information determined relevant by authoritarian instructors/parents.
Because instructors are the central subjects and transmitters of knowledge,
they function as parental figures able to restrict student autonomy because
students are infantile: they know nothing. Instructors are parental: they know
truth.

Consider this common example: "I need to put my kid gloves on when talking to my class about diversity issues." Rather than competent individuals capable of participating in complex dialogues, students are instead rendered as less than and in need of delicate handling. Here, an instructor must equip themselves with a special tool, kid gloves, capable of meeting students where they are—which is somehow distinct from the instructor. Students are assumed to be lacking, like an empty vessel, in need of nurturing and proper infantile handling from an instructor. This pacifies students, reducing them to pre-determined associations of "child-ness" and diminishing their complex histories, experiences, and contributions. Breunig (2005) reminds that the banking model "supports the dominant educational ideology that silences and marginalizes students' voice and experience" (115). Very similar to the colloquial language that "kids should be seen and not heard," the banking model renders students unknowing; if you know nothing, your voice, perspective, and thoughts are valueless, while the instructor becomes gatekeeper of that which should be knowable and thus valuable.

Similarly, the differing identities amongst students are erased in favor of an ontology of sameness. A parental approach, reliant on the banking-model, priorities "kid" as the central and integral identity category for pedagogues to address. This pre-supposes that all students are the same—in need of the same types of knowledge, access, and relationality despite intersectional differences. While, certainly, interpersonal communicative patterns may emerge from, for example, communities of color that facilitate child-like references, our argument is that infantilization can be linked to the broader and systemic history of academic whiteness.

Second, viewing instructors as parents prioritizes pedagogical enactments of White civility. Like we mentioned, students-as-kids co-constitute instructors, making good parenting synonymous with good pedagogy. This, in turn, presupposes that educational interventions aimed at reducing unsocialized behavior should be pedagogically prioritized. However, transitioning a "kid" to a productive member of society is reliant on pre-supposed perceptions of behavior—and a pre-supposed framework on what progress looks like. The question remains: What does good socialization mean? What constitutes "good" parenting? As we've mentioned in the section above, infantilization exists through distancing kids from adults—a distance that collapses when children learn correct and civil behaviors. So being a good pedagogue means being a good parent and being a good parent means creating civilized citizenry.

In turn, student/kids who fail to acclimate toward normative whiteness are promptly expunged from the educational social order. In other words, through parental infantilization, student/kids "are socialized into the proper way of behaving and those who do not adhere to the norm are considered deviants in the social order" (Hillier 2012, 57). To be blunt: to name students as kids is to interpellate individuals into narratives of white respectability that standardize socialized behaviors as good or bad (LeMaster and Mapes 2020; Rudick and Golsan 2018). Hillier (2012) reminds that kids who are unable to properly socialize—those "who are not product citizens in a capitalist society"—are quickly disciplined and labeled as degenerate or lazy (57). Unfortunately, producing deviant student kids is evidence of bad parenting, of bad pedagogical enactments that failed to follow normative pathways of whiteness.

This is infuriating. We do not want kids—as a queer, feminist, non-child-bearing woman and a mixed-race Asian/white queer non-childbearing trans scholar, the presumption that pedagogy somehow mirrors normative parental responsibility is, quite frankly, nauseating. In fact, such a construct relies on a cishetero-futuristic fantasy that instructors must produce correct citizen-subjects that can properly assimilate into society, perpetuating a legacy of toxic parenting pedagogues.

REFUSING INFANTILIZATION

Choosing to pursue higher education is an "adult" decision. In the United States, choosing to pursue higher education is an especially risky "adult" decision, in light of: increasing tuition costs and attending student loan debts; the shift from a service economy to a "gig economy" enabled less by education and more by the technological capacity to commodify the whole person; exacerbated mediated representation and amplification of gun violence in learning environments (which are also work environments); decreasing access to regular and gainful employment or to healthcare and retirement as options let alone as "benefits"; intensifying global climate change and resulting environmental catastrophes leading to increasing displacement and death; and a surge in global fascism manifesting near and far in ethnocentric and nationalist projects defined through anti-Muslim racism (Yousuf and Calafell 2018), anti-indigeneity, antiblackness, and racialized cisheterosexism, for instance. Moreover, we are writing in the United States and on colonized land at the cusp of 2020, which means many of the students (and soon many of our colleagues) that we encounter in our classrooms were raised in a country always at war. Choosing to pursue higher education today is very much an "adult" decision, and the adults who we work with in our classrooms are very well aware of their precarious locations in this shrinking global economy. And as diversity initiatives open space for increasing numbers of first-generation and low-income students to enter academe—including the authors of this chapter—the materiality defining the "typical" student experience is shifting. As such, communication pedagogy must reflect changing student needs rather than continuing to assert curriculum devoid of humanity.

The picture we paint is gloomy because the global scene in which many of our students are laboring to survive is equally so. Though the core of communication curriculum continues to persist as if nothing in our sociocultural worlds have changed. And with it, communication instructors operate under the false assumption that their training in communication studies holds within it the key for student enrichment sans lived life. Infantilizing discourse, in turn, rhetorically justifies and exacerbates the communication instructor's self-appointed position as a paternalistic figurehead. To infantilize the adults with whom we work in our classrooms is to belittle and dismiss the affective—and sometimes terrifying—complexities many of our students are navigating as adults already: working multiple jobs, racist violence, debt, illness, caretaking. Failure, further, to center these mundane and intersectional complexities asserts a curriculum that coercively predetermines that which allegedly matters to students, when it really merely reflects a specialized, contained, and ahistorical understanding of the communicative world. Such an education reflects, in Freire's (1970) terms, a banking model of education in which

> the educator's role is to regulate the way the world 'enters into' the students. The teacher's task [in a banking model] is to organise a process which already occurs spontaneously, to 'fill' the students by making deposits of information which [they] consider [. . .] to constitute true knowledge. And since people 'receive' the world as passive entities, education should make them more passive still, and adapt them to the world. The educated individual is the adapted person, because [they are] better 'fit' for the world. Translated into practice, this concept is well suited to the purposes of the oppressors, whose tranquility rests on how well people fit the world the oppressors have created, and how little they question it. (76)

The result is a docile student dependent upon teachers to "teach" that which matters—regardless of its importance to students' needs or lives. This dependence is the result of a paternalistic logic that positions students and teachers in an oppressive orientation such that teachers (communicatively constituted as paternalistic figureheads) determine what's best for students (communicatively constituted as "kids") who are constrained by their "absolute ignorance" (Freire 1970, 72).

Conversely, critical pedagogy fosters dialogue between students and teachers such that "both are simultaneously teachers *and* students" (Freire 1970, 72). The goal is humanization of both the student and the teacher. To refuse infantilization is to conceptualize students as dialogical equals—as fully capable subjects navigating life and who have turned to higher education as a "site of class mobility," which, regardless of cases for or against a liberal arts education, may be tangential to student needs for more immediate survival and navigating a brutal world at best (Salaita 2015, 178). They are, indeed, adults, making adult decisions. And we, communication instructors, are adults, who have the power to choose to facilitate student needs through communication curriculum or serve as oppressive gatekeepers asserting means that suit our own ends—and that of the Ivory Tower—as professional academics. To that end, we turn to Freire to articulate a path away from the dehumanization that infantilizing discourse asserts. Humanization is realized through dialogue, which is founded upon *love*, *humility*, and *faith*. Taken together, Freire provides a heuristic means by which we might labor to refuse infantilization. Because, in Freire's words, "the oppressed must see examples of the vulnerability of the oppressor so that a contrary conviction can begin to grow within them," we turn to autoethnographic insight to illustrate our unique and collaborative attempts to refuse infantilization through *love*, *humility*, and *faith*—as students and as educators (Freire 1970, 64).

Love

> Because love is an act of courage, not of fear, love is commitment to others. No matter where the oppressed are found, the act of love is commitment to their cause—the cause of liberation.
>
> (Freire 1970, 89)[1]

***

"It's in the syllabus. It's in the syllabus. It's in the syllabus." This loaded refrain chafes. I (Benny) remember the first time I entered a professor's office. At that time, I was designated a "junior" though I was in my 7th year of undergraduate education and a "non-traditional" student by institutional standards. Being a first-generation college student working a full-time job and multiple part-time gigs coupled with life i t s e l f meant the monotony of higher education was the least of my concerns. Indeed, I did not avoid office hours; rather, my 60+ hour work weeks did not align with the small window of advising time set aside for students. On this day, I called out sick to work—a loss in wages that would inevitably mean a late bill in the subsequent month: a cost to acquiescing to higher ed's middle-class formation.

"Hi, prof. Can you tell me what sort of sources count for this project? And, can you tell me when it's due exactly?"

"It's in the syllabus." The professor refuses rolling their eyes, swiveling their chair back around to items of larger importance. I am but another stu-dent, *another* burden.

Or, in the telling words of a fellow graduate teaching assistant years later—when I had greater access to the inner threshold of academe—a "privileged and lazy brat." I could not comprehend syllabi as the binding documents higher ed alleges largely because professors flippantly altered the "set" document to accommodate their own poor planning. Teaching is hard. And institutional minutiae make it harder effectively alienating the humans behind the "student" and "teacher" descriptives. To love our students, to commit to their cause, to their liberation, is to decenter our institutional demands as being "more important" than the fight it takes to navigate higher education as a first-generation student, specifically. In the words of Rachel Griffin (2012), this love provides a "humanizing means to render the invisible visible, offer compassion when there seems to be none, and extend empathy beyond previous boundaries" (218).

***

Humility

> Someone who cannot acknowledge himself to be as mortal as everyone else still has a long way to go before he can reach the point of encounter. At the point of encounter there are neither utter ignoramuses nor perfect sages; there are only people who are attempting, together, to learn more than they now know.
>
> (Freire 1970, 90)

***

I (Benny) learned in my communication courses that my trans identity was invalid; at least according to the cissexist research my professors chose to assert effectively refusing to update their knowledge reserves; their comfort as non-trans folks depended upon my discomfort as a trans person. After all, as one professor offensively asserts a common refrain my family of origin continues to enjoy, "It's probably just a phase they'll grow out of." The "they" referencing a theoretical and developmentally defunct—indeed, immature—trans subject detached from my own materiality as a trans adult in the communication classroom. The "phase" asserting a cisheteronormative reproductive futurity on to my person—onto the allusive "they" located elsewhere among the other temporal freaks. I do not exist to this professor. My people do not exist to this professor. We are but children who need to grow up and out of our gender fantasies.

Years later, I am facilitating a course in intercultural communication. Today's discussion engages whiteness.

A transsexual woman of color offers, "Whiteness implicates both my race as a Latina and my gender as a transsexual woman."

I respond, "Yes, yes. An important intersectional point!" I pose the point to the class, "Based on their *insight, how does whiteness implicate both your race and your gender in similar and different ways?"*

A hand or two raises before the student jumps back in, "Um, do not use 'they' pronouns to describe me. I am a woman. A transsexual woman who fought to be who I am."

I am stunned. Implicated. And wrong.

"Thank you for correcting me. My apologies. I will do better."

I am a non-binary trans person who messes up a lot. The adults who enter my classrooms are well aware of who they are. Even those who are "figuring shit out" need merely loving and critical support as they materialize terrains of their own design set against a broader terrain of cultural conscription and denial—even as they enter our communication classrooms but for a semester or two. To act with humility is to decenter professorial authority and to work in service of facilitating, in the words of Jack Halberstam, "futures [that] can be imagined according to logics that lie outside of those paradigmatic markers of life experience—namely, birth, marriage, reproduction, and death"(Halberstam 2005, 2).

***

Faith

> Without this faith in people, dialogue is a farce which inevitably degenerates into paternalistic manipulation . . . Faith in people is an *a priori* requirement for dialogue.
>
> (Freire 1970, 90; 91)

***

A colleague feigns paternal concern, "Aren't you worried about not teaching them how to respect deadlines?"

I respond, "It sounds like you're worried about that. I am more concerned with facilitating a space in which students can request extensions as life demands. Deadlines are not of my design, they are of institutional design and things don't deserve respect as humans do. I trust they are doing their absolute best, which should look and feel different than my very best."

The pre-occupation with deadlines reflects instructor constraints and institutional demands for productivity: Tight grading deadlines, the drudge of endless grading generally, and the presumption that a deadline distinguishes a moment of alleged mastery. To lead with faith is to accept the adults in our classrooms are, indeed, doing their very best given their material circumstances.

RELINQUISHING PARENTAL RIGHTS, OR RATHER, WORKING WITH ADULTS

As teachers, we get it. Our teacher-stories often center teaching as being helpful. "You are making a difference," our 3 a.m. brains chant. One teacher blog describes the reasons to become a teacher, noting that "a great teacher wants to help students along [their] path and to play a part in shaping the person they will ultimately become" (Mano 2012). This insight is profound, identifying teaching as a profession accountable to the development of persons. Teachers strive to shape students, and a *great* teacher wants to move students along their path to becoming. But what *kind* of difference emerges when students are animated through rhetorics of infantilization? For us, such mundane enactment centers histories of colonial and racist violence, suturing teachers to parental expectations, and animating pedagogy through disciplinarian means. Instead, love, humility, and trust are three embodiments that may subtly disrupt the paternalistic and violent history of our educational upbringing.

NOTE

1. See also Bernadette Marie Calafell and Robert Gutierrez-Perez, "(Critical) Love is a Battlefield," in *Critical Intercultural Communication Pedagogy*, eds. Ahmet Atay and Satoshi Toyosaki (Lanham, MD: Lexington, 2018), 49–63; Rachel Alicia Griffin, "Navigating the Politics of Identity/Identities and Exploring the Promise of Critical Love," in *Identity Research and Communication*, eds. Nilanjana Bardhan and Mark P. Orbe (Lanham, MD: Lexington, 2012), 207–222.

REFERENCES

Báez, Kristiana L., and Ersula Ore. 2018. "The Moral Imperative of Race for Rhetorical Studies: On Civility and Walking-in-White in Academe." *Communication and Critical/Cultural Studies*, 15, no. 4: 331–336. https://doi.org/10.1080/14791420 .2018.1533989.
Breunic, Mary Breunig. 2005. "Turning Experiential Education and Critical Pedagogy Theory into Praxis." *Journal of Experimental Education*, 28, no. 2: 106–122. https ://doi.org/10.1177/105382590502800205.

Demby, Gene Demby. 2018. "When Boys Can't Be Boys." *National Public Radio*, November 2, 2018. https://www.npr.org/sections/codeswitch/2018/11/02/4175 13631/when-boys-cant-be-boys.

Eshet, Dan. 2015. *Stolen Lives: The Indigenous Peoples of Canada and the Indian Residential Schools*. Brookline, MA: Facing History and Ourselves, n.p.

Fassett, Deanna, and John T. Warren. 2006. *Critical Communication Pedagogy*. Thousand Oaks, CA: Sage Publishing.

Freire, Paulo. 1970. *Pedagogy of the Oppressed*. New York: Continuum.

Griffin, Rachel Alicia. 2012. "Navigating the Politics of Identity/Identities and Exploring the Promise of Critical Love." In *Identity Research and Communication*, edited by Nilanjana Bardhan and Mark P. Orbe, 207–222. Lanham: Lexington.

Halberstam, Jack. 2005. *In a Queer Time and Place: Transgender Bodies, Subcultural Lives*. New York: New York University Press.

Hillier, Harold Chad. 2012. "Foucault and Education: Power, Pedagogy, and Panopticon." *Didaskalia*, 23. https://digitalrepository.trincoll.edu/cgi/viewcontent. cgi?article=1564&context=theses.

Koops, William. 2012. "Infantilization, Civilization, and Child Abuse." *European Journal of Developmental Psychology*, 9, no. 1: 11–20. https://doi.org/10.1080/1 7405629.2011.627189.

LeMaster, Benny. 2018. "Pedagogies of Failure: Queer Communication Pedagogy as Anti Normative." In *Critical Intercultural Communication Pedagogy*, edited by Ahmet Atay and Satoshi Toyosaki, 81–96. Lanham, MD: Lexington Books.

LeMaster, Benny, and Meggie Mapes. 2020. "Embracing the Criminal: Queer and Trans Relational Liberatory Pedagogies." In *Queer Intercultural Communication: The Intersectional Politics of Belonging in and Across Differences*, edited by Shinsuke Eguchi and Bernadette Marie Calafell, 63–78. Lanham: Lexington.

Mano, Michelle. 2012. "Reasons for Becoming a Teacher." *Teach: Make a Difference*, May 2, 2012. https://teach.com/blog/reasons-for-becoming-a-teacher/.

Pratt, Yvonne Poitras, Dustin W. Louie, Aubrey Jean Hanson, and Jacqueline Ottmann. 2018. "Indigenous Education and Decolonization." *Oxford Research Library*.

Rudick, C. Kyle, and Kathryn B. Golsan. 2018. "Civility and White Institutional Presence: An Exploration of White Students' Understanding of Race-Talk at a Traditionally White Institution." *Howard Journal of Communications*, 29, no. 4: 335–352.

Salaita, Steven. 2015. *Uncivil Rites: Palestine and the Limits of Academic Freedom*. Chicago, IL: Haymarket Books.

Yousuf, Shereen, and Bernadette Calafell. 2018. "The Imperative for Examining Anti-Muslim Racism in Rhetorical Studies." *Communication and Critical/Cultural Studies*, 15, no. 4: 312–318. https://doi.org/10.1080/14791420.2018.1533641.

Chapter 3

Empath(olog)ic Pedagogy

An Autoethnography of Health, Class, and the Classroom

Brandi Lawless

My mother's house, where I am forced to move back into from my aunt's home, is under construction. There is a curtain blocking the exposed construction area from the older part of the house that will remain intact. I'm sleeping on a futon that carries the stench of mildew, and the wind is blowing the curtain and the dust it carries toward me.

I have recently been diagnosed with asthma by a school physician while I was trying out for the volleyball team. There is a history of asthma on my dad's side of the family (my father and two paternal sisters have it). I am having my first attack. I feel like my throat is collapsing. I am breathing through a straw. My eyes start to swell from the dust. I have a reconstructed tear duct from a childhood dog bite so any irritation makes water run down my face. I'm also crying. My mother responds, "You're a hypochondriac! I don't want to hear it again. I'm not wasting the fucking money to take you into the emergency room. I don't care what they said at the physical. You faked it. You don't have asthma. You're trying to get attention. Why are you rubbing your eyes? I know you're trying to make it worse so everyone will think I'm a bad mother. Get out of my face."

My mother's boyfriend goes against her wishes and drives me to the emergency room where I was given a breathing treatment and diagnosed with pneumonia. I was also given a prescription for an albuterol inhaler and Singulair, a medication that should improve my asthma and allergies. The prescriptions are never filled. We could neither afford them, nor, in my mother's opinion, was there a need for them. I'm sure this was also a punishment for making her look bad in front of her boyfriend. Yet, at the time, I was asking myself, "Am I a hypochondriac? How would I know?"

***

As a child, I had neither medical insurance nor money for doctor visits, prescriptions, or therapies. When I was ill, I was told I was being a hypochondriac. I now believe this was my mother's coping mechanism to help weed out times I was seriously ill or not. Because of this, every time I thought I was sick or getting sick, I would second guess myself. I suffered at home with Tylenol or some soup. This dismissal now terrorizes my body. I struggle to understand when a "normal" person would/should seek medical intervention, how to use the resources I now have, and how to decode the messages that I received as a child. For example, I rarely make preventative-care appointments because I have it in my head that I am wasting my doctor's time when they can be helping the *real* sick people. I am embarrassed to ask my practitioners health-related questions because they might not take me seriously. I may have serious physical ailments that I have written off as no big deal and wouldn't have thought otherwise had a friend not told me, "Those symptoms are not normal."

I worry that I am not only failing my body, but I am also failing my students. I cannot trust what my body tells me and therefore I cannot trust theirs either. Rather than perpetuate health disparities for lower and working-class students or those marginalized because of their health status, this chapter explores pedagogical possibilities for communicating with students about health. Traditional writing and scholarship have failed to help me explore these intersections or offer an understanding of these embodied epistemologies (i.e., those knowledges that are felt and performed in/through the body) in my work. Thus, I have turned to auto-ethnography, hoping to make sense of how "critical-pedagogical-performative-autoethnography" belongs together and can elucidate otherwise invisible materialities and practices (Johnson-Mardones 2015). This process allows for the systematic recall of emotion, the writing of experiences as stories, and exploration of such experiences as a way to generalize others' experiences (Ellis and Bochner 2000). I use these experiences as fodder for better understanding best pedagogical practices in communicating about mental and physical health with students.

I follow Diana Taylor (2003) in claiming the metatheoretical assumption that performance "is/as." Taylor utilizes this marking as a way to note that the body *is* an epistemology and exists *as* an ontology. In other words, the body itself produces knowledges that cannot be produced by other methods. Embodiment is communication manifested in both everyday, mundane, taken-for-granted performances of self and community as well as height-ened performances in specially bounded communication contexts, such as the classroom. A theorization of the body and lived experience adds to the literature on material conditions of social class, structures that produce class, and psychological reactions and attitudes about social class. As I reflect on these theories of the body and my experiences of health, class, and embodi-ment, several questions come to mind: How do embodied knowledges create a sense-making schema for how we interpret the world? How have those childhood experiences shaped my health for years to come?

I also heed the call by Nainby and Pea (2003) that "we working-class academics speak publicly about our relationship to institutional cultures, that we let our colleagues [and students] know without shame" (27). Following this call, I try to simultaneously make my class background known and make sense of the ways in which that background informs my own understandings of the body as a site of knowledge production and the ways in which I com-municate with students about their own embodied knowledges with regard to mental and physical health. First, I explore the medical industrial complex and its influence on health disparities. Next, I articulate theories of embodi-ment as they relate to health, knowledge, and pedagogy. To clarify these intersections, I offer the concept of *epistemological incongruence*. Finally, I describe the reflexive process educators must undergo in order to develop more empathetic pedagogies. Throughout this chapter, I weave autoethno-graphic reflections as a practice of embodied sensemaking.

(DE)PATHOLOGIZING AS A (POOR) TACTIC

Time and again throughout my childhood, my mother compared me to my Aunt T. Aunt T was in a car accident that left her in severe pain. She had a box surgically placed in her body that emitted electro-pulses to help stop neurological pain. I remember watching other family members roll their eyes when she couldn't walk through the metal detector at the local amusement park, holding up the line. She was spoiling their fun. Her own life was spoiled when she became addicted to pain pills and her drug use later took her life. Nobody in the family believed that Aunt T was really in pain. They all called her a hypochondriac behind her back. Whenever I complained of an ailment, I was told, "Stop being a hypochondriac like your Aunt T. I mean, Jesus, we don't need another one." Regardless of whether or not Aunt T was a hypo-chondriac, she was clearly deeply depressed. But nobody took her seriously enough to be concerned. When my mother found her dead in her bed with empty pill bottles nearby, it was too late to believe her.

***

Those in poverty have long-term health disparities, regardless of whether they achieve social mobility (Cohen et al. 2010; Evans and Cassells 2014). Researchers have found a strong correlation between access to health care and utilization of health services, meaning low-income families without health insurance are less likely to use health services, resulting in long-term health disparities (Andrulis 1998). As a result, lack of affordable health care has long-term effects on the body and the psyche. My experience tells me that this results in communicative coping mechanisms such as minimizing health emergencies or second-guessing symptoms. When you cannot afford medical advice or intervention, you make the best of your situation and reconstruct reality. You are interpellated into discourse that is dominated by the medical-industrial complex (MIC)—a system in which corporate profits are valued over the health and wellbeing of individuals (Relman 1980).

Rather than fight for an equitable system in which everyone has a right to affordable or free healthcare, this reconstructed reality is one in which the poor risk their lives by rationing insulin because they cannot afford the exponential increase to their medication (see for example Altucker 2019). The MIC has given economic and political power to corporations, while severely limiting health agencies of individuals—particularly those who cannot pay to play. All-the-while, the MIC thrives on victim-blaming and deficit thinking (Isbell et al. 2018)—ideologies that assume people in poverty (a) have access to health care but are too lazy, uninformed, or incapable of taking advantage of social services[1] or (b) don't work hard enough to earn a job that comes with health benefits.[2] Thus, private insurance reproduces a status-based hierarchy that influences quality of care and likelihood of seeking medical treatment and prevention (Parsons 1975). Within such a framework, healthcare does not exist as a human right, but instead is earned through hard work—a pull-your-body-up-by-the-bootstraps mentality. Thus, there is no empathy for those who cannot/do not obtain health insurance, regularly visit a provider, and maintain their health through proper usage of medications. These larger social discourses, which limit access to medical care, also challenge the body as a site of knowing.

EPISTEMOLOGICAL INCONGRUENCE AND RESISTANCE

From the ages of five to seventeen, I fanaticized about being a singer. I was good. I made All-District chorus, was a soloist in the vocal jazz ensemble, and played the lead role in *Annie Get Your Gun* as a high school sophomore. By the time senior year rolled around, I noticed my voice changing and so did my instructors. After an audition for a district musical, the person who walked into the audition room after me overheard my choral director say to her co-director, "Something is wrong with her voice. It's too breathy." They weren't wrong. I knew that my voice was changing too quickly for this to be puberty. I was basing my future on my voice and would not take it for granted. I forced my mother to take me to the local Ear, Nose, and Throat doctor. The doctor sprayed a numbing solution into my nose and stuck a camera through my nostril into my throat. They were looking for vocal nodules, but only had basic equipment. The doctor explained, "We think there are nodes but you'll need to see a specialist in Pittsburgh." My mother retorted, "I'm not going to Pittsburgh or to a specialist. You have the camera and you see something, but you aren't telling us. You just want more money!" Despite the doctor's insistence that Pittsburgh would just have better equipment to diagnose the problem, my mother stood firm. We were not going. We never did. Instead, I changed my major and never sang in public again.

***

I have been conditioned to believe that what my body tells me is a lie. I can see that and am trying to reclaim my own epistemologies, but I continue to question myself. I wonder how far I have let these threats to embodied ways of knowing seep into other aspects of my life. To what extent can I really know and resist such discourses? How are these memories and knowledges inter-personally and systematically erased? I find myself battling *epistemological incongruence*—a liminal zone in which my avowed bodily epistemologies do not match ascribed or dictated ways of knowing. Like identity incongruence, when epistemologies do not match those expressed and impressed upon us, confusion and lower self-esteem arise. Think of this as a type of embodied imposter syndrome—second guessing illness because it doesn't fit an under-standing of illness that has been impressed upon us. When described in the context of embodiment, epistemological incongruence is detrimental to the body, feeding misunderstanding and fueling depression, dysmorphia, anxiety, and frustration. To experience epistemological incongruence is to know and not be known. It can fuel projection and displacement of incongruence onto others, despite knowledge that contradicts the reiteration of such harmful discourses.

When my mother told me that I was lying about being sick, even when I knew that I was, I still questioned the extent to which I needed care. As an adult, I second guess myself every time I am sick. I have insurance and don't comprehend where the line is for using it. I constantly worry that I am being one of "those patients" who overuses the system. I ask my partner, "You believe me, right?" and am met with annoyance over the absurdity of my worry. *"Of course, I believe you. Why wouldn't I?"* This has framed the way I interact with students and meet their needs.

When my students tell me they are sick, I know it is possible, but I will question the extent to which it is true and whether or not they need my care and accommodation. My colleagues and I will often regale in tales of the most absurd excuses without documentation: *"So and so won't come to class once a month because she has debilitating cramps. TMI!"* *"If I show up to class sick, then I expect them to make it to class!"* *"I know she can't breathe, but then if you're really THAT sick, why wouldn't you just drop the class?"* We laugh and roll our eyes at the inconvenience this causes us for providing undocumented accommodations. In the back of my mind, I am taken back to a time when I couldn't forgive myself for giving the original doctor's note to my school office for an excused absence, wishing I had it to prove to my sneering classmate that I did indeed have walking pneumonia, which can exist without a debilitating cough. That was/is me. I've been deeply injured by this incongruence and now must ask myself, "What would happen if I break the cycle of epistemological incongruence?"

In addition to epistemological incongruence around physical illness, I am deeply concerned about the way I think about my/others' mental health. Am I imagining this? Am I not strong enough? Do I just want attention? Should I just suck it up? Bernadette Calafell (2017) reminds us that depression is "part of the job description" for academics, particularly at the intersections of race, class, and gender. I, too, know this to be true; yet, this embodied epistemology is challenged by my mother's ghost who continues to argue that depression is a man-made excuse exacerbated and commodified by the pharmaceutical industry.

"You put me in therapy!" This punctuated one of the last times I spoke to my mother before she died of an overdose from self-medicating on pharmaceutical opioids. In her undiagnosed bipolar state, she left me twenty-six voicemails before my cheap Nokia 2003 mailbox was full, all bolstering conspiracy theories that I had fallen into the trap of making "sadness" clinical—a first step to blaming my sorrows on everyone but myself. This was followed by a series of failed therapeutic and psychological experiments, including trials of Zoloft, a generic mood stabilizer, and a counselor who kept calling me "Brenda" instead of my real name. Did these approaches not work because my mother was right—I didn't have depression and anxiety—or had I not found the right solution for my specific body? The incongruence between knowing that my body was improperly functioning and being told from a variety of sources what would "really" fix things, left me feeling isolated and confused. I am embarrassed to admit that I have thought the following things about students when they disclose their mental health status to me:

Do they really have anxiety or do they just not want to do the work?

Why should I give them a deadline extension when it would cause less anxiety to just finish the paper? I know exactly how they feel and yet I did it. If I can, so can they.

Wow, so many students are claiming to have depression and anxiety these days? Do they actually have it or are they just trying to get undue accommodations?

I find myself asking these questions, despite both my personal experience and the data that suggests that "severe" psychological problems have indeed increased for college students over the past two decades (Gallagher 2015, 5).

I am embarrassed because I am participating in discourse that creates and exacerbates epistemological incongruence. I am an active participant in systems of privilege that operate to keep people in their place. It is my whiteness and cisgender, heterosexual privilege that open spaces for me to ignore the incongruence I experienced and project logical fallacies onto others' bodies. It is my whiteness and cis-het privilege that reproduce the same systems that keep me from acknowledging the health needs of myself and my students. I recognize and actively teach about the dismantling of these systems; I so badly want to believe that I am not what I so desperately tried to flee and disavow, but truthfully, I unintentionally reproduce the very discourses that exert(ed) control over my body. I am the system. I am the problem. Can I move beyond this discourse and operate solely from my embodied perspective on health, class, and well-being in my own pedagogies?

PERFORMING (DE)PATHOLOGIZING PEDAGOGIES IN THE CLASSROOM

My mother died in 2009. In the months following her death, I tried to pick up the pieces in my life. I wanted to know how she really died. The toxicology report declared that there were several different drugs in her system, including oxycodone, cocaine, and marijuana, among others. Of course, there were drugs in her system; she was an addict. But, what did she really die from? I could not afford an autopsy. I was gifted the next best thing. . .an appointment with an intuitive (ok, ok, she was a psychic). I needed closure. I gave my mother's name and birthdate while E sat there with her eyes closed, tuning in. Immediately, she could feel my mother's pain. E explained that my mother felt buildup in her liver and an immediate explosion in her brain. E continued to tune into my mother's attitude (I recorded the session):

E: "She has her own rules. She wants everyone to follow by those rules. She is
actually very smart." Yes, and manipulative. I felt affirmed. When I was done
asking about my mother, I asked about my own health.

Me: "My mom always thought she had . . ."

E. "I know she did. But you don't. Try taking a probiotic or eating more
yogurt."

(So, I AM a hypochondriac?)

My mother always thought that she had Crohn's, but refused to be seen
by a doctor. In recent years, I had begun seeing blood in my stool. I wanted
a family medical history, but had none both because my mother had passed
away and she refused to see doctors while she was alive. Before she died,
I urged her to see a doctor. I wanted her to think my health was worth it
enough for her to go. She didn't. I literally had to take the word of a psychic, rather than have my mother go to the doctor to find out if she had this
inheritable disease. I couldn't trust her judgment. I had to start trusting my
own. And, I had to start trusting others' autonomy over their own embodied
knowledges.

***

The personal is pedagogical. The classroom is a context in which my history of communication informs the way I teach and care for students. I
view my students through the lens of my own lived experience. My pedagogical responses to students are also entrenched within a broader discourse
that shapes how class should be performed in academia. As LeCourt and
Napoleone (2011) explain, "Working-class bodies perform in response to
academic spaces in a variety of ways, frequently manifesting in affective
responses that we knew would seem 'unacceptable' in academic contexts
where mind is privileged over body" (81). These affective, or pre-cognitive
embodied responses are first and foremost linked to our pedagogies. Thus,
we must deeply contemplate and try to make sense of the responses before
linking them to those pedagogies that are more cognitively informed. This
reality prompts these scholars to ask, "How did our backgrounds and working-class identities emerge in our teaching, in our academic work, influencing
both in ways we do not completely understand?" Likewise, I ask, how does
epistemological incongruence, steeped in a context of classism, inform my
pedagogies?

When I find myself defaulting to a position that students are making
excuses for why they were absent or why they cannot submit an assignment
on time, I must be reflexive about my own epistemological truths as well as

the research that indicates that students with disabilities or illness (i.e., physical or mental) are already less likely to disclose their health status and are more likely to drop out of school because of real or anticipated lack of faculty accommodations regarding their health status (Greenbaum et al. 1995; Quick et al. 2003). These students often take on the additional burden of negotiating self-disclosure, accommodations, and downplaying their avowed identities in order to save face in the classroom (Barnar-Brak et al. 2010; Corrigan and Matthews 2003).

I am reminded to participate in critical reflection for the purposes of "culturally relevant pedagogy" (Howard 2003, 195). Though his remarks were aimed at white teachers of diverse students, I find the point applicable to issues of social class and health. I, too, must deconstruct the differences that I am encountering with students who have different health experiences. Howard pushes me to reflexively ask: *How frequently and what types of interactions do I have with individuals from different health statuses? How were my perspectives about health and illness shaped by people around me? How were their opinions formed? Am I, or have I ever, harbored prejudiced thoughts about students who advocate for health accommodations? Do I create negative profiles of students who seek accommodations for health or disability status?* While it's difficult to answer these without drawing from my own discounted experiences, I must be open to dialogue that challenges my privilege and resituates my experiences within a broader context.

Critical communication pedagogies are, in part, defined by reflexivity, "the process of exploring how we, as teachers and researchers, create the phenomena we observe, through our assumptions, values, past experiences, language choices, and so on" (Fassett and Warren 2007, 51). Reflexivity has been theorized and extended in a variety of ways. Critical approaches to reflexivity invite the individual to explore context, participate in dialogic engagement with others about positionalities, build an understanding of cultural differences, examine intersectionality, and problematize power and hierarchies—each of which is important in pushing back against the reproduction of epistemological incongruence. Pedagogical responses to student communication about mental and physical health should also incorporate *reflexive caring*—a process of recognizing power, building relationships, rejecting heteronormativity, and promoting vulnerability (Harris and Fortney 2017). This approach is vital in pedagogical spaces that make room for multiple understandings of health in that reflexive caring is projected both inward and outward. Caring for students' embodied realities can also reaffirm embodied ways of knowing for the instructor who experiences epistemological incongruence and call out the ways in which we "socially prioritize" particular identities and experiences to which we assign power and privilege (Harris and Fortney 2017, 22).

Moreover, pedagogy is informed by positionalities. In the process of reflexivity, I must contemplate not only my experiences growing up in poverty with a single mother, but also how those experiences always already exist in my white female body. Whiteness both makes my lower-class background less visible (Lawless 2012) and allows for a heightened level of agency in responding to students' needs and accommodation requests. My projection of epistemological incongruence around issues of health and mental well-being are both a response to my perceived powerlessness over my own embodied knowledges and an enactment of white authority. I must challenge this enactment of authority over students as a way to reclaim my own sense of embodied knowing and acknowledge students who are risking their own understandings of themselves in disclosing information about their physical and mental health status. I am also deeply reflective of the fact that I can speak from my position of a white woman who is still affected by her lower-class upbringing, and still not know how epistemological incongruence is experienced by queer, trans, and differently abled bodies. I will never know what epistemological incongruence looks like at the intersections of class and race for a woman of color. These realities in themselves should challenge the way I communicate with my students about health accommodations.

To assume that students do not understand their own bodies and to imply that the instructor knows what is best for said students, reproduces the harmful practices of *biopedagogies*—an ironic practice that draws from a "modern subject who believes that her body is a site of agency, freedom, and empowerment" but nonetheless reproduces Foucauldian articulations that individuals are "increasingly subject to control, surveillance, and regulation" (Rail and Jette 2015, 328). I should not be the arbiter of such knowledge and at the same time should create space for agency that exists outside of the limited discourse of accommodations. The classroom should be a space where students are free to communicate about how their bodies are limited by the constraints of classroom discourse and can add to the broader discourses about who can access education. These bodies and subsequent knowledges should not be regulated by me, regardless of their (albeit differing) experiences with health subjugation and the inflection of a lower-class background. Biopedagogies are fueled by rampant individualism, as is the notion, "If I did it, then you can too!" and should be countered through deep reflexivity.

Finally, depathologizing pedagogies manifest through deep connection with students. Building individual relationships with my students establishes a sense of trust, affirmation, and empathy that dissolves the need to question sincerity and motive. Understanding the *context* in which students enter our classroom affirms individual knowledges and minimizes epistemological incongruence. Research also shows that relational closeness (immediacy) between students and instructors increases satisfaction and classroom performance (Witt et al. 2004). This approach can be limited for colleagues who teach classes with rosters approaching and exceeding 100 students. The neoliberalization of the university infringes upon our responsibility to humanize students, as opposed to treating them like a number or cog in the educational machine. Such structures create a limitation for depathologizing pedagogies and may exacerbate epistemological incongruence.

CONCLUSION

I am slowly coming to terms with my body, my class, my health, and my heart. I want to feel "normal" when it comes to understanding and using health systems instead of feeling a shade of imposter syndrome in yet another aspect of my life. My understanding of health is akin to dysmorphia. I'm confused. I'm unsettled. This reality should fuel my desire for students to feel healthy in my classroom. And, yet, it does the opposite. In theorizing epistemological incongruence, I hope to engage a set of reflexive questions and actions that improve students' relationships to the classroom, with instructors, and with their own bodies. Empowerment in the classroom cannot reject students' knowledge of their health needs. Rather, I must make a stronger effort to challenge the discourses of distrust around health (both physical and mental) and accommodation. I have little to gain from my disbelief but much to offer and learn from in a more deeply reflexive pedagogy.

NOTES

1. For example, in his comments about why the Affordable Care Act should be repealed, Republican Congressman Roger Marshall claimed the poor "just don't want health care" and later suggested they are more preoccupied with having the best iPhone. See Phillips (2017).

2. Although many politicians have asserted that there are too many able-bodied people on Medicaid that don't work, "only 7.5 percent of Medicaid's non-elderly, non-disabled adult beneficiaries aren't working, and can't cite school, family, or physical ailment as a reason." See Spross (2018).

REFERENCES

Altucker, Ken. 2019. "Struggling to Stay Alive: Rising Insulin Prices Cause Diabetics to Go to Extremes." *USA Today*, March 27. https://www.usatoday.com/in-depth/news/50states/2019/03/21/diabetes-insulin-costs-diabetics-drug-prices-increase/3196757002/.

Brandi Lawless

Andrulis, Dennis P. 1998. "Access to Care is the Centerpiece in the Elimination of Socioeconomic Disparities in Health." *Annals of Internal Medicine*, 5, no. 129: 412–416.

Barnard-Brak, Lucy, DeAnn Lechtenberger, and William Y. Lan. 2010. "Accommodation Strategies of College Students with Disabilities." *The Qualitative Report*, 2, no. 15: 411–429.

Calafell, Bernadette Marie. 2017. "When Depression is in the Job Description #realacademicbios." *Departures in Critical Qualitative Research*, 1, no. 6: 5–10. https://doi.org/10.1525/dcqr.2017.6.1.5.

Cohen, Sheldon, Denise Janicki-Deverts, Edith Chen, and Karen A. Matthews. 2010. "Childhood Socioeconomic Status and Adult Health." *Annual of New York Academy of Science*, 1186: 37–55. https://doi.org/10.1111/j.1749-6632.2009.0533 4.x.

Corrigan, Patrick W., and Alicia K. Matthews. 2003. "Stigma and Disclosure: Implications for Coming Out of the Closet." *Journal of Mental Health*, 12, no. 3: 235–248.

Ellis, Carolyn, and Art Bochner. 2000. "Autoethnography, Personal Narrative, Reflexivity." In *Handbook of Qualitative Research* (2nd ed.), edited by Norman K. Denzin and Yvonna S. Lincoln, 733–768. London: Sage Publications.

Evans, Gary W., and Rochelle C. Cassells. 2014. "Childhood Poverty, Cumulative Risk Exposure, and Mental Health in Emerging Adults." *Clinical Psychological Science*, 3, no. 2: 287–296. https://doi.org/10.1177/2167702613501496.

Fassett, Deanna L., and John T. Warren. 2007. *Critical Communication Pedagogy.* Thousand Oaks, CA: Sage.

Gallagher, Robert P. 2015. "National Survey of College Counseling Centers 2014." *The International Association of Counseling Services.* http://d-scholarship.pitt.edu /28178/.

Greenbaum, Beth, Stephen Graham, and William Scales. 1995. "Adults with Learning Disabilities: Educational and Social Experiences During College." *Exceptional Children*, 5, no. 6: 460–472.

Harris, Kate Lockwood, and James Michael Fortney. 2017. "Performing Reflexive Caring: Rethinking Reflexivity Through Trauma and Disability." *Text and Performance Quarterly*, 1, no. 27: 20–34. https://doi.org/10.1080/10462937.2016 .1273543.

Howard, Tyrone C. 2003. "Culturally Relevant Pedagogy: Ingredients for Critical Teacher Reflection." *Theory into Practice*, 3, no. 42: 195–202. https://doi.org/10.1 207/s15430421tip4203_5.

Isbell, Janet Kesterson, Julie C. Baker, Lisa Zagumny, Amber Spears, and Alice Camuti. 2018. "Maintaining the Myth: How Tennessee Perpetuates Deficit Thinking About Recipients of Government-Sponsored Health Care." *Journal of Poverty*, 22, no. 1: 23–41.

Johnson-Mardones, Daniel F. 2015. "Understanding Critical-Pedagogical-Performative Autoethnography." *Cultural Studies ↔ Critical Methodologies*, 3, no. 15: 190–191. https://doi.org/10.1177/1532708614562884.

Lawless, Brandi. "More Than White: Locating an Invisible Class Identity." In *Our Voices: Essays in Culture, Ethnicity, and Communication* (5th ed.), edited by

Alberto Gonzalez, Marsha Houston, and Victoria Chen, 247–253. New York, NY: Oxford.

LeCourt, Donna, and Anna Rita Napoleone. 2011. "Teachers With(out) Class: Transgressing Academic Social Space Through Working-Class Performances." *Pedagogy*, 1, no. 11: 81–108.

Nainby, Keith, and John B. Pea. 2003. "Immobility in Mobility: Narratives of Social Class, Education, and Paralysis." *Educational Foundations*, 3, no. 17: 9–36.

Parsons, Talcott. 1975. "The Sick Role and the Role of the Physician Reconsidered." *The Millbank Memorial Fund Quarterly: Health and Society*, 3, no. 53: 257–278. https://doi.org/doi:10.2307/3349493.

Phillips, Kristine. 2017. "The Poor 'Just Don't Want Health Care': Republican Congressman Faces Backlash Over Comments." *Washington Post*, March 9. https://www.washingtonpost.com/news/powerpost/wp/2017/03/09/the-poor-just-dont-want-health-care-republican-congressman-faces-backlash-over-comments/.

Quick, Don, Jean Lehmann, and Terry Deniston. 2003. "Opening Doors for Students with Disabilities on Community College Campuses: What Have We Learned? What Do We Still Need to Know?" *Community College Journal of Research & Practice*, 27: 815–827.

Rail, Geneviève, and Shannon Jette. 2015. "Reflections on Biopedagogies and/of Public Health: On Bio-Others, Rescue Missions, and Social Justice." *Cultural Studies ↔ Critical Methodologies*, 5, no. 15: 327–336. https://doi.org/doi:10.1177/1532708615611703.

Relman, Arnold S. 1980. "The New Medical-Industrial Complex." *New England Journal of Medicine*, 17, no. 303: 963–970. https://doi.org/doi:10.1056/NEJM198010233031703.

Spross, Jeff. 2018. "Don't Make the Poor Work for Healthcare." *The Week*, January 9. https://theweek.com/articles/747297/dont-make-poor-work-health-care.

Taylor, Diana. 2003. *The Archive and the Repertoire: Performing Cultural Memory in the Americas*. Durham, NC: Duke University.

Witt, Paul L., Lawrence R. Wheeless, and Mike Allen. 2004. "A Meta-Analytical Review of the Relationship Between Teacher Immediacy and Student Learning." *Communication Monographs*, 2, no. 71: 184–207. https://doi.org/doi:10.1080/036452042000228054.

Chapter 4

"Bad Hombre" in the Classroom

Pedagogical Politics of Performing "Brown Man" in a Conservative Time

Antonio T. De La Garza and
Andrew R. Spieldenner

"I almost killed a white person today," referencing one of my favorite lines from a study of racial battle fatigue as I slip into his office and close the door (Smith et al. 2009). He laughs and shakes his head, "It must be Thursday, what happened?" I shake my head and we begin a ritualized dragging of the politics of toxic whiteness that opens up space for reflecting and healing. I don't know what I would do without these brief but crucial reprieves from the institutionalized pressure to perform civility and harmlessness.

We are two men of color teaching at a Hispanic Serving Institution that has a low density of faculty of color. In 2018, the California State University system served 481,210 students: more than half of those students were people of color, yet "across the 23 campuses, the median ratio of Latin[x] students to Latin[x] tenure line faculty is 200.3 to 1. This is in comparison to 14.3 white students per white tenure line faculty" (California Faculty Association 2019). These demographic inequities persist and present particular challenges to faculty of color whose labor in this regard is often invisible (University of Oregon 2017). Research on cultural taxation demonstrates that faculty of color experience greater service burdens (Joseph and Hirschfield 2011); and students from marginalized communities ask more of scholars of color than they do of white faculty, and scholars of color typically step up (Canton 2013). We teach in the same department and have found that our burden is lessened by being able to create a space of recognition and understanding for each other. We also recognize that our situation is unique. Due to horrendously low numbers of men of color in tenure track lines, scholars of color in tenure track positions often find themselves alone, isolated, and without proper support (Nadal 2019).

We started working at this public university in Southern California a year apart from each other (Fall 2016 and Fall 2017, respectively): with the election of Donald Trump as the forty-fifth president of the United States looming in the background. His framing of immigrants, Latinx communities, migration and the US/Mexico border grew and has become entrenched in public discourse (Mendoza-Denton 2017). This is the backdrop to our work: in 2016, in the last Presidential debate with Hillary Clinton, Donald Trump insisted on "building the wall" because "we have some bad hombres here and we're going to get them out" (CNN 2016). The "bad hombre" taps into tropes of Latinx threats that include "the construction of 'illegal aliens' as criminals, . . . the Mexican invasion and *reconquista* (reconquest) of the United States, an unwillingness to learn English and integrate into U.S. society, out-of-control fertility, and threats to national security" (Chavez 2013, 25). Since Trump took power—and continues to be given support from a far Right religious base, legislators, media and the wealthy, the larger public seems to have adopted many of his rhetorical devices and discursive intrusions (Theye and Melling 2018). The context where people are brought into higher education also becomes significant in how people navigate and negotiate the space with colleagues and students. The "bad hombre" circulates as a way to frame us in the university and classroom. In this chapter, we offer our experiences and analysis through narrative; we purposefully blur the "I" and "We" in our writing to play with these experiences as individual and communal.

Her eyes roll when I speak, at faculty meetings my contributions are followed by snorts and moans. After two years of trying to head off the brewing conflict, I do not back down, I respond to these microaggressions, "what is your problem with me?" Ever since my first month at this job this full professor has been on me about my performance of masculinity, admonishing me for even the behavior of other male faculty members. When I ask what's wrong with it she replies that I, "don't make myself vulnerable enough." As if someone like me, a man of color who has spent the last twenty years in higher education owes her my vulnerability. The hostility of academic spaces to men of color is well documented, and I have lived it.[1] *Between three degrees and 4 years at a tenure track job I've experienced racial battle fatigue, hyper-sexualization, the Latinx threat narrative, and racial profiling on campus. I've been accused of being lazy, of being too ambitious, of being cowardly, of being overly confrontational, of being angry, and of being violent. Once again, I am required to justify myself to a white person.*

At a forced social happy hour—since named the "Unhappy Hour"—this same senior colleague picks a fight with me. I ask her to stop rolling her eyes, she responds with "stop treating me like I'm just another white woman,

I've done my work." As it gets heated, she taunts "what are you going to do, beat me up?" I'm confused by this shift: she has a long history of critical work on race in our discipline but is unable to reflexively look at the power in our interactions. She is a full professor who continues to undermine me. I recognize the irony of being hired into a university and department whose mission is social justice but repeating the marginalization of people based on race, gender and sexuality. I put my hands on the table and look down. A hand reaches out in support, another arm wraps around my shoulder. Two colleagues of color showing support the only way they feel safe to do so. Her appalling racism is clear, but none of us have tenure. What would you do? Do I have the right to be angry? Apparently not, I'm not allowed to access this emotion anymore due to race and gender.

This chapter is an attempt to intervene in the structures of toxic whiteness that alienates and abuses bad hombres by sharing our experiences of Brownness in the university at this particular time and place. The chapter will proceed in three parts. The first part consists of a description of our subject position as bad hombres and our particular pedagogical projects. The second section explores the pathologizing and stigmatizing discourses that produce feelings of precarity and racial battle fatigue, and how toxic whiteness informs our relationship to our students, peers, and the university. The third section is about the counternarratives and tactics that we employ to subvert white supremacist discourse and find power and healing in owning our identity as bad hombres.

THE BROWN SUBJECT

As professors, we all have an opening to set the tone of the semester. Mine is: I'm here at this school because I believe in what it's about. Seventy percent of you are first-generation, 50% are Pell Grant eligible, 50% of you are Latinx, and all of you have been underserved in K–12 (Yasso et al. 2009). You're probably here because you are trying to break out of the cycle of poverty and miseducation. I am going to teach you how to think and write with the voice of authority, and to understand how elites play this game. I am going to be hard on you because you have to learn a lot in these four years.

I'm a bad hombre; I am not afraid of naming and confronting racial microaggressions. I insist on being referred to as Dr. or Professor, I refuse to accept late work, I take attendance, assign homework on the first day, and dare my students to drop. I also refuse to pretend that I am anything but a flawed, complicated, and real person in the classroom. In addition to learning about my field, my students also get a lot of stories about the mistakes that I have made. At one time I was a terrible student, I partied too much, was

*academically ineligible to attend my first university and had to go to commu-
nity college to earn my way back into a university. I believe that in order to
be an effective teacher I have to be part of the community I serve. To me that
means publishing with my students, organizing politically with my students,
attending their weddings, and even the occasional quince. It also means
acknowledging and speaking from my lived experience. My lived experience
as an activist, student of color and educator taught me that, "we must always
attempt to lift as we climb."(Davis 2011, 12) I push my students because I
want to help them survive in a system that pushes out so many. At the same
time being unapologetic about confronting whiteness and being close to your
community invites precarity.*

Being a teacher is often a performance, not just a matter of transmitting
information (Calafell 2007). Instructor pedagogy emerges as the framework
that determines roles and power of all participants—including students, teachers, school institutions, and materials covered (Hsu 2019). Communication
patterns are integral in reinforcing positions, as identities and roles are constantly affirmed or corrected. When the professor in a college setting also has
a socially marginalized identity, this performance becomes complicated by
student expectations and institutional support (Spieldenner and Eguchi 2020).
As tenure-track faculty of color, we are conscious of both the privilege of
being tenure-track academics and the precarity of being pre-tenure faculty of
color. We utilize critical communication pedagogy to engage the university
and our students in ways that recognize and challenge hierarchical modes of
power.

Critical communication pedagogy centers issues of power, identity, and
culture in the classroom. As a process, critical communication pedagogy
deals directly with issues of marginalization and power in the syllabus,
assignments, class conversations, and interactions. Within this framework,
knowledge is co-constituted among all parties, and position is acknowledged
and reflected on regularly (Fassett and Warren 2007). It assumes that communication is a process that reifies identities, roles, and power. Through critical communication pedagogy, we pay attention to the "body, where identity
meets the politics, the assumptions, the policing of the other, remains the site
of power's enactment, where disciplinary mechanisms play out in our flesh,
our hearts, and our minds" (Fassett and Warren 2007, 59). We are both cisgender men of color who are easily raced as brown in the United States.

As a racial assignation, brownness is a useful category in the bad hombres
discourse. Black/white racial dialectics have limited use in determining how
bad hombres are constructed and circulated in the university. Hiram Pérez
offers brownness as a "category . . . to mark a position of essential itinerancy
relative to naturalized, positivist classes such as white, black, Asian" (2015,
103). Pérez situates the ambiguity of brownness firmly within the political

domains of colonialism and globalization, acknowledging that brown bodies have multiple currencies as servant and threat within this scope. Brownness is not apolitical. It is a strategic intervention in a restrictive racial discourse. We use brownness as an intentionally ambiguous category to understand, perform, and critique identity in the university, especially in conservative times where brownness is a signifier of threat connecting multiple racial, ethnic, religious, sexual, and gender groups.

I understand brownness as a convention where I am both rewarded and often misunderstood. I was a go-go boy while I was in my Masters program. One night, I was approached at the now-defunct Latinx gay club Circus and asked if I wanted to be a dancer. I thought "in 10 years, no one will ask you to dance in a gay club" so I agreed to do it. Over the course of the year, I performed at every Latinx gay night in Los Angeles and Long Beach. I worked out every day, bought ridiculously skimpy underwear, did a lot of drugs, and developed a core group of friends amongst the dancers. In the university where normative identities are rewarded, these acts—working as a go-go boy, doing drugs, being part of gay nightclub scene—constitute a bad hombre. I am a bad hombre.

Willy and I worked four to five nights a week together. Short, muscular, tatted up and popular in the circuit, he showed me the ropes and took me underwear shopping. He taught me how to get more tips out of men, and how to identify which guys were never going to tip. One Sunday, after a long weekend dancing, we all met at Willy's for a BBQ. Willy's mother made pupusas, and his cranky boyfriend manned the grill. His roommate and I flirted as we always did in social situations, discomfiting some of the other guys who wanted a shot at one or both of us. After several beers, Willy and the other guys circled me and decided to have an intervention. Willy said, "we want you to stop telling people you're half-Asian and White. It's okay to admit you're Mexican."

I offer this story as a way into my misinterpellation as Latinx. I also want to point out that it has been a consistent mis-reading and performance for much of my life. Within the go-go boy world, I was constantly booked for Latinx nights and part of my success was with the deployment of a purposeful ambiguously brown performance. We invoke James Martel's notion of misinterpellation here. Playing off Althusser's interpellation—where subjects and identities are formed in the context of communication, Martel explores what happens when a "people respond to perceived calls (calls to freedom, calls to sacrifice, calls to justice, calls to participation, calls to identity) that are not meant for them, and how the fact that they show up anyway can cause politically radical forms of subversion" (2017, 4). Institutions and people gain power through naming and categorizing people in certain ways which limit our perception of what is possible, changeable, and disruptable.

In the classroom setting, this serves as a bridge to students who see them-selves reflected in their own brown skin and dark hair. They never ask where I am from: only the white students do. The brown ones have gone so long without an instructor that looks like them that they are hungry for it. I do not respond to the student queries about my race. Rather, I tell them their questions say more about them than it does about me. I resist the easy pull of clarification. I make a gesture of my brownness in the classroom. Juana María Rodríguez notes ". . . gestures are always relational; they form con-nections between different parts of our bodies; they cite other gestures; they extend the reach of the self into the space between us; they bring into being the possibility of a 'we'" (2014, 2). I want my students to feel seen and heard, no matter what the subject material is so I gesture to them through pedagogy. I want them to see from my pedagogical choices that we are in commu-nity by bringing in examples from African American, Latinx, Asian Pacific American, Native American, global, queer and feminist contexts to explicate communication phenomenon. When a student asks me how he's supposed to watch a film in Spanish for the class, I pause until he realizes the films would have subtitles. Then I jokingly reply "learn Spanish." The class and this stu-dent laugh; the Spanish-speaking students snap an "ok" in being affirmed. I refuse easy boundaries of us/them; I want my students to experience a disrup-tion in the educational system that attempts to indoctrinate them into believ-ing in systems of power and knowledge that privilege only a certain kind of knowing, where rote learning is prized or who can read the most knows best. What kind of analysis can their experience, culture or embodied knowledge provide? I invite them to fathom what feels wrong or right and explore that.

TIRED OF THREATS/BEING THREATENING

We work and teach in an environment where brown men are configured as "bad hombres," meaning threatening to social norms and politeness. Where this discourse is racialized, then, sex becomes part of this danger. We are read as threats that must be policed and controlled to ensure that white normative comfort and civility are protected. This means that whenever we interact with white women we must be aware that whiteness has constructed us as something to be feared and that patriarchy has constructed white women as possessions that must be protected from us. In her essay "Reflections on Race and Sex," bell hooks argues that the maintenance of white supremacy partially relies on the construction of the black male body as threatening, particularly to white women. This construction justifies enslavement or incar-ceration by the state in order to protect innocent, defenseless, white women. The construction is both rooted in patriarchal notions of female inferiority, and racist assumptions of hostility and threatening sexuality. hooks writes, "Mainstream white supremacist media make it appear that a black menace to societal safety is at large and that control, repression, and violent domination are the only ways to address this problem" (1994, 231). She continues, "[this construction of the black male] is also about the overwhelming desperate longing black men have to sexually violate the bodies of white women" (229). While the bad hombre exists at a different social valence than African American men, we argue that the signifier of the bad hombre similarly cites embedded cultural narratives of MS13 gang bangers, Mexican rapists, and hyper sexuality to channel fear and white resentment into political power. However, the paranoid fantasy of the Latinx rapist does not stop at the border or the ballot box. Instead these tropes become part of the cultural narrative that stick to men of color inside of the academy.

In my time at CSUSM I have found myself misinterpellated as both a sexual object and sexual predator, sometimes simultaneously. Even though the image circulated for nearly a week, I wasn't aware of it until a group of female students approached me after class. They appeared nervous, I had a feeling this was going to be a difficult conversation, but I had no idea it was going to be about me. "Excuse us professor, we, um, think there is something you should see." I ask what and they hedge, one tells me it could be a joke, one can't make eye contact, one just sighs and hands me her phone. The image reminded me of Baywatch, my head, photoshopped onto a topless male body against a beach backdrop. They are quick to tell me they had nothing to do with it. One of them asks me quite directly, "how does it make you feel?" They pause, waiting for an answer. In this moment, I find myself reliving from the outside my cis-performance of masculinity. Even as I continue to negotiate between my attraction and close intimate relationships with men, my sport, Brazilian jiu jitsu which has taught me to appreciate my and other male bodies. In public I benefit from my conformity to normative expectations of gender. At the same time, I am keenly aware of how race and gender intersect in my experience, moving between privileged and stereotyped depending on context, sometimes multiple times a day. I let out a sigh, "embarrassed, and disrespected?" By the way they all look at the ground, it was the answer they were afraid of. They tell me that the image was airdropped in another professor's class, a large lecture of 135 students. They rush to tell me that they don't think it's ok, and my professor persona slips. We talk about hypersexualization, racism, and workplace harassment. I find myself thinking they probably know much more about this sort of thing than I do. I love them for having my back. I am embarrassed by this situation and concerned about the potential impact this event could have on my classroom environment. I contacted my Dean and let her know about the image because I was afraid of rumors spreading about students having nudes of me on their phone.

My Dean and university were supportive and took steps to intervene. However, this type of harassment functions synergistically with the "Mexican rapist" trope to undermine my legitimacy in the workspace by making it appear that this attention is my fault. Even before the incident of the cropped picture, a group of white female students referred to me as the "department daddy" referencing the BDSM trope of the Daddy Dom. Again the inter-section of race and gender script my gruffness, dad bod and graying hair as a particular fetish. Rather than discourage such discourse, I have had colleagues and co-workers use the term Daddy to refer to me, comment on how "popular I am with the ladies," and even going so far as to ask me why female students so heavily outnumber male students in my classroom (as if I have any power to determine who enrolls in my class). This hypersexual narrative that I have done nothing to encourage has even led senior female colleagues to suggest to each other that they "need to keep an eye on me."

For several weeks after the image was circulated, many of my students seemed to be intentional about making overtures of support. Only one ever mentioned the image directly, she wanted me to know that she was taking steps to "interrupt that shit, because it's immature and hypocritical." The conversations about my body and my sexuality continue but I've learned that there are colleagues and students who speak up for me when I am not present, and I've tried to be more attuned to the ways that race, power and sexuality operate in my workplace. The bad hombre is a signature that is firmly attached to my body; it is not a frame I get to escape. Rather, the bad hombre produces a network of stereotypes, significations, and expectations that contextualize how my actions and words will be interpreted. However, like all structures of meaning the bad hombre holds room for play. I expect that learning to take ownership of the signifier, how to make it, bend it, and break it is the most affirming and restive tactic.

This hope for a better future is embodied in Ioanide's description of the ethical witness, "identifies and challenges the logic of discipline, punishment, and pleasurable spectatorship on which the projects of racism and sexism depend. S/he dis-identifies with forms of power that necessitate others' deni-gration" (2007, 21–22). By identifying and criticizing acts of white suprema-cist violence, teaching can move beyond the realm of the academic and into a politically useful tool that creates challenges to white supremacist institu-tions of power. We talk about our pedagogy with our colleagues: how they teach and how they assess various learning objectives. Assessment is another vehicle where brown bodies are disciplined. We try to build other ways of demonstrating competence than the dreaded thirty-five-page research paper that privileges a certain kind of learning and voice. We want our students to feel emboldened by taking risks and learning, building on the knowledges they already have through their survival. This means repeating instructions in multiple ways and allowing that our syllabus description may not be clear to students who were not raised by middle-class college-educated parents. We encourage open dialogue in class including conflict with us. We use the platform to break down academic concepts into everyday relatable notions that they may experience. Students should not need a Ph.D. to understand concepts we discuss in class: we see our role as a professor to co-create knowledge with the students.

BREAKING BAD

I watch him as a professor and marvel at the ways that he is disciplinarian and coach to his students. He succeeds at a formality I will never have. I am the messy professor, who will talk about sex and drugs and mistakes. I try to make a space for students to explore identity formation and choices, but I question if my unorthodox style works (Spieldenner and Booker 2020). By comparison, he performs "professor" in a way that encourages his students' hard work. When he recognizes their improvement, they glow. He strives to make them better warriors in a world that will constantly undermine most of them. When I visit his office, he often has a student in his office, trying to clarify his feedback so they can become better readers and writers. Sometimes there are tears. He has a box of tissues on his desk.

The bad hombre has become a modern trope about brown men. The way that we are interpellated within this trope—aggressive, stupid, criminal and rapists—is problematic. The bad hombre is also a way of connecting to other brown students who face similar readings in the US society. We demonstrate how to manage and even thrive in white supremacist institutions. As people of color, we have found a way to survive by being comfortable in the conflict. We hold tenure-track jobs in an increasingly tenuous academic environment; we build friendships rather than compete with each other for what little resources are available; we work to shift the narrative for others like us.

Our students have particular pedagogical needs. When interviewing potential faculty, we ask about diversity and they often reply with similar phrases—"I believe in the importance of diversity," "my classroom is inclusive," "I want every student to feel accepted"—without giving practical ways they expand or restructure the classroom. How does one build courses that meet the needs of first-generation, majority students of color? How does one build a classroom where students of differing capacities and resources are supported? Have you ever taught students whose second (or third) language is English and how did you adapt feedback? Are you deliberate in identifying students who are less comfortable in participation and strategizing mechanisms for them to participate? Our processes are different: one encourages discipline, skill, and confidence as a way to equip students with the challenges ahead; the other disrupts what students take for granted as norms in order to transform their vision of the world and their place in it.

We believe that part of our role is to open up possibilities, to envision a world where they are not always interpellated in the ways that they have become accustomed. Misinterpellation is a politic that can work in an anarchistic way. Rather than invest in liberal universalizing norms of capitalism and success, misinterpellation offers political moments in the daily life where power is disrupted. Misinterpellation offers confusion, delight, and potential wonder as the rules do not work so well, where chains and systems of surveillance are revealed as looser than expected. The retail worker who lives check-to-check in a world where malls are slowly disappearing goes to college and is identified "smart" for the first time. In our classrooms, she is not seen as "dead end" or "entry-level." Rather she has a moment where she is meant to see possibilities. What does she do? What can she do next? Martell notes, "[s]eeing that resistance is, in fact, constant and ubiquitous helps us to see that the power and authority of states and other institutions under liberalism are much weaker and more tenuous than they appear" (2017, 13). Institutional and discursive powers are not as all-encompassing as they would like us to believe.

I slip into his office, to once more about to begin my account of the weekly, slights, aggressions, and outrages, when I notice that brown men occupy every single surface and wall. They come from a range of demographics but all of them share the characteristic of being brown and shy. They are laughing, teasing each other and talking about basketball. They seem so relaxed and alive. In my time at a HSI I have come to understand that brown men who appear disengaged and sit silently in my classroom are the ones who escaped the school to prison pipeline by making themselves small. I shake my head in wonder at his ability to draw them out. I think he does this because he's a bad hombre. The way he is misinterpellated means that he has learned to cope and thrive in the presence of stigma. As a result he is very good at making people feel safe. One of the men asks me about the difference between great players and great coaches, I respond with something half-baked and the conversation continues. The daily outrages fade into the back of my mind, the wounds close a bit and I remember why I am a teacher.

NOTE

1. People of color are highly surveilled in academia by their white counterparts, see, for example, Andrew R. Spieldenner and Shinsuke Eguchi, "Different Sameness: Queer Autoethnography and Coalition Politics," *Cultural Studies Critical Methodologies*, 20, no. 2 (2020): 137–138. At the intersection of race and gender,

men of color are often looked at as sexually desirable and a threat to the community. For hyersexualization, see Hiram Pérez, *A Taste for Brown Bodies: Gay Modernity and Cosmopolitan Desire* (New York and London: New York University Press, 2015), 25–30. For racial battle fatigue, see Antonio De La Garza, "A Critical Eulogy for Joaquin Luna: Mindful Racism as an Intervention to End Racial Battle Fatigue," in *Racial Battle Fatigue: Insights from the Front Line of Social Justice Avocacy*, edited by Jennifer L. Martin (Santa Barbara, CA: Praeger, 2015), 183–185. For the trope of the Mexican gangster, see Norma Mendoza-Denton, "Bad Hombres: Images of Masculinity and the Historical Consciousness of US-Mexico Relations in the Age of Trump," *HAU: Journal of Ethnographic Theory*, 7, no. 1 (2017): 425–427 and Leo R. Chavez, *The Latino Threat: Constructing Immigrants, Citizens, and the Nation* (Palo Alto: Stanford University Press, 2013), 25.

REFERENCES

Calafell, Bernadette M. 2007. "Mentoring and Love: An Open Letter." *Cultural Studies <-> Critical Methodologies*, 7, no. 4: 425–441.

California Faculty Association. 2019. "Continuing the Conversation on Cultural Taxation." *California Faculty Association*. Last modified April 24, 2019. https://www.calfac.org/headline/continuingconversation-cultural-taxation.

Canton, Cecil. 2013. "The "Cultural Taxation" of Faculty of Color in the Academy." *California Faculty Magazine*, December 9–10.

Chavez, Leo R. 2013. *The Latino Threat: Constructing Immigrants, Citizens, and the Nation*. Palo Alto: Stanford University Press.

CNN. 2016. "Donald Trump: We Need to Get Out 'bad hombres.'" *YouTube.com*. Last modified October 29, 2016. https://www.youtube.com/watch?v=Aneeacsv NwU.

Davis, Angela. 2011. *Women, Culture & Politics*. New York, NY: Vintage.

De La Garza, Antonio. 2015. "A Critical Eulogy for Joaquin Luna: Mindful Racism as an Intervention to End Racial Battle Fatigue," in *Racial Battle Fatigue: Insights from the Front Line of Social Justice Avocacy*, edited by Jennifer L. Martin, 177–190. Santa Barbara, CA: Praeger.

Eguchi, Shinsuke, and Mary Jane Collier. 2018. "Critical Intercultural Mentoring and Allying: A Continuing Struggle for Change in the Academy." *Departures in Critical Qualitative Research*, 7, no. 2: 49–71.

Fassett, Deanna L., and John T. Warren. 2007. *Critical Communication Pedagogy*. Thousand Oaks: Sage Publications.

hooks, bell. 1994. *Feminism Is for Everybody: Passionate Politics*. Boston: South End Press.

Hsu, Stephanie. 2019. "Notes on a Pedagogy of Debility." *QED: A Journal in GLBTQ Worldmaking*, 6, no. 3: 81–87.

Ioanide, Paula. 2007. "The Story of Abner Louima: Cultural Fantasies, Gendered Racial Violence, and the Ethical Witness." *Journal of Haitian Studies*, 13, no. 1: 4–26.

Joseph, Tiffany D., and Laura E. Hirschfield. 2011. "'Why Don't You Get Somebody New to Do It?' Race and Cultural Taxation in the Academy." *Ethnic and Racial Studies*, 34, no. 1: 121–141.

Martel, James R. 2017. *The Misinterpellated Subject*. Durham: Duke University Press.

Mendoza-Denton, Norma. 2017. "Bad Hombres: Images of Masculinity and the Historical Consciousness of US-Mexico Relations in the Age of Trump." *HAU: Journal of Ethnographic Theory*, 7, no. 1: 423–432.

Nadal, Kevin. 2019. "Queering and Browning the Pipeline for LGBTQ Faculty of Color in the Academy: The Formation of the LGBTQ Scholars of Color National Network." *Journal of Critical Thought and Praxis*, 8, no. 2: 1–19.

Pérez, Hiram. 2015. *A Taste for Brown Bodies: Gay Modernity and Cosmopolitan Desire*. New York and London: New York University Press.

Rodríguez, Juana Maria. 2014. *Sexual Futures, Queer Gestures, and Other Latina Longings*. New York and London: New York University Press.

Smith, William A., Tara J. Yosso, and Daniel G. Solórzano. 2006. "Challenging Racial Battle Fatigue on Historically White Campuses: A Critical Race Examination of Race-Related Stress," in *Faculty of Color: Teaching in Predominately White Colleges and Universities*, edited by Christine A. Stanley, 299–327. Bolton: Anker Publishing.

Spieldenner, Andrew R., and Jahnasia Booker. 2020. "The Queer Act of Talking Sex: Pedagogical Challenges in a Communication Course on Pornography," in *Queer Communication Pedagogy*, edited by Ahmet Atay and Sandra L. Pensoneau-Conway, 151–165. New York: Routledge.

Spieldenner, Andrew R., and Shinsuke Eguchi. 2020. "Different Sameness: Queer Autoethnography and Coalition Politics." *Cultural Studies <-> Critical Methodologies*, 20, no. 2: 134–143.

Theye, Kristen, and Steven Melling. 2018. "Total Losers and Bad Hombres: The Political Incorrectness and Perceived Authenticity of Donald J. Trump." *Southern Communication Journal*, 83, no. 5: 322–337.

University of Oregon Social Sciences Feminist Network Research Interest Group. 2017. "The Burden of Invisible Work in Academia: Social Inequalities and Time Use in Five University Departments." *Humboldt Journal of Social Relations*, 39, no. 1: 228–245.

Yosso, Tara J., William A. Smith, Miguel Ceja, and Daniel G. Solórzano. 2009. "Critical Race Theory, Racial Microaggressions, and Campus Racial Climate for Latina/o Undergraduates." *Harvard Educational Review*, 79, no. 4: 659–691.

Chapter 5

What Difference Does It Make?

Navigating the Privileged Halls of Academia as a Queer Black Woman Professor

Elizabeth Whittington

As a graduate student starting out as a Teaching Assistant, I had no idea what lie ahead of me. I started my teaching career at a four-year institution that classifies as a predominantly White institution (PWI) in North Texas. As a graduate student, my pedagogy class started me on a journey of being a more critical professor, where I would question how power operates in my class, how I would best facilitate discussions around power dynamics in our society, and how, as a marginalized instructor, I would not try to control and dictate in my classroom as I saw many of my White male professors do. The following chapter is a critical autoethnography of narratives of my teaching experiences and pedagogy surrounding my navigation within the halls of academia.

I situate these narratives to tell my different stories of teaching at a variety of institutions as an instructor. I use autoethnography as a researcher to provide an intimate look into experiences of representation and authenticity (Wall 2008, 39). I employ a critical autoethnographic approach of various narratives of my experiences in the classroom as a Black Queer Woman. Autoethnography is "a critical methodology or approach to doing critical cultural examinations that might shape the mode of investigating experience, but not establish a standard of experience" (Alexander 2012, 141). I am not arguing for my experiences to be seen as the established norms of all Black, Queer women professors, but as a continuation of the narratives of Queer people of color's ongoing struggle to find their place in the normative cis-gendered, heteronormative, White space of Academia. Through autoethnography, I seek to disrupt the notions of what it means to be a professor and teaching in the traditional lecture formats. Shinsuke Eguchi (2020) reinforces "that autoethography is a powerful and radical method to disrupt normative systems of knowledge productions to investigate historically marginalized experiences." They continue, "autoethnography is about the way in which the self-implicates the complexities and contradictions of ideological and material environments" (Equchi 2020, 107–122). The use of autoethnography allows me to reimagine what being an inclusive, engaging, and challenging professor looks like inside and outside of the classroom. Autoethnography provides a tool for me to investigate how my teaching has progressed through the years, but also provides a space for the reader to understand and analyze their own teaching. My personal narratives provide a landscape of how my teaching links to the cultural and social (Ellis 2004). I label this a critical autoethnography because I also examine how power influences the social interactions between student and professor (Alexander 1999).

As of Fall 2020, I started teaching sixteen years ago and through the years, I realized how my pedagogical focus has developed to one that resembles bell hooks's revolutionary feminist pedagogy and Gloria Joseph's Black feminist pedagogy (hooks 1989, 25; Joseph 1995, 464). Both have influenced my way of teaching and helped to create a diverse, safe space for students to engage. Throughout the various institutions I have taught at, I have incorporated Black feminist pedagogy to help students critically analyze and question the information they receive. To accomplish these objectives, I incorporate several strategies in any class that I teach: (1) motivate students in the classroom by creating a learner-centered environment by using innovative teaching styles to cater to all students learning styles; (2) motivate students to develop a classroom community in order to feel comfortable communicating their ideas, thoughts, and beliefs through the implementation of Black feminist pedagogy and; (3) incorporating components of revolutionary feminist pedagogy through self-reflexive teaching tools. Next, I will explain how these statements operate in my classroom.

REVOLUTIONARY FEMINIST PEDAGOGY

bell hooks' revolutionary feminist pedagogy came from an elementary school teacher she had while growing up in a segregated south. hooks states

> Miss Moore knew that if we were to be fully self-realized, then her work, and the work of all our progressive teachers, was not to teach us solely the knowledge in books, but to teach us an oppositional world view—different from that of our exploiters and oppressor, a world view that would enable us to see ourselves not through the lens of racism or racist stereotypes but one that would enable us to focus clearly and succinctly, to look at ourselves, at the world

around us, critically—analytically—to see ourselves first and foremost as striving for wholeness, for unity of heart, mind, body, and spirit. (1989, 49)

While reading the previous section in her book *Talking Back*, as a graduate student, I realized my teaching had to be more than what was in the textbooks that students were forced to buy. If I wanted them to engage in a learning experience that required them to engage with myself and their classmates, I had to implement these pedagogical perspectives. hooks continues to list the tenants of revolutionary feminist pedagogy. This includes, instructors must "relinquish our ties to traditional ways of teaching that reinforce domination," also, "we must first focus on the teacher-student relationship and the issue of power," and lastly "we cannot have a revolutionary feminist pedagogy if we do not have revolutionary feminists in the classroom" (hooks 1989, 52–54).

During my time at a predominantly White Instituion (PWI) in the Pacific Northwest, I was responsible for teaching classes on race, gender, and relationships. I was teaching an advanced interpersonal communication class when I received an email from a student stating that my class was "anti-White heterosexual male." I thought this statement was completely accurate and I was unsure as to how this was a negative critique. Using hooks' first tenant, relinquishing the connection to reinforce domination, means that my class brings in perspectives that value and validate relationships that mainstream society does not deem valuable (i.e., polyamorous relationship, same sex relationships, interracial relationships, etc.). I took the student's comment as a compliment that I was implementing revolutionary feminist pedagogy. I created spaces in which this White heterosexual male student felt uncomfortable and made him question his own ideas on which relationships were privileged in our society. I challeneged his power of which relationships were privileged and by introducing him to different types of relationships I was illustrating an "oppositional worldview," one that opened his lens to more marginalized relationships (hooks 1989, 49). However, many students complained in my classes about my style of teaching, the articles I choose to incorporate, and the assesments I used.

During my second year at this institution, the chair was replaced by a White male cisgender heterosexual. He embodied so much White privilege but did not realize that every interaction with every complaint by students was his White male privilege constantly oppressing my Black girl magic. Many times, he sided with the student(s) or tried to get me to see the ways I was wrong in the situation. Being at this university, I never felt protected, respected, or appreciated. I tried to do my job and not ruffle feathers, but it felt that my body was unwanted and on display under that leadership. Sometimes when using revolutionary feminist pedagogy, especially in a marginalized identity, there is a lot of emotional labor in teaching courses that challenge students to unpack their privilege and encourage them to use lenses that help them understand and empathize with those that are different.

In hooks' second statement about power in the classroom she says "We can use that power in ways that diminish or in ways that enrich and it is this choice should distinguish feminist pedagogy from ways of teaching that reinforce domination" (hooks 1989, 52). This is the power of feeling that, as a professor, I am the all-knowing instructor. Meaning I am expected to know everything when asked or through my lectures. Also, this encompasses the idea of having to keep control of my classroom in ways that limit my students owning to their learning experience. Feminist pedagogy fights against the "I know everything" mentality that some professors may have when it comes to their classroom.

Early in my teaching career, a mentor, one of my first young Black female professors, responding to a question I had, said, "I don't know but I would be happy to find the information for you, or direct you on where to find the information." This was more than an acceptable response; it was transformative. I thought professors must know everything. Later I would learn that part of feminist pedagogy is by letting go of the power of knowing everything, the enrichment begins. To students, it may appear as though professors are unprepared, especially professors of color, and why many professors shy away from saying they do not know. Being able to give up control and own that knowledge is not about knowing everything, illustrates that learning is on-going and forever for everyone. hooks states, "it is important to make clear to students that we are prepared and that willingness to be open and honest about what we do not know is a gesture of respect for them" (hooks 1989, 52).

Along with the ability to show vulnerability and transparency, I focus on the embodiment of appreciation and affirmation in the classroom. As a Black woman in the classroom, my evaluations have always been slightly below the average expectation of "good" (Wallace et al. 2019; Smith 2009; Storage et al. 2016). I also know from the research that being a woman of color and queer, students will automatically rate me lower than they would a White male professor (Meritt 2008). At one PWI in the Pacific Northwest, the chair required that our evaluations were within the average range of the department, a 4 out of 5. Research also shows that professors of color are judged before students even taken a class with them on evaluations based on competence, legitimacy, and interpersonal skills (Bavishi et al. 2010). When race is combined with gender, sexual orientation, and other marginalized identities, the numbers continue to decrease (Merritt 2008; Sinclair and Kunda 2000). At this university, they assigned me classes on race, gender, ethnicity, and culture and how communication operates within these various identities. In classes like these, I realize students come into the classroom in a defensive stance if they represent any part of the dominant group. This caused many challenging conversations, but it also caused many students to get defensive. These interactions made them question their long-held values, their strong held beliefs, and made them dig deeper in unpacking why they believed what they believed. I wanted them to understand that until they knew why they held these beliefs they could not begin to figure out if their values were long-held stereotypes that needed to be acknowledged.

Because of these challenging interactions, my evaluations suffered semester after semester. I received qualitative statements that called me derogatory names that were racialized and gendered, and lied about misbehaviors I never exhibited in the classroom. I grew thick skin quickly. My students who appreciated what I was teaching sent me emails praising what they were learning and applying in their own lives. I received these emails years after I left the institution.

I have learned that I will not always be valued or affirmed by students and/or other faculty, but the work I am doing is not about affirmation. As hooks states, "I began to see that courses that work to shift paradigms, to change consciousness, cannot necessarily be experienced immediately as fun or positive or safe and this was not a worthwhile criterion to use in evaluation" (1989, 53). Students come to realize that it is not that the class was difficult, but that the class challenged them in a unique way that they were not expecting. The uncertainty is what made them feel they disliked the class. I could not use their dislike of the class or them saying derogatory names as an evaluation of if the class was effective and if students were learning. Many times, the learning started but they did not recognize it until semesters or years later and then I would usually receive an email. I could no longer think that I had to have affirmations in the classroom to determine if I was making a difference because it was about a bigger picture. The bigger picture means that being liked is nice, but transforming how students view the world is more important.

In the last tenant, we cannot have a revolutionary feminist classroom without revolutionary feminists teaching the classes. It reminds me of my place in the classroom. hooks suggests collaborating and working together with other feminists to continue to "challenge issues of sexism and sexist oppression both by what we teach and how we teach" (1989, 54). I am thankful for my colleagues and friend-tribes that have come together to help each other create spaces for students that continue to challenge and transform the way that they think about power in the classroom and society at large. Through deconstructing these power dynamics with my tribe of women within academia (all marginalized identities), I have allowed the space to continue in this emotional labor of challenging, changing, and creating new approaches to learning in the classroom (hooks 1989, 54). Before this tribe, I found teaching a lonely space, where classroom territoriality existed and colleagues would not help or even engage in conversations on how we could collaborate. My question: How can we expect students to work together if as colleagues we cannot come together to create radical and subversive spaces?

BLACK FEMINIST PEDAGOGY

Gloria Joseph states "Black feminist pedagogy is designed to raise the political consciousness of students by introducing a worldview with an Afrocentric orientation to reality, and the inclusion of gender and patriarchy as central to an understanding of all historical phenomena" (Joseph 1995, 465). One of the key components of Black feminist pedagogy requires the integration of the history of Blacks, Latinos, and Native Americas (Joseph 1995, 463). To truly understand America's history, students must understand the beginnings of how America got its start. In Joseph's essay, she quote's Robert Moore, who states that "an understanding of history is critical in shaping an awareness of the present and the vision for a viable future" (Joseph 1999, 463). The more students, especially marginalized students, can see themselves in the curriculum and dominant group students can see how dominant group ideology has impacted the way students learn and what they learn, the more classrooms can be a place where marginalized students can feel validated and dominant groups can learn how harmful their ideology can be.

The following example is just one of my experiences in trying to get to a place where I could be a face for marginalized students. I was in a Skype interview for an instructor position for a school in South Texas. The quote at the beginning of this chapter was on top of my teaching philosophy at one point in time. The Dean in the interview said to me, "You don't really believe that you weren't supposed to be here [academia]." I explained to him that I have many stories to tell that make it obvious that even if I thought I was supposed to be here, many people felt that it was their job to show me they could get me out of my position. From students going over my head to report me to the legal department at a university, to a Dean changing a grade that a student deserved. "By and large, the literature tells us that Afro-American women have a realistic, commonsense, rational view of their relationship to the dominant society and do not operate on false illusions about their chances" (Joseph 1999, 464). Realistically, I do understand that how I teach and the experiences with some of my students do not lead to tenure track positions especially at PWIs. Student evaluations matter and when a university may feel I could threaten their numbers or cause tension with calling out their -isms, they tend to offer me contracts but not tenure track positions (see some of the studies mentioned above).

Recently, at a workshop on emotional labor for marginalized women and marginalized identities, many participants talked about how hard it was to do the work of being a person of color or part of the LGBTQ community, or a woman, in an institution. They saw how their colleagues treated them differently when they challenged the dominant ideologies that oppressed marginalized groups at their institution. In this workshop, I was reminded I am not alone, but it is difficult work that sometimes makes it hard to advance a teaching career. These moments help as I continue to navigate my place in academia and to not feel alone so I can continue to do the "hard" work even when I am not understood or appreciated. Although, I embody Black feminism within my pedagogy it is a lonely place that is not always supported by institutions.

These narratives influence my pedagogy as I try to transform and liberate my students from a dominant ideology that causes them to oppress those that are different than them. They demonstrate to my students that what I teach comes from a place of transparency and by sharing these stories it creates a space for them to share their own experience; to allow their voices to feel validated. My goal is to create authentic spaces that allow students to challenge and maybe transform their lives, communities, and/or society, into an accepting place where difference is acknowledged and appreciated. These are all ideas I have learned with using both Black feminist pedagogy and a revolutionary pedagogy.

I do not have any false illusions about my place in academia because of these experiences. I have learned that as an educator my job is to share my knowledge and instill in students that I should be here. My temporary future at an institution is complicated by the privilege that somehow the students deserve to be there, and I do not. The privilege of them feeling that I am dispensable also seems to entitle them to challenge my knowledge and my place at the institution at different times. I chose to take these moments of challenge as teachable moments where I can question their privilege and, sometimes, help those who did not realize what they were doing. The other? I hope I planted a seed that may one day grow into a better understanding of my pedagogy.

Black feminist pedagogy at its center examines gender and patriarchy in the construction of society to understand that patriarchy reflects White male's worldviews, perspectives, and interest (Joseph 1995, 465). The philosophy is one of liberation. Liberating all people to understand the journey with Black feminist pedagogy is not "exclusively Black or exclusively African. It is a journey toward wholeness that requires seeing the world not black or white, but in its full spectrum" (Joseph 1995, 466). As a Black feminist incorporating Black feminist pedagogy, I realize if I create spaces and building blocks for students to become "true agents of radical change" I will come into contact with students who do not agree with this perspective or want to be an agent of change, and that may cause them to take more extreme measures

(Joseph 1995, 467; Lane 2017, 21). Black feminist pedagogy can serve as a catalyst for creating a blueprint that requires radical change in the educational social movement. This is not an overnight change and many times there are consequences, but for those students who take the opportunity to unpack their privilege their lens can be altered to make the changes for a more trans-formative future. And as Joseph shows, "It is fitting to have black feminist pedagogy as the theoretical construct for educational change" (1995, 471).

UNDERSTANDING THROUGH MOTIVATION

When it comes to teaching, I incorporate both conventional methods of teach-ing such as lectures and discussion, but also through interactive methods that employ mass media, pop culture, and/or hands-on activities that illustrate how communication is incorporated in their lives daily. I find that students need more than just my experience as a queer woman of color in the class-room. They need to see it in the shows and movies they watch, have thought about watching, or have heard about.

One semester, my students and I watched *Moonlight*. The movie provided various perspectives on sexual orientation, class, race, and gang life (Jenkins 2016). My students admitted this was not a movie that they would have watched. We discussed it in terms of intercultural communication and the different theo-ries from class. Students typically do not get to encounter the perspective of a closeted, gay Black gang member in various contexts. The students did not understand why Chiron, the main character in the movie, felt the need to do this or do that, but it was a good opportunity for me to explain the various complex natures of identity in different societies. They asked about my coming out expe-rience and how it impacted my career and other aspects of my life.

Using my experiences in the classroom was an opportunity for me to also bring in a religious context to the conversation. One semester, I had a student ask me how I reconcile my faith with my sexual orientation. This began a very transparent and vulnerable conversation of how the church turned their backs on the student and her girlfriend when they became involved in a relationship. They were kicked out of the church. My heart broke in that moment because I did not experience this in my church. I did understand the student's struggle to create an identity that for many seems contradictory. In that moment, together we were able to understand my own identity and that my faith was about my relationship with God and not with what people in my church thought. I also expressed to her that there were churches that were affirming and could also help her.

Conversations like these help students feel safe enough to discuss topics that may be more controversial. Through these conversations, I apply some of the concepts of liberating the space of taboo topics and allowing students to explore their experiences in relation to the ideas in the class. If they tend to fall a little short, I am there to guide them back to how it all comes together. The idea is to motivate students to feel that they are in control of the conversations in the classroom and throughout the semester. My goal is for students to feel that they are the center, the most important part of their learning experience. I want them to walk away with feeling that learning does not start and end in the classroom but it is a lifelong process.

CLASSROOM COMMUNITY THROUGH BLACK FEMINIST PEDAGOGY

When the classroom is a community, students are not afraid to ask questions, engage in discussion, or speak about their beliefs. My goal is for the classroom to feel like a place where different opinions are welcomed, not ridiculed. In a community, people need to feel open, trusting, and that an investment is being made by all parties involved. I understand that although I am able to let go of some of my power in the classroom, I ultimately can harness my power to help students discover who they are. An aspect of recognizing the power I have within the classroom is that I can create an environment where my students have a voice; a safe space in which their voice will be recognized and may be challenged but not in a vindictive way, but a critical way. This pedagogical method allows them to begin to understand why they think or believe the way they do and either own it or challenge it. The goal as hooks states is "to enable all students, not just an assertive few, to feel empowered in a rigorous, critical discussion" (hooks 1999, 53). Building a community within my classes is one of my most important goals in getting students to feel that they are more than just a face in the crowd.

One semester, a student asked me "where did my kids come from?" At a time, I was married to a woman and the student was perplexed that I had children. The school was in the deep south and this student had never met someone in a same-sex couple who biologically had children. This was a learning moment on what community members can look like and experience when we minimize power dynamics. These students had a moment to learn about sexuality and motherhood in ways that are not always present in the classroom. I can model by not ridiculing or making fun of my student for asking an obvious question to me, and take it as a moment to allow them to feel comfortable in the classroom space to ask anything.

I have come to realize that it is important that I create an environment for change and what better course than a college course that gets them to focus on how they communicate with others, challenge their perceptions, understand intercultural communication, and how they can become more effective communicators. A valuable lesson I learned was to relinquish the desire to be the most liked teacher by every student. It was later when students came back to thank me for what they were able to learn in my class that helped me to continue in my goals.

CONCLUSION

This chapter highlights my narratives of teaching in the walls of academia as a Black queer woman. I have experienced great moments where I was able to awaken in students the desire to be change agents in this world; to critically think about how information happens and how they can contribute to a more robust and diverse society. I have had dark moments, where my teaching evaluations suffered terribly, not receiving a renewed contract and feeling discouraged with my teaching path. The semesters have been long as I have learned and come to the realization that I will have to work much harder than my counterparts who teach in a more traditional way and look more like the "traditional" professor. Many outside of academics and teaching believe that as instructors, our work is easy. We walk into the classroom, teach, and then go home and live lives where work is minimal.

However, as a Black feminist, a revolutionary instructor, I have never taught the same lesson twice, I am always prepping and revising based on my student demographics that semester, that class. This requires time, energy, and lots of emotional labor that many discount as "real" work. I conclude this chapter with one more quote by Joseph: "The presence of an independent black woman's point of view using an alternative epistemology is fundamentally significant because its existence challenges not only the content of what currently passes as 'truth,' but simultaneously challenges the process of arriving at that truth" (Joseph 1995, 465). Added to my layers of being queer are my rich and diverse experiences in the classroom. I am so thankful to facilitate students' coming to their truth as they learn how the multiple layers of their identity impact how they learn and their experiences in the classroom. I am more thankful that I have chosen to teach predominately Black and Brown students, who may struggle with some of my other identities, but at least appreciate seeing a face that looks similar to them.

REFERENCES

Alexander, Bryant. 2012. *The Performative Sustainability of Race: Reflections on Black Culture and the Politics of Identity.* New York: Peter Lang.

Alexander, Bryant K. 1999. "Performing Culture in the Classroom: An Instructional (Auto)Ethnography." *Text and Performance Quarterly*, 19, no. 4: 307–331. https://doi.org/10.1080/10462939909366272.

Bavishi, Anish, Mikki Hebl, and Juan Madera. 2010. "The Effect of Professor Ethnicity and Gender on Student Evaluations: Judged Before Met." *Journal of Diversity in Higher Education*, 3, no. 4 (Winter): 245–256. https://doi.org/10.1037/a0020763.

Eguchi, Shinsuke. 2020. "Queer Lonliness, Queer Hopefulness: Toward Restaging the Intersectionality of Gay + Asian/American from the Southwest." In *Home and Community for Queer Men of Color: The Intersection of Race and Sexuality*, edited by Jesus Gregorio Smith and C. Winter Han, 107–122. Lanham, MD: Rowan & Littlefield.

Ellis, Carolyn. 2004. *The Ethnographic I: A Methodological Novel About Teaching and Doing Autoethnography*. Walnut Creek, CA: AltaMira.

Freire, Paulo. 2018. *Pedagogy of the Oppressed, 50th Anniversary Edition*. New York: Bloomsbury Academic.

Gabriel. 2016. "Why Is School So Boring?! 3 Ways Black Feminist Pedagogy Can Radically Improve Our Learning." *Medium: Black Feminist Thought 2016*, April 14, 2016.

hooks, bell. 1989. *Talking Back: Thinking Feminist, Thinking Black*. Boston: South End Press.

Jenkins, Barry, dir. 2016. *Moonlight*. Miami, FL: Plan B Entertainment and A24, 2017. DVD.

Joseph, Gloria. 1995. "Black Feminist Pedagogy and Schooling in Capitalist White America." In *Words of Fire: An Anthology of African American Feminist Thought*, edited by Beverly Guy-Sheftall, 462–471. New York: The New Press.

Lane, Monique. 2017. "Reclaiming Our Queendom: Black Feminist Pedagogy and the Identity Formation of African American Girls." *Equity & Excellence in Education*, 50, no. 1 (Winter): 13–24. http://dx.doi.org/10.1080/10665684.2016.1259025.

Merritt, Deborah J. (2008). "Bias, the Brain, and Student Evaluations of Teaching." *St. John's Law Review*, 8, no. 1 (Winter): 235–287.

Sinclair, Lisa, and Ziva Kunda (2000). " Motivated Stereotyping of Women: She's Fine If She Praised Me but Incompetent If She Criticized Me." *Personality and Social Psychology Bulletin*, 26, no. 11 (Winter): 1329–1342. https://doi.org/10.1177/0146167200263002.

Smith, Bettye P. 2009. "Student Ratings of Teaching Effectiveness for Faculty Groups Based on Race and Gender." *Education*, 129, no. 4 (Summer): 615–624.

Storage, Daniel, Zachary Horne, Andrei Cimpian, and Sarah-Jane Leslie. 2016. "The Frequency of 'Brilliant' and 'Genius' in Teaching Evaluations Predicts the Representation of Women and African Americans Across Fields." *PLos One*, 11, no. 3: 1–17. https://doi.org/10.1371/journal.pone.0150194.

Wallace, Sherri, Angela K. Lewis, and Marcus D. Allen. 2019. "The State of the Literature on Student Evaluations of Teaching and an Exploratory Analysis of Written Comments: Who Benefits Most?" *College Teaching*, 67, no. 1 (Winter): 1–14. https://doi.org/10.1080/87567555.2018.1483317.

Chapter 6

Teaching While Vulnerable

Connection through Shared Vulnerability as a Pedagogical Stepping Stone to Queer Consciousness

Richard G. Jones, Jr.

A PIVOTAL DAY, PERSONALLY AND PEDAGOGICALLY: #SAYHERNAME

It's spring semester of 2017. The teaching assignment I am most excited about is a graduate seminar I created titled "The Body, Performance, and Identity." We are in week four of a fifteen-week semester. I've worked hard to build a supportive and inclusive climate as I, along with many of my students, are still working through our emotions regarding the outcome of the 2016 presidential election. This week, for our discussion of intersectionality, I'm doing something new that I'm a little nervous about.

Only a few months earlier, Kimberlé Crenshaw delivered a TED Talk titled "The Urgency of Intersectionality" (Crenshaw 2016). This is my first chance to use it in my classes and I'm eager to show the video to my graduate students. The day before, when I re-watched the video and created the in-class worksheet and reflection questions, I sat at my desk and cried, deeply cried, for several minutes. Will I be able to control my emotions? Should I try to control my emotions? Will my students get emotional?

I get to class and we discuss the readings for that day which focus on the body. Building on the previous week's readings that focused on intersectionality and self-reflexivity, I explain to the students that our bodies are materially affected by our identities, even though our identities are socially constructed (Alcoff 2006, 102). The material advantages that come with white skin, such as higher-paying jobs and better health outcomes, stand in stark contrast to the economic and health disparities experienced by people of color. We have good small-group and full-class discussions for the first half of the class. I know the students are "getting it" as we move toward the activity that I've been nervous about. We are going to confront how bodies also become targets, or not, based on identities. Aside from discussing the connection between embodiment and identities, we also discuss the connection between embodiment and performance. We consider how each of us perform our cultural identities through everyday actions, and how putting our bodies into action as allies can be an empowering learning experience. I hope the students will appreciate the embodied component of Crenshaw's talk. I hope they'll make deep and visceral connections to what she's saying, to the video that she shows her live audience, to our course content, to the current cultural and political climate, and to their own identities. Am I hoping for too much?

At the beginning of Crenshaw's talk, she does an interactive activity. She says, "I'd like to try something new. Those of you who are able, please stand up. OK, so I'm going to name some names. When you hear a name that you don't recognize . . . I'd like you to take a seat and stay seated." Then she reads off some names: "Eric Garner. Mike Brown. Tamir Rice. Freddie Gray." At the end of that list, a list of men of color who were killed by police, about half of the audience is seated. She continues, "Michelle Cusseaux. Tanisha Anderson. Aura Rosser. Meagan Hockaday." At the end of that list, a list of women of color who were killed by police, there are only about four people standing. Crenshaw skillfully uses this activity to set up the remainder of her talk which focuses on intersectionality, particularly between race and gender.

At fifteen minutes into the talk, near the end, Crenshaw says, "So we have the opportunity right now—bearing in mind that some of the images that I'm about to share with you may be triggering for some—to collectively bear witness to some of this violence . . . And as we sit with these women, some who have experienced [acts of] violence and some who have not survived them, we have an opportunity to reverse what happened at the beginning of this talk, when we could not stand for these women because we did not know their names."

I stop here, as I had planned. In preparing for this part of the video, I couldn't come up with an answer to the question: Will I ask the students to participate in the interactive portion of the video as if we were part of Crenshaw's live audience? I decide to observe, to read the mood of the room, to try to feel the emotions and read the expressions of the students as we watch the video to this point. They seem engaged and I know, after four weeks with them, that this will be a powerful shared experience for us all, so I invite them to imagine that we are part of Crenshaw's audience. To imagine that we are there with her. And, I invite them to follow the instructions that Crenshaw is about to give. During this pause, I tell them that I'm not going to speak at the end of the video. Instead, I ask them to take a few moments after the video to silently reflect on what they saw and what they are feeling. I remind them that they have some questions on the handout I distributed earlier that I would like them to answer after they have taken a few moments of silence. I resume the video.

Crenshaw goes on, "So at the end of this clip, there's going to be a roll call. Several black women's names will come up. I'd like those of you who are able to join us in saying these names as loud as you can, randomly, disorderly. Let's create a cacophony of sound to represent our intention to hold these women up, to sit with them, to bear witness to them, to bring them into the light."

At this point, singer Abby Dobson comes on stage and begins singing, in a haunting, beautiful, and spiritual voice, "Say, say her name" and Crenshaw plays the video for her live audience. The video starts with a still image of a group of people marching in the streets with #sayhername centered as a graphic overlay. This image, which is only displayed for a little over one second abruptly shifts to a somewhat grainy cell phone video of a law enforcement officer straddling a black woman who is lying flat on her back, on the ground, on the side of a busy highway. The officer is punching the woman, full force, on her upper torso and/or face. That video quickly slides into the next which was recorded on a security camera inside a jail. A group of officers enter the room with a black woman in handcuffs and then throw her, with her hands still cuffed behind her, headfirst into a wall. There are two more video clips, both showing black women being assaulted by police. The four video clips only last for fourteen seconds. The next part of the video is pictures of black women who were killed by police with their name, their age, and the date and place of their death. As prompted, audience members begin saying, then shouting the names of the women shown in the video: Shelly, Kayla, Michelle, Gabriella, India, and so on.

I stand when Crenshaw asks her live audience to stand, which prompts the students to stand. Although I thought I might have to start saying names to get them to join in, some of them are already participating. They are into it. I am into it. As I say the names my voice cracks with emotion.

Abby Dobson sings, "Say her name. For all the names I'll never know, say her name." And then a list begins to scroll, like movie credits, with the names of more black women who have been killed or assaulted by police. The audience continues: Aiyanna Stanley Jones, Kathryn Johnston, Rekia Boyd, Yvette Smith, and so on. In my graduate class, we continue to say the names as well. As I look at the class, trying not to bring attention to myself, I see that some of them are emotional. At this point, I am just mouthing the names. My voice won't come.

Abby Dobson sings her last refrain of "Say her name." Crenshaw concludes: "So I said at the beginning, if we can't see a problem, we can't fix a problem. Together, we've come together to bear witness to these women's lost lives. But the time now is to move from mourning and grief to action and transformation. This is something that we can do. It's up to us."

I mute the projector from my seat in the back of the classroom. I don't want to move, to distract them from the powerful moment we just shared. I sit and reflect along with the students. Unlike them, I am not reflecting as much on the content of the video as I am on the experience we just shared. These moments don't happen very often, so I want to take it in. I take one more look around the classroom. Some students are sitting, processing internally. Some are crying. Some are already writing. I close my eyes. I feel my heart beat. I hear my heart beat. I breathe in the emotions that are circulating in the room. I'm reminded of why I teach, of why I embrace critical pedagogy. We are learning and feeling together. We are activating and expanding our critical consciousnesses. I open my eyes and jot down some responses on the worksheet. The first question is: What are you feeling right now? The other two say, "I stand for . . ." and "I stand with . . . "

I share this narrative at length because this was one of the most powerful and moving days of teaching that I have ever experienced. I already felt a special bond with these graduate students. Creating this class was cathartic because it connects my academic, personal, and political passions for critical inquiry and social justice. In our first four weeks together, we have engaged in mutual self-disclosure and discussed difficult topics associated with power, privilege, and oppression. Standing and speaking the names of black women who were killed by police is a powerful moment that extends beyond that evening's class. Students approach me after class to discuss this activity. It comes up in class discussion throughout the rest of the semester, and students discuss it at length in their written assignments.

In the intervening time since this pivotal pedagogical and personal moment, I have engaged in self-reflection and changed, or perhaps evolved, as a scholar and practitioner of critical communication pedagogy. In the remainder of this chapter, I further contextualize the experience described above through my personal narrative in conversation with relevant literature. I then share some reflections on the intentionality with which I infused intersectional reflexivity into the class, on the pedagogy of vulnerability, and on how this experience has changed me and what I learned from it that may help other educators as they prepare for, encounter, and/or reflect on similar experiences.

A MOMENT OF INTERRUPTION: AN
OPENING FOR VULNERABILITY

The timing of this pivotal day of teaching is salient, and influenced, I believe, the special moments of queer consciousness that unfolded within me and within my classrooms. In other scholarship, I have conceptualized queer consciousness as inherently critical, reflexive, and intersectional and theorized that embodied moments of incongruency are germinal seeds that develop queer consciousness (Jones 2015, 773). I have also traced through personal narrative how lived experiences with queer theory and critical pedagogy can create shared queer consciousness that facilitates alliance building (Jones and Calafell 2012, 957–981). In this chapter, I reflect on the connection between pedagogy and vulnerability, and explore how moments of connection through shared vulnerability can also develop queer consciousness.

Now, let's flash back to November 8, 2016. Election day in the United States. I pose for a selfie outside of my local polling place with a big smile and my "I voted" sticker on. I go through my work day and then go, along with my partner, to another gay couple's home to watch the election results come in. It's fun. We take pictures with our Hilary signs and celebrate each victory that is announced. We feel like we are on our expected trajectory toward a democratic win and the first female president. We *know* she's the most vetted presidential candidate in history and we've seen eagerly and excitedly watched her debate a man that we *know* is unfit for the office of the president. There are some state win projections that give me pause, but I am again comforted by my certainty that voters will not elect Donald Trump as president. Now, it's 10:32 pm. I'm sitting on our friends' guest bathroom floor facing a full-length mirror. I cry. I try to catch my breath. I look at myself in the mirror. I eventually find the strength to pull myself from the floor to a standing position. I return to my partner and friends in the living room and deliver a somewhat coherent impromptu speech about how a pendulum always swings back and how dying beasts, in this case whatever beastly forces led to Trump's election, can still get one win in before they die. But, this is just a performance, my psyche, my life has been interrupted.

Poulos (2012), writing about interruption notes that "there are moments in life when *something*—an insight, an epiphany . . . a trauma, a loss, or even a shadow . . . seems to just 'break through' into the ordinary flow of everyday life . . ." (323). He goes on to say that not all moments of interruption are like sudden epiphanies. That they can first emerge as "fear, or grief, or pain, or anger—emotion [that] just sweeps over us, and life is . . . interrupted" (323).

I, like many, experienced such a moment of interruption on November 8, 2016. It was not an epiphany but more like the emergence of a mix of emotions just described. I spend the rest of that semester going through the motions at work and trying to keep things together as much as I can within myself and in my relationships. I rely on intrapersonal communication. I don't want to process my thoughts or emotions with anyone. I want to pretend it didn't happen, but I can't escape the reality. I don't do a good job of holding it together for myself or anyone else.

Things are not good at home. My partner's reaction to the election results is much more expressive and volatile. He regularly gets angry at me, himself, and others in ways I have never seen before. He drinks more. He cries more. One night he yells at me and a friend who we had invited for dinner: "It doesn't matter anymore! We are going to end up having our marriage invalidated and we'll be put in a concentration camp!" I know he knows that's irrational. I try to be there emotionally for him.

Things are arguably worse for me, even though most people wouldn't be able to tell. I have struggled with mental health issues including chronic depression for twenty years. I get a letter from my psychiatrist, a man just a couple years older than me who I had come to like and identify with. The letter lets me know that he is no longer seeing patients for outpatient treatment. He'll be working at the hospital and focusing on acute patients with emergent needs. After reading the letter twice, I rip it up, throw it away and think, "Well, if he'll only see me if I'm acute, maybe I should do something drastic so I get taken to the emergency room!" After the anger wears off, the truly dark nature of that internal comment strikes me. I need to do something. I need to do something for myself, for my partner, and for my students.

I decide that I'll think of my coming semester as a gift. I can use my classes, especially my graduate seminar, to engage with concepts directly related to the current and volatile cultural and political climate—to engage with these concepts to help my own processing and to help my students process. This is when the moment of interruption that occurred on election night ceases being a black hole of negativity and I begin to see, in the distance, a window that opens to a new and different consciousness, to "a world of transcendence, of spirit, of possibility" (Poulos 2012, 323). I, however, am still not sure that I'll be strong enough to follow through with my commitments to critical communication pedagogy. Am I too fragile, emotionally and psychologically? I decide to deal with that later. I use my time over winter break to find some renewal and motivation as I draw upon my experience with critical theories and pedagogies and prepare for a new semester and a new year.

REFLECTIONS ON INTENTIONALITY

I intentionally, even more than usual, incorporated my commitments to critical communication pedagogy and intersectional reflexivity into my classes. For years I have intentionally infused my classes, especially those that focus on culture and identity, with the commitments of critical communication pedagogy outlined by Fassett and Warren (2007). Some of the most salient are: a constitutive understanding of identity, an understanding that power is fluid and complex, the centrality of culture, an embrace of social critique, the importance of self-reflexivity, and a nuanced understanding of human agency (39–54). These commitments are evident in my course objectives, course readings, and assignments.

I was also ready to teach about, model, and assess intersectional reflexivity in my classes. I conceptualized intersectional reflexivity in my dissertation and have expanded on it in subsequent publications (Jones 2010, 122–125; Jones and Calafell 2012; Jones 2015, 766–775; Jones 2014, 23–45). Intersectional reflexivity "requires one to acknowledge one's intersecting identities, both marginalized and privileged, and then employ self-reflexivity, which moves one beyond self-reflection to the often uncomfortable level of self-implication" (Jones 2010, 122). I believe that intersectional reflexivity should also be incorporated into critical scholarship as a paramethodological commitment that guides researchers as they unpack their positionalities in the research process and in the final scholarly product (Jones 2015, 767). At the level of lived experience, I have explored, in conversation with Calafell, how intersectional reflexivity can be useful as people marked as "other" navigate their way through neoliberal discourses within the academy (Jones and Calafell 2012, 963). The 2016 election results, although shocking and difficult for me, gave me new motivation to return to my previous scholarly and applied work with intersectional reflexivity. I was reminded of the seventh commitment of CCP that notes that reflexivity is an essential element of critical communication pedagogy (Fassett and Warren 2007, 50). I wondered how, in what seemed and felt like a new world to me, intersectional reflexivity might look and feel different as part of my course preparation and teaching praxis. The question I asked earlier, but decided to leave unanswered until I finished my course preparations—Am I too fragile, emotionally and psychologically?—was still needling me.

REFLECTIONS ON PEDAGOGY OF VULNERABILITY

Brantmeier states that "a pedagogy of vulnerability challenges teachers to render their frames of knowing, feeling, and doing vulnerable" (Brantmeier 2013, 95). Brantmeier (2013) admits that the concept of pedagogy of vulnerability is simple: "open yourself, contextualize that self in societal constructs and systems, co-learn, admit you do not know, and be human" (95). He goes on to say that such a simple statement might be indicative of naiveté, because a pedagogy of vulnerability is a complex and tangled terrain.

Although I was familiar with vulnerability as an important part of responsive pedagogy and being the "whole professor" I had not yet intentionally embedded a pedagogy of vulnerability into my teaching praxis. In my graduate seminar on communication pedagogy, I bookended the course with a discussion of the "whole professor," having students reflect on the fact that educators and students bring their minds, bodies, and spirits with them into the classroom (Palmer 2017, 12). I engaged in self-disclosure in the classroom, disclosing for example, my lower-working-class origins and my experiences as a first-generation college student, which I hoped would build immediacy and rapport and prompt reciprocal disclosures. I expressed a wide range of emotions over the years in classes but, still buying into and reinforcing the idea that displaying strong emotions would detract from my credibility in the classroom, I usually tried to control or soften the expressions.

Expressing vulnerability is risky. I have had some amazing mentors who have modeled a pedagogy of vulnerability. Chris Poulos was a mentor to me in my MA program and was instrumental in transitioning me to a doctoral program. He was mentored by Roy Wood who later also mentored me. Poulos (2010) often quoted the philosopher Levinas, and one his oft-cited quotes, included on syllabi, assignments, and in several of his publications is: "Communication with the other can be transcendent only as a dangerous life—a fine risk to be run" (68). In 2001 I was an undergraduate student of Poulos and I emailed him after an early morning trip to the doctor on September 11 to let him know I wouldn't be in class because I had an abscess in my tonsil. I sent the email before I knew what was going on. It was just a normal 9/11 for me. Around noon, he emailed me back. It said, "Today there is an abscess in the soul of this country." He totally changed his approach to the class after 9/11 and for the rest of that semester modeled a pedagogy of vulnerability that I unfortunately could not fully appreciate at the time.

Poulos wasn't afraid to show his emotions or vulnerability following the tragic and traumatic interruption that was 9/11. Brown (2012) notes that "vulnerability is at the core, the heart, the center, of meaningful human experience," and that we take emotional risks when we allow ourselves to be vulnerable (12). Emotions are also part of our classroom experiences from kindergarten through college. As Palmer (2017) notes: "In every class I teach, my ability to connect with my students, and to connect them with the subject, depends less on the methods I use than on the degree to which I know and trust my self-hood—and am willing to make it available and vulnerable in the service of learning" (10).

Sharing emotions is a key part of building close relationships and bonding, and those moments can and do happen in and out of the classroom. However, as scholars from marginalized groups have recognized, close relationships, especially loving relationships, threaten the hierarchy on which institutions of higher education are built (Calafell 2007, 426). These relationships, especially between faculty of color and students of color are especially powerful and meaningful in that they create an affective and discursive homeplace. I am not a person of color, yet I am a faculty member who is often sought out by students of color as an instructor, advisor, and mentor. While this is due to the large underrepresentation of faculty members of color at my institution in comparison to the diversity of our student body, I also credit some of it to the fact that I was mentored in my doctoral program by two women of color, one of them, Bernadette Marie Calafell, who has since been a co-author and a dear friend and colleague. They provided me with the tools I needed to excavate my identities and to acknowledge and work with my privileges. And once I had done that, it was clear that I had a mandate to use those tools and teach those tools to others for the rest of my life. I also think students who are marginalized seek me out because of my openness in class and outside of class to talk about issues of race, to label my whiteness and my privilege, while at the same time avowing my alliances with people of color, women, people who are trans*, and people with disabilities. Although these actions do open me up for some scrutiny, my white, male, cisgender privileges have and continue to insulate me from material harmful effects of such open alliance.

One of the most powerful emotional experiences that followed our #say-hername activity was with a black female graduate student. After our moment of silence and reflective writing, we sit in our circle to process. This student is the first to speak. She is eager. She gets through the first few words before huge tears began falling, yet she continues to speak. She tells us that the first name that came up at the end of the video is the same name she gave her daughter, who was four years old at the time. She speaks for a while longer and we thank her for sharing and continue our discussion. When we take a break about five minutes later, I want to follow-up with her. I go out into the hall where she was surrounded by three other students. They are hugging. When they broke off I also thank her for sharing. And, through our tears we embrace. Later in her journal entry, she writes, that seeing her daughter's name in that context "hurt me but the TED Talk was meant to touch all of us, and I believe it did."

REFLECTIONS ON OUTCOMES AND IMPLICATIONS

The moment of interruption, the results of the 2016 presidential election, didn't strike everyone as a traumatic event. However, looking back on the spring semester of 2017, I can now see that my decision to turn that moment of interruption into an opportunity for personal and pedagogical growth was successful overall. I can demonstrate confidently that using this moment of interruption, most often without naming it, as an opportunity to employ my commitments to critical communication pedagogy and intersectional reflexivity in new ways helped develop a new or nurture an existing queer consciousness among my students and myself.

Queer consciousness develops as people experience incongruency between and among identities and social and discursive forces and then reflect on those experiences in intersectional and reflexive ways. In my previous work, I have acknowledged that my conceptualization of queer consciousness is informed by the work of queer scholars of color (Jones and Calafell 2012, 973). I have also explored queer consciousness in the context of lived experience in the academy and in how queer men think about their bodies (Jones and Calalfell 2012, 973; Jones 2015, 773). I have also traced the individual, academic, and activist roots of queer consciousness (Jones 2014, 24–29). LeMaster (2020) has since insightfully extended my research by conceptualizing and operationalizing how we can foster an emerging queer consciousness in mentoring relationships (171–74). Queer consciousness is inherently evolving, dynamic, and unfixed.

I continually remarked to my partner and to my colleagues about the depth and quality of my students' work. Both classes had weekly reading reactions or journal prompts. I was often moved to tears, either empathetic tears, due to something difficult or traumatic they shared in their writing, or tears of joy, as I read their nuanced connections between theory, practice, the personal, and the political. Both classes ended the semester with an activism unit in which they engaged in culture jamming. Although this is an assignment I've done many times over the years, the critical depth and the level of intersectional reflexivity in the final products were inspiring and exceptional.

The spring semester of 2017 was indeed a gift. Aside from the graduate seminar I have discussed throughout this chapter, I also taught an upper-level undergraduate course on gender and the body. Over half the students in both classes had at least one marginalized identity that they discussed openly in the class. I was also directing two graduate student thesis projects that semester, one with a black male student doing a creative thesis on incarceration because his brother is in long-term incarceration and one black female whose thesis focused on identities and needs of students of color. These classes and mentoring relationships helped me process through some of my post-election emotions and thoughts. These students supported me a lot with their strength but they probably didn't know that. Should I have told them? How should I have told them?

What did I learn that I can try to do better, do differently? My main disappointment in myself is that I didn't make myself as vulnerable as I would have liked. I did make myself vulnerable in more private and implicit ways. For example, when giving feedback on journals or reading reactions I would reciprocate self-disclosure about a wide range of topics that students brought up from racism to mental health issues to surviving sexual assault and an abusive relationship. But, I didn't open myself up as much as I wanted in class. Upon reflection, I think I channeled my energy into emotionally supporting my students and creating and delivering content and activities that were creative and engaging so I wouldn't have to deal with my own emotions. Putting myself into my work and into my students though was therapeutic, but it didn't live up to the standards of a pedagogy of vulnerability that I have since learned.

I did however reach new levels of understanding about my identities through intersectional reflexivity in the new political and cultural context. I was able to skillfully, confidently, and successfully (for the most part) teach students about complicated concepts related to intersecting identities, power, privilege, the body, and activism. That success is due in part to the unearned privileges that come with my identities. Like Whitworth, I spent time thinking about how "inhabiting a male-read body means my authority as a teacher is rarely second-guessed and that" the privileges that come along with my gender and race offer me "a generous and initially unearned reading of capability, authority, and adequacy from my students" (Whitworth and Wilcoxen 2020, 215). I did share many things about my identities including that I identify as gay, queer, and a first-generation college student. I also shared that I spent the early years of my life in poverty. Even as I made myself vulnerable with those disclosures, I still knew that I could always pull back. This sentiment is captured by Hobson (2020) who notes that she, as a faculty member, has the power to decide not to share her identities when she doesn't want to do the emotional work that comes with such disclosures (196). She acknowledges however that students are socialized to follow the rules and that educators often require and expect students to self-disclose and show vulnerability in assignments and activities without critically evaluating the pedagogical soundness or ethical implications of those activities (196).

Additionally, even though I was more emotionally expressive than I had normally been to that point as a teacher, I still regularly made efforts to control those emotions while also realizing that I'm given much more leeway to express those emotions should I choose to or be moved to, due to my layers of privilege. Stern (2018) notes that even though displaying emotions is a vulnerable stance, the display "might work in those educators' favor who have certain privileges of gender, sexuality, or tenure" (45). Similarly, Yep and Lescure (2018) state "If a white person is challenging whiteness, then whiteness must be real and must be challenged!" This however can have a boomerang effect as "using privilege to critique privilege can subsequently reinforce privilege" (122). Stern (2018) has only begun to theorize what she calls privileged vulnerability but I think this is a promising concept that warrants more study (47).

In the years that have followed I have pushed myself more as I have continued to reflect on that spring semester of 2017. I haven't been able to teach either of those classes again due to other commitments and a much-needed sabbatical. But, as I prepare to teach the undergraduate class on gender and sexuality again, as I write this, I am eager to take what I've learned and try to implement it. I have, over these three years, made myself vulnerable and expressed emotions in more public ways. I have become a more outspoken advocate for mental health awareness and suicide prevention after earning a certification in adult mental health first aid. I have talked about my depression in presentations to student groups and at workshops. I recently started doing SafeZone trainings again and have found that I am much more likely to get emotional and provide personal examples than I used to be. I can't and won't complain about the emotional labor that I exert as I strive and struggle to embody more a pedagogy of vulnerability. My emotional labor isn't comparable to the epistemic violence faced daily by people with multiple marginalized identities and I can always retreat back to the spaces of privilege that my white, male, and cisgender identities afford me.

My pedagogy is a reflexive work in progress. I am a reflexive work in progress. Our students are works in progress. Crenshaw's TED Talk was a moment I shared with my students that was more powerful because of the post-election social and political climate, the intentionality with which I infused intersectional reflexivity into the class, and a willingness to express and invite vulnerability. Although vulnerability involves varying levels of risk, I hear the voice of one of my mentors, paraphrasing Levinas, reminding me that transcendent communication with others is dangerous, but that it is a fine risk to be run.

REFERENCES

Alcoff, Linda M. 2006. *Visible Identities: Race, Gender, and the Self.* Oxford: Oxford University Press.

Brantmeier, Edward J. 2013. "Pedagogy of Vulnerability: Definitions, Assumptions, and Applications." In *Reenvisioning Higher Education: Embodied Pathways to Wisdom and Social Transformation*, edited by Rebecca L. Oxford, Jing Lin, and Edward J. Brantmeier, 95–106. Charlotte, NC: Information Age Publishing.

Brown, Brené. 2012. *Daring Greatly: How the Courage to be Vulnerable Transforms the Way We Live, Love, Parent, and Lead.* New York: Avery.

Calafell, Bernadette Marie. 2007. "Mentoring and Love: An Open Letter." *Cultural Studies <-> Critical Methodologies*, 7, no. 4: 425–441.

Crenshaw, Kimberlé. *The Urgency of Intersectionality*, TED Women 2016, October 2016, video, 18:41. https://www.ted.com/talks/kimberle_crenshaw_the_urgency _of_intersectionality.

Fassett, Deanna L., and John T. Warren. 2007. *Critical Communication Pedagogy.* Thousand Oaks, CA: Sage.

Hobson, Kathryn. 2020. "Hesitant to Walk: Affective Interventions in Queer Communication Pedagogy." In *Queer Communication Pedagogy*, edited by Ahmet Atay and Sandra L. Pensoneau-Conway, 189–206. New York: Routledge.

Jones, Jr., Richard G. 2010. "Putting Privilege into Action through Intersectional Reflexivity: Ruminations, Interventions, and Possibilities." *Reflections: Narratives of Professional Helping*, 16, no. 1: 122–125.

Jones, Jr., Richard G. 2014. "Divided Loyalties: Exploring the Intersections of Queerness, Race, Ethnicity, and Gender." In *Critical Articulations of Race, Gender, and Sexual Orientation*, edited by Sheena C. Howard, 23–46. Lanham, MD: Lexington Books.

Jones, Jr., Richard G. 2015. "Queering the Body Politic: Intersectional Reflexivity in the Body Narratives of Queer Men." *Qualitative Inquiry*, 21, no. 9: 766–775.

Jones, Jr., Richard G., and Bernadette Marie Calafell. 2012. "Contesting Neoliberalism Through Critical Pedagogy, Intersectional Reflexivity, and Personal Narrative: Queer Tales of Academia." *Journal of Homosexuality*, 59, no. 7: 957–981.

LeMaster, Benny. 2020. "Fostering an Emerging Queer Consciousness." In *Queer Communication Pedagogy*, edited by Ahmet Atay and Sandra L. Pensoneau-Conway, 170–188. New York: Routledge.

Palmer, Parker. 2017. *The Courage to Teach: Exploring the Inner Landscape of a Teacher's Life*. San Francisco, CA: Jossey-Bass.

Poulos, Christopher N. 2010. "Transgressions." *International Review of Qualitative Research*, 3, no. 1: 67–88.

Poulos, Christopher N. 2012. "Life, Interrupted." *Qualitative Inquiry*, 18, no. 4: 323–332.

Stern, Danielle M. "Privileged Pedagogy, Vulnerable Voice: Opening Feminist Doors in the Communication Classroom." *Journal of Communication Pedagogy*, 1, no. 1: 40–51.

Whitworth, Colin, and Anna Wilcoxen. 2020. "Disclosing Lives, Reading Bodies: A Duo-Autoethnography of Queerness in the Classroom." In *Queer Communication Pedagogy*, edited by Ahmet Atay and Sandra L. Pensoneau-Conway, 209–222. New York: Routledge.

Yep, Gust A., and Ryan M. Lescure. 2018. "Obstructing the Process of Becoming: Basal Whiteness and the Challenge to Critical Intercultural Communication Pedagogy." In *Critical Intercultural Communication Pedagogy*, edited by Ahmet Atay and Satoshi Toyosaki, 115–136. Landam, MD: Lexington Books.

Chapter 7

Queer-Femme-Pedagogy
Telling Our Tales // Confessing Our Truths
Bri Ozalas and Kathryn Hobson

the podium is a stage, a performance for which i did not audition.
cheshire cats grins side-stage, menacing until i put the *drinkme* bottle to my lips.
drinkme drinkme drinkme.
wear the mask, rub salt in the wound. down the rabbit hole.
do i dare go off script?
secure the puppeteer strings, smile and laugh.
the cheshire cat grins seal my fate.
see? we're all MAD *here.*
salt in my lungs, salt in the wound. smile and laugh.
i wear the mask, ready for curtain call.

***

"Do you come out to your students?" you ask me. We sit in my office—a dimly lit refuge from the outside world. For both of us.

"It depends on the class and the group of students," I say. "I rarely tell my large lecture because they do not deserve to know, and if they find out, they are likely to hold it against me. Smaller classes? Sometimes. If the vibe is right, and if I have students I know in the class, then I generally do."

"Do you?" I ask.

"I want to," you say. "But I'm too anxious about it so I typically just avoid the topic altogether."

***

When we enter the classroom and are queer and femme, with our long curly or wavy hair, tight black pants with Dr. Martens, and made-up faces with strongly arched brows, it would seemingly be easy, we could just pass for a couple of basic cisgender, white, feminine presenting curvy women. However, passing is complex because it is based on outdated stereotypes of what it means to "look queer" and often feels more like erasure as queer femmes. Yet, we know that there is complex privilege for some of our identities and marginalizations for others. Because of the way white, US-based, cisheteronormative culture is structured, for our students to "find out" we are queer, we have to speak up and confess our truths to them. To make our queerness known, we have to constitute our sexuality in the classroom by confessing to the students "who" and "what" we *really* are—even when we may be unsure and at times, wavering.

Picking up where Johnson and Calafell (2020) left off in their piece on public pedagogies of bisexuality, we suggest that the act of confessing who we are is promising in order to foster honest and open relationships between professors and their students. However, the confession of our sexuality is also problematic because we must continually confess and come out about our sexual desires and relationships. Drawing on theories of the flesh (Moraga and Anzaldua 1981), Johnson and Calafell (2020) suggest, "As femme-performing bisexual women ... femmes must consistently fight for legitimacy (much like bisexuals) in the academy, which privileges performances of masculinity" and heterosexuality (67).

On these pages, we use our personal narratives as a means of building on critical and feminist pedagogy (Freire 1970; hooks 1994). Critical pedagogy is the act of balancing power relationships between students and teachers (Freire 1970), while feminist pedagogy extends this theory to address the intersectional identities of marginalized folks empowering themselves through education (hooks 1994). Both scholars view education as a liberatory practice (Freire 1970; hooks 1994).

We use Foucault's notion of the "confessional" as a lens to problematize truth-telling about our sexualities in the classroom. Foucault claims that "Western man has become a confessing animal" (Foucault 1978, 59). As such, the confession of one's sexual desire, according to Foucault, is the very discourse that constitutes the truth of one's sexuality. The confession is a central "technology of the self" (Foucault 1988, 16) "through which we come to know who we are" (Fejes and Nicoll 2015, 5). Thus, in Western society, the confessional has become *the* primary way of expressing the truth of the self and of a person's sexuality. Without confessing the truth of our bisexuality, our queer femme-ness, are we bisexual, queer and femme at all, and how much do these identities matter when it comes to our critical and feminist communication pedagogy? We call upon critical and feminist pedagogy (Freire 1970; hooks 1994) to provide a lens through which to critique the confessional as both liberating and limiting in the classroom.

In this chapter, we build upon existing scholarship that addresses the challenges queer femme instructors face within the classroom. We further examine the internal struggle of grappling with the decision queer instructors, like us, face—the decision of whether or not to "out" ourselves to our students. We reference our own experiences, our own internal struggles, to take a closer look at the intersections of queer femme identity, disclosure, and confession, ultimately questioning the ways in which heteronormative institutions create and perpetuate this predicament in the first place. We explore the confessional as it relates to our gender and sexual identities in the classroom in order to forge relationships and alliances within the classroom, while continually problematizing what it means to come out and stay out as part of such a confession.

***

University classrooms are spaces that co-construct learning through interactions between instructors and their students (Frisby et al. 2014; Goldman and Goodboy 2014; McKenna-Buchanan et al. 2015). Although self-disclosure holds importance for the relational and educational aspects of the classroom, the utilization of self-disclosure is a challenge and overall complicated for LGBTQ+ (queer) instructors with stigmatized identities (McKenna-Buchanan et al. 2015; Mottet et al. 2006; Warren and Davis 2009). This unique pedagogical challenge forces us to weigh our options as to whether or not to disclose our sexual orientation. This disclosure might trigger identification between us and students, or it might create barriers between instructors and students. In all likelihood, it creates some of both, rather than an either/or scenario.

The unique intricacies of individual identities undoubtedly have an influence on (non)disclosure of queer identities in the classroom. Thus, our exploration of our bisexual queer femme identities in the classroom is informed by intersectional theory. Intersectional theory contends that social phenomena are often best understood by examining the overlap of institutional power structures such as race, class, gender, and sexuality (Choo and Ferree 2010; Crenshaw 1991; Hill-Collins 2000; Meyer 2012). We both understand our bisexual identity to encompass attraction to at least two genders, with the potential to be attracted to more. Addressing intersectional identity is pertinent to this work, as we view this project from the perspective of white, cisgender, university-educated, bisexual, queer femme women. However, between us, age, able-bodiedness, and experiences bring differences in our perspectives, even though our struggles to come out in the classroom continue in similar ways. Bringing these facets of our identities to the forefront and acknowledging how they shape our experiences is essential to our work.

We have come to these identities from differing life experiences, and identify with them differently. As such, we acknowledge the complexity of privileges and marginalizations we face because of our intersectional identities.

When it comes to femme, following Ortiz (2014), we understand femme as the "reclaiming of attributes associated with femininity that have so often been used against us individually and collectively and using them for our own benefit and pleasure" (92). Queer femme or the queering of femme alludes to the fact that our femme-ness is not a singularity, but a precarity. Our femme identities are in flux because they are in constant evolution. For different femmes, femme-ininity is performed differently in all contexts, including the classroom. Taking into account our different identity constructions and cultural backgrounds, and acknowledging institutionalized power structures and multiple axes of oppression, provides a gateway into reflective inquiry about positionality and queer identities in the classroom.

***

penance, reconciliation starts with a mouthful of *"forgive me, father, for i have sinned"*

while sitting in a small dark room, a thin curtain dividing the space between you and

the pastor. you feel the pressure to say *something*, you don't want to, but you feel like

you have to, so you do. you don't want to, but you do. you speak into the dark nothingness.

afterward you're supposed to feel the ease of diffused pressure, freed of your wrongdoings.

the utterance of your blunders absolves you of them, as long as you promise to say your prayers. *forgive me, father, for i have sinned*

***

"Do you identify as femme?" you ask me. We sit in the office—a rare quiet moment from the hustle and bustle of the outside world. For both of us.

"I don't know," I say. "I've never really thought about it."

I consider the champagne shimmer on my cheekbones, lips painted mauve. Then say, "I guess I do—I just didn't have a word for it before."

***

As suggested earlier, femme-identified folks embrace femininity as liberatory. Femme is not *just* femininity, but its own entity: "[femme is] femininity's rebellious sibling. Fiercely uncompromising and unapologetically all-encompassing" (Hoskin and Hirschfeld 2018, 85). However, queer femme as an identity is a complicated one, as it is an "identity full of contradiction" (Hobson 2015, 102). Hobson (2015) further explains that queer femme "is a complicated identity because those who identify as femme often appear invisible" (102). This invisibility stems from the supposed advantage of occupying a space that appears to be normative, stereotypical femininity (Hobson 2013; Ozalas 2020).

Many femmes face institutional oppression of femmephobia both from broader culture and queer communities. While words like misogyny and sexism express the role of patriarchy and oppression against cisgender women, the significance of our focus on femmephobia specifically acknowledges that femme-ininity is rooted in political ideology. For example, femmes can be cisgender, transgender, gender non-conforming, non-binary folks who embrace the transgressive politics of embodied femme-ininity. Hoskin (2019) elaborates, "Femmephobia refers to the systematic devaluation of femininity as well as the regulation of patriarchal femininity. Femmephobia operates by policing feminine transgressions as they relate to race, class, sexuality, ability, and so on" (2). We have experienced the institutional devaluation of femme identity with comments about our bodies, clothes, tattoos, and piercings, as well as students disrespecting our authority and personal space in the classroom. Too often have young male students wanted to go in for the hug. Tried to shift for a side hug. Stood a little too close. Lingered a little too long. However, we also recognize that sometimes our femme identities are read as relatable, hip, and as such the students are willing to disclose and be vulnerable. We experience femme identity as liminal between liberation and constraint.

Johnson and Calafell (2020) explore queer femme pedagogy and bisexuality and note that their excessive femininities are policed both in the classroom and in the academy more broadly. In combination with bisexuality, queer femme pedagogy is often rejected for more masculine relational styles, similar to the traditional confessional. These relational styles default to the assumption of monosexism, the idea that individuals cannot be attracted to more than one gender, thus invalidating bisexuality. Instead, as bisexual and queer femme instructors, we queer the confessional with our bodies because the catharsis that is supposed to come from outing ourselves rarely happens. Instead, we have to continually come out, prove our queerness, our sexuality, and our gender dissonance. The monocisheterosexist and masculinist confession does not work for us.

***

Foucault's conceptualization of confession and the confessional frames our analysis of teaching while bisexual and queer femme. This concept stems from a famous scene in which a psychiatrist forces, through the use of repeated cold showers, one of his patients to "confess" his own mental illness (Foucault 1978, 2014; Lorenzini and Tazzioli 2018). This recognition of "madness" from the patient was, essentially, viewed as the "cure" to this patient's mental illness, based on the "idea of the incompatibility between madness and recognition of madness" (Lorenzini and Tazzioli 2018, 73). This instance, according to Foucault (1978, 2014), is the utilization of a very old "religious and judicial procedure" in which power lies within "truth-telling" and, particularly, "truth-telling about oneself," as summarized by Lorenzini and Tazzioli (2018, 73). This notion of confession (or "avowal," "truth-telling") encompasses the "complex set of relations between subjectivity, discourse, truth, and coercion" in our society (Lorenzini and Tazzioli 2018, 73). Ultimately, Foucault's (1978, 2014) analysis of the concept of confession reveals the ways in which the act has transformed throughout history while also problematizing the normalized notion of confession as a means through which individuals can heal, be saved, or find salvation.

Foucault (1978, 2014) notes that confession is one of the main rituals or practices that is utilized for the production of "truth" and "from its original religious and judicial framework it has spread its effects far and wide, in medicine, education, family, and love relations, and—in general—in almost every circumstance of our everyday life" (Lorenzini and Tazzioli 2018, 73). Foucault conceptualizes confession as a technique of power and not one that is imposed on an individual from the outside nor whose effects only produce a certain discourse about a preexisting or fixed individual. Foucault views avowal as the procedure of individualization by power because, through this, the individual is "*constituted* as a subject who bonds himself or herself to the truth he or she verbalizes" (Lorenzini and Tazioli 2018, 74).

The act of confession or avowal essentially speaks *something* into truth. An individual says it out loud (whatever "it" may be), and speaking it into truth makes it real, which in itself is an act of individualization by power. Further, confession is something that is a choice and isn't imposed or pressured by outside forces or individuals. The confession therefore situates and provides a specific meaning or understanding of a specific individual once they speak it into truth. The truth is verbalized and then the subject or individual is paired with that truth, through which others can understand them. For example, if we, as bisexual queer femme pedagogues, were to "out" ourselves or "confess" our "truths," then that truth will be utilized by our students as a means through which they will understand and conceptualize us as individual subjects.

***

SCOM 349. Ethnographic approaches to communication. Twenty students, several I know and have had before, while others are brand new to me. We are reading Minge's (2012) book, *Concrete and Dust*, in which she comes out as bisexual and feminine-performing. Taylor, a white, cisgender, woman with a feminine, hippie aesthetic says, "I'm bisexual, too, and this book really resonates with me."

I weigh my options. Leave her hanging. The *ONE* who is out in the classroom. I cannot do that, it is part of my training in performance. We have to put our bodies on the line. The classroom is one of those spaces where teachers of difference have to be cautious. As Young (2020) explains, "Not all feel safe coming out in the classroom for fear of poor course evaluations, negative repercussions on the tenure process, losing control of future disclosures, or cultural differences" (45). We fear retribution from students who may think our queerness invalidates our teaching credentials; we fear the Department Chair, Dean, University Provost, or President being called *again* because our class is too political; and we fear being stuck in a car with a colleague telling us how our tall, curvy body just looks different in our clothes as compared to our thinner, much more petite Asian, female colleague. Apparently, she has better boundaries with her students, too. The fear of confessing is real.

I take a deep breath and say, "Thank you for trusting us with that information, Taylor. I, too, identify as a queer woman and I am currently with a queer partner." I exhale. They do not say anything. Later I find out that one of the students, a white, hetero, cis male texted the class GroupMe. "I got our professor to come out today. It's so cool that she felt comfortable enough to share." A couple of my queer students "LOL," and say, "Dr. H has always been out. You did not *get her* to come out. She came out in Intercultural Comm and have you seen her office? It is full of gay stuff." He apologizes for his insensitivity, and later becomes my advisee, and one of the best student allies to several of my trans, non-binary, bisexual, and queer students. But as Young (2019) suggests, once you out yourself there is no telling where that confessional discourse will end up. I am left with the metallic taste of bile in my mouth, worried that my sexual orientation will be my demise.

***

Upon entering a classroom, queer instructors "enter with bodies that tell tales, that speak for them, even if those readings are beyond their control or, as is sometimes the case, incorrect" (Warren and Davis 2009, 307). In other words, queer instructors enter the classroom and are instantly the subject of their students' perceptions—their students make judgments and draw conclusions based on the outward appearance of their instructors. "As queer teachers, it is about what happens when we walk into this classroom space (as we do in any space) that is already marked by language, by institutional norms, by so many reminders of heteronormativity" (Warren and Davis 2009, 319). For example, an instructor's whiteness proceeds their entrance into the classroom, and perception of this is not necessarily within the realm of the control for the individual (Warren and Davis 2009).

Revealing information that is unknown by most people (self-disclosure), regardless of the context, carries some degree of risk (Derlega et al. 1993; McKenna-Buchanan et al. 2015). As such, disclosing identities that exist outside the heterosexual-homosexual binary (bisexuality, pansexuality, queer, etc.) adds another layer of difficulty. For some, thinking beyond the binary unsettles the common limits of our minds and the way we think (Britzman 1995; Warren and Davis 2009). Frequently, bisexuality is conceptualized as a "third space" that exists, somehow, outside of this hetero-homo binary that is indoctrinated as the social norm in our society (Garber 1995). Young (2020) notes that this "third space" exists because bisexuality is a hybrid identity, one that is "betwixt and between" heteronormativity and homonormativity (40). We, however, conceptualize our bisexuality as a liminal space without binary ends on a spectrum, that encompasses our personal experiences of attraction and desire, while adhering to an intersectional understanding of both sexuality and gender.

***

SCOM 123. Introduction to fundamental human communication. Twenty-nine first-year college students. We are all at a crossroads, betwixt and between—my students, new to college life, and me, adjusting to my role as an instructor of record as a graduate student. I stand at the front of my classroom and wait for twenty-nine pairs of eyes to look somewhere in my relative direction.

"Today is National Coming Out Day," I say before starting the lecture. I smile but my voice shakes. I weigh my options, as queer instructors must continually do. The possibility of "outing" ourselves forces us to catalog our fears: the fear of our students conflating our queerness, especially bisexuality, with a hyper-sexualized body; the fear of vulnerability; the fear of confession, of speaking the words, "I'm queer."

Do I "out" myself? (do it do it do it) My femme-ness masquerades my queerness. Why am I so afraid? (you should be ashamed of your own apprehension) I want to do this. I know I do (just *DO IT*). Why do I feel like I need to "prove" my queerness? I've been dropping hints all semester, though—discussing the importance of proper pronouns, using "they" when referring to my (female) partner, and even adding a rainbow flag to my damn email signature. Hints aren't enough, we have to *say it*. While the flag implies more than an ally "safe zone" symbol. So many allies have co-opted the flag for their own optical allyship that it does not communicate my queerness as loudly as I had hoped. But I can't force my vocal cords to utter a sound, my tongue to shape the words.

I take a deep breath and instead conclude with: "Make sure to show some love and support for your LGBTQ friends, family, and peers."

***

It's been a long day and it has not even started. I am in a class of 160 students teaching intercultural communication. The sheer number of students makes for a less-than-ideal way to teach this particular class. Having intimate analytical conversations about the politics of race, class, gender, sexuality, and disability tends to make the class more profound. Embracing critical and feminist pedagogy in the classroom means being willing to recognize each other's humanity while having these vulnerable discussions. With 160 students, several of whom are shopping online, doing other homework, or watching sporting events, it is challenging to teach concepts, let alone acknowledge each other's subjectivities.

I told the class I was queer during our Social Identity Wheel exercise where we go through and talk about all of our social identities: race, class, gender, gender identity, sexuality, ability, age, religion, ethnicity, language, and the nation of origin, and so on. Who knows how closely they pay attention in such a large lecture hall? However, today is the day the Supreme Court makes its ruling on whether or not discriminating against LGBTQ folks in the workplace should be legal, or, should employers be allowed to fire us for our gender and sexual identities.

Like Johnson and Calafell (2019), "I'm done. I'm done trying to discipline my body," and for me, I'm also done policing my tone and my tongue even when it means that I may come out with negative evaluations (I mean, who reads those things anymore anyway?). Even more, I will likely be termed as part of the liberal gay agenda trying to convert the seemingly innocent undergraduate students into my seductive lair of ideas and knowledge. The air swells pregnant with tension. With each passing moment, the heat rises from my stomach, to my chest, to my face, and I cannot hold back any longer.

Fuck it; this is when my hard, edgy, white working-class femme comes out.

"I could be fired from this job for being queer in Virginia. If you all organized against me, you could probably advocate to fire me." Why am I saying this? I don't know? It's just coming over me. Stop. Giving. Them. The. Tools. Fortunately, as of this moment, June 2020, the Supreme Court has ruled that it is no longer legal for businesses and workplaces to discriminate or fire queer and transgender employees (de Vogue and Cole 2020).

"Why the fuck should a bunch of straight people get to decide the fate of my community, my people?" I exclaim.

I am obviously angry, or "passionate," as I am often labeled.

"This is a serious issue. Yet, most people do not even know that I could be fired from my job for being queer--for having pictures of my partner in my office, for my gay postcards and bumper stickers." My bright orange "I Can't Even Drive Straight" sticker is burning in my mind. I was worried when I put it up, now I cannot even grip a steady pulse. Why am I bringing this attention to myself? Why am I saying "fuck" so much? That is likely all the students will hear. But I cannot let it go. I have to be honest about what is happening even if it is to my detriment. This is an Intercultural Communication issue.

"Nobody gets to decide whether or not to discriminate against straight folks. Granted, we, queer people, cannot discriminate against straight people, but that is beside the point. It is not fair that one's identity could preclude them from receiving equitable treatment." I end with, "Regardless, now that the Supreme Court has made their ruling, we have to wait months to know the results. The justices do not reveal their rulings right away."

I'm out to around 160 students. Now what? I wait for their judgments as I wait for the Supreme Court reeling over whether or not I did the right thing. Did my confession work? For them? For me?

***

Queer femme pedagogy is often rejected for more monocisheteromasculine relational styles, like the traditional confessional. Foucault (1988) suggests that the confessional is contentious because of the power differentials between the confessor and the confessee. While we are supposed to experience catharsis from outing our "madness," our sexuality, to those who are a part of the heteronormative social order, it rarely happens in quite that way. Instead, because students and teachers are in a continual push and pull of power dynamics like, "I grade you" and "I pay your salary" there is no one psychiatrist and patient, we exist as both simultaneously. Thus we find it imperative for femme confessionals to unilaterally balance power relations.

The masculinist discourse of confession puts undue burden on people with marginalized identities. Because we are queer femmes, we have to out ourselves over and over again often without benefit to us. Thus, we critique Foucault's (1978, 2014) confession as the main way of constituting one's self. Our own experiences detail the ways in which utterance of an individual's "truth" falls short—queer femme identities encompass more than the ways in which we verbally identify or "out" ourselves. While we do not discredit the significance of individuals speaking their truths, we note that this is more than a speech act—this is a queer femme embodiment act. An embodiment act that allows both queer and straight students and teachers to co-create empowered spaces of learning while deconstructing the existing masculinist confessional discourse and hegemonic structures within the classroom.

REFERENCES

Brewster, Melanie E., and Bonnie Moradi. 2010. "Perceived Experiences of Anti-Bisexual Prejudice: Instrument Development and Evaluation." *Journal of Counseling Psychology*, 57, no. 4: 451–468. https://doi.org/10.1037/a0021116.

Britzman, Deborah P. 1995. "Is There a Queer Pedagogy? Or, Stop Reading Straight." *Educational Theory* 45: 151–165. https://doi.org/10.1111/j.1741-5446 .1995.00151.x.

Choo, Hae Yeon, and Myra Marx Ferree. 2010. "Practicing Intersectionality in Sociological Research: A Critical Analysis of Inclusions, Interactions, and Institutions in the Study of Inequalities." *Sociological Theory*, 28: 129–149. https ://doi.org/10.1111/j.14679558.2010.01370.x.

Crenshaw, Kimberlé. 1991. "Mapping the Margins: Intersectionality, Identity Politics, and Violence Against Women of Color. *Stanford Law Review*, 43: 1241–1299.

Derlega, Valerian J., Sandra Metts, Sandra Petronio, and Stephen T. Margulis. 1993. *Self Disclosure*. Newbury Park, CA: Sage.

deVogue, Ariane, and Devan Cole. 2020. "Supreme Court Says Federal Law Protects LGBTQ Workers from Discrimination." *CNN*, June 15, 2020. https://www.cnn .com/2020/06/15/politics/supreme-court-lgbtq-employmentcase/index.html.

Fejes, Andreas, and Katherine Nicoll. 2015. "An Emergence of Confession in Education." In *Foucault and a Politics of Confession in Education*, edited by Andreas Fejes and Katherine Nicoll. New York, NY: Routledge.

Foucault, Michel. 1978. *The History of Sexuality, Volume 1: An Introduction*. New York: Pantheon Books.

———. 1988. *Technologies of the Self: A Seminar with Michel Foucault*. Edited by Luther H. Martin, Huck Gutman, and Patrick H. Hutton. Amherst: The University of Massachusetts Press.

———. 2014. *Wrong-Doing, Truth-Telling: The Function of Avowal in Justice*. Edited by Fabienne Brion and Bernard E. Harcourt. Translated by Stephen W. Sawyer. Chicago: Universityof Chicago Press.

Freire, Paulo. 1970. *Pedagogy of the Oppressed*. New York, NY: Herder and Herder.

Garber, Marjorie. 1995. *Bisexuality and the Eroticism of Everyday Life*. New York, NY: Routledge.

Goldman, Zachary W., and Alan K. Goodboy. 2014. "Making Students Feel Better: Examining the Relationships Between Teacher Confirmation and College Students' Emotional Outcomes." *Communication Education*, 63: 259–277. https://doi.org/10 .1080/03634523.2014.920091.

Hill-Collins, Patricia. 1990. *Black Feminist Thought: Knowledge, Consciousness, and the Politics of Empowerment*. Boston: Unwin Hyman.

———. 2000. *Black Feminist Thought*. New York: Routledge.

Hobson, Kathryn. 2013. *Performing Queer Femininity: Passing, Playing, and Camp.* PhD diss., University of Denver.

———. 2015. "Sue Sylvester, Coach Beiste, Santana Lopez, and Unique Adams: Exploring Queer Representation of Femininity on Glee." In *Glee and New Directions for Social Change*, edited by Brian C. Johnson and Daniel K. Faill, 95–107. Brill: Sense.

hooks, bell. 1994. *Teaching to Transgress: Education as the Practice of Freedom.* New York, NY: Routledge.

Hoskin, Rhea Ashley. 2019. "Femmephobia: The Role of Anti-Femininity and Gender Policing in LGBTQ+ People's Experiences of Discrimination." *Sex Roles*, 81, no. 11–12: 1–18. https://doi.org/10.1007/s11199-019-01021-3.

Hoskin, Rhea Ashley, and Katerina Hirschfeld. 2018. "Beyond Aesthetics: A Femme Manifesto." *Atlantis: Critical Studies in Gender, Culture, & Social Justice*, 39, no. 1: 85–87.

Johnson, Jessica A., and Bernadette Marie Calafell. 2020. "Disrupting Public Pedagogies of Bisexuality." In *Queer Communication Pedagogy*, edited by Ahmet Atay and Sandra L. Pensoneau-Conway, 62–72. New York, NY: Routledge.

Johnson, Julia R. 2013. "Cisgender Privilege, Intersectionality, and the Criminalization of CeCe McDonald: Why Intercultural Communication Needs Transgender Studies." *Journal of International and Intercultural Communication*, 6, no. 2: 135–144. https://doi.org/10.1080/17513057.2013.776094.

Lorenzini, Daniele, and Martina Tazzioli. 2018. "Confessional Subjects and Conducts of Non Truth: Foucault, Fanon, and the Making of the Subject." *Theory, Culture, & Society*, 35, no. 1: 71–90. https://doi.org/0.1177/0263276416678291.

McKenna-Buchanan, Tim, Stevie Munz, and Justin Rudnick. 2015. "To Be or Not To Be Out in the Classroom: Exploring Communication Privacy Management Strategies of Lesbian, Gay, and Queer College Teachers." *Communication Education*, 64, no. 3: 280–300. https:/doi.org/10.1080/03634523.2015.1014385.

Meyer, Doug. 2012. "An Intersectional Analysis of Lesbian, Gay, Bisexual, and Transgender (LGBT) People's Evaluations of Anti-Queer Violence." *Gender & Society*, 26, no. 6: 849- 873. https://doi.org/10.1177/0891243212461299.

Minge, Jeanine Marie. 2012. *Concrete and Dust: Mapping the Sexual Terrains of Los Angeles.* New York, NY: Routledge.

Moraga, Cherrie, and Gloria E Anzaldua. 1981. *This Bridge Called My Back.* London: Persephone Press.

Mottet, Timothy P., Virginia P. Richmond, and James C. McCroskey. 2006. *Handbook of Instructional Communication: Rhetorical and Relational Perspectives.* Boston, MA: Allyn & Bacon.

Ortiz, Lisa. 2014. "Dresses for My Round Body." In *Femme: Feminists, Lesbians, and Bad Girls*, edited by Laura Harris and Elizabeth Crocker. New York, NY: Routledge.

Ozalas, Bri. 2020. *The (In)Visible Woman: A Performative Autoethnographic Exploration of Queer Femme-ininity and Queer Isolation.* Master's thesis, James Madison University.

Warren, John T., and Andrea M. Davis. 2009. "On the Possibility of (Some) Critical Pedagogies: Critical Positionalities Within a Binary." *Cultural Studies - Critical Methodologies*, 9, no. 2: 306–320. https://doi.org/10.1177/1532708608321517.

Wood, Julia T. (2009). "Feminist Standpoint Theory." In *Encyclopedia of Communication Theory*, edited by Stephen W. Littlejohn and Karen A. Foss, 397–399. Thousand Oaks, CA: SAGE Publications.

Young, Stephanie L. 2020. "Bi and Bi: Exploring the Transgressive Potential of the Bisexual Biracial Identity in the Queer Classroom." In *Queer Communication Pedagogy*, edited by Ahmet Atay and Sandra L. Pensoneau-Conway, 44–61. New York, NY: Routledge.

Chapter 8

Pedagogy, Passing, Privilege

Rachel Silverman

INTRODUCTION: SITUATING MYSELF

To begin this chapter, I want to situate my pedagogy and myself by explaining first where I teach and then who I am. I am a tenured, associate professor of communication in the Department of Humanities and Communication (HU/COM) at a private, southern, STEM school focusing specifically in the fields of aviation and aerospace. As of fall 2019, the university's student body is approximately 80 percent male, 50 percent white, 30 percent military affiliated (we have the third largest ROTC program after the US Naval Academy and WestPoint), 30 percent in-state, 13 percent international (primarily from Korea, China, and India), and less than 1 percent communication majors. The communication major is housed in HU/COM department and is comprised primarily of athletes and children of staff and faculty who attend the university for free. HU/COM is the only department on campus with a predominantly female faculty, and the department's chief responsibility is to teach general education courses in the humanities (including writing and speech). Students love and hate our courses—love them because we offer a reprieve from their engineering/physics/math homework and hate them because we take away from their "important" classes.

There is an undeniable sexism associated with our classes and research. Because of the high ratio of female faculty as compared to the university as a whole, the subjects and the department are seen as feminine. Additionally, our research and classes are "soft," disposable, and have questionable value unlike the hard sciences with measurable professional and monetary value. We don't receive the same sorts of grants as other fields of research, we are not teaching specifically for professional development, and while writing and speaking are skills, they are often seen outside our department as immeasurable compared to an aviator's check ride or an engineer's successful project development. All of this results in the marginalization of our department by the administration, other faculty, and students.

One example of this marginalization is our research and teaching load. All full-time faculty are assigned a 4-4 load; however, research releases are regularly given, allowing many faculty to teach as few as two courses per semester. Unfortunately, to receive regular releases, the research must be in line with the mission of the university or be grant-funded. As a communication scholar who studies women's health and the social construction of identity in popular culture, my research never aligns with the university's focus on aviation and aerospace nor receives grants. Neither does the research of my departmental peers. As such, I have a 4-4 teaching load that involves a 3-3 of Speech Communication and a 1-1 of a communication course in support of the major. I do my best to bring my research into each of the classes I teach, albeit Speech, as a general education course with strict learning outcomes, only allows for so much flexibility

INTERSECTIONALITY AND QUEER JEWESS-NESS

When it comes to who I am and how my identity fits into my pedagogy, admittedly, I want to go to my minority identities first. To do so would be to ignore my most privileged identity, the one that allows me to "pass," and that is my whiteness. I privilege from all that comes with the history and current practices of the systematic racial oppression of people of color. I am also Jewish, and Jewish whiteness is "not quite white" (Brodkin 1998). It is both white and different. My whiteness is not the whiteness of Christonormative US whiteness (Ferber 2012); it is a whiteness that corrupts from within (Dyer 1997); it is a whiteness that invites many who doubt it to look for and find a "Jewish difference" (Gilman 1991). And yet, I am undoubtedly white, and I benefit from all that comes with the privilege of my skin color. My whiteness is complex but is nonetheless white.

I am a woman, specifically a cis-gendered woman. Being a woman is the only one of my three minority identity categories always visible to the people around me. My Jewishness and my queer sexuality can be, and often are, invisible, requiring that I come out as Jewish and/or queer on each new occasion (Silverman 2016). I prefer the term Jewess rather than Jew when describing my Jewishness. This preference is not something associated with my pedagogy but my own sense of self and feminist ideology. According to Prell (1999), the word Jew is synecdochically male and ignores the gendered reality of being Jewish. The term Jewess, which can be found in literature as early as 1292, is an Orientalized, racially ambiguous, and exotic other (Nirenberg 2007); she is an "unruly woman" (Rowe 1995), and she is an empowered subject who puts herself first regardless of normative social boundaries. She is and has long been a feminist within patriarchal culture.

I use the term queer Jewess to mark the entirety of my identity. The terms Queer and Jewess carry hatred alongside them and I reclaim those labels. Queer means strange and was a slur thrown at the LGBTQ community for decades if not centuries. Queer also means radical and transformative and has been embraced and reappropriated by the same community of people it was used to harm. Queer allows for a fluidity of identity and I believe it embraces the intersectionality of my identity.

The term "intersectionality," coined by feminist scholar Crenshaw (1989), has become the imperative analytic framework for which feminist conceptions of identity and feminist theory now operate. Intersectionality recognizes that all aspects of identity co-construct each other and the embodiment of different social categories interacts with different forms of oppression. Likewise, privileged categories interact with minority identities rendering varying combinations of privileged and oppressed identities depending on context and construction.

Beyond identity frameworks, intersectionality also contends feminists must accept discomfort when their identity or category of oppression doesn't easily coalesce with their peers. We must lean into the discomforts of differences rather than allow them to separate us. However, thus far, neither feminist theory and as a result, nor queer theory, have viewed Jewishness as a critical site of difference or included Jewish theories of gender, sexuality, and race into their projects of analysis (Antler 2018; Branfman 2019; Brettschneider 2016; Kaye/Kantrowitz 2007). In fact, Jewishness is regularly excluded from feminist texts, feminist pedagogy, and feminist action. For example, after the Charlottesville riots in 2017, the National Women's Studies Association made a statement, which omitted antisemitism[1] from the list of violence and hatred happening at the event.

Beck (1988) claims this specific form of feminist antisemitism, where "Jewish themes are systematically excluded" is seen when "Jewish women's lives continue to remain so conspicuously absent from the majority of introductory Women's Studies texts as well as most feminist and lesbian-feminist anthologies" (94). Pegueros (2004) further describes feminist antisemitism as "amorphous" claiming most feminist antisemitism is "Willful ignorance (is) coupled with an unconscious hatred of Jews" (178). Similarly, queer people of color critiques, which argues for the intersectionality of oppression amongst LGBTQ people within colonialist discourses of stigmatized racial difference, also ignore Jewishness (Ferguson 2004; Morgensen 2011; Muñoz 1999; Nguyen 2014).

While other Jewish cultural studies scholars and I discuss the varying ways gender, race, sexuality, and class are co-constructed with Jewishness; the work of including Jewishness into feminist and queer theory is far from complete.

By excluding Jewishness as a site of difference, a long history of oppression and genocide is ignored. Integral to a productive understanding and practice of intersectionality is the inclusion of Jewishness as a site of difference. Intersectionality is recognizing all people are interconnected and in order for social progress to occur; we must accept the discomfort of different identities and standpoints. Intersectionality is my knowing I am privileged *and* I am othered, and any participation in some sort of "Privilege or Oppression Olympics" will "never get [us] anywhere until we find more effective ways of talking through difference" (Gay 2014, 19). In this space of effectively "talking through difference" and engaging in critical communication pedagogy, I work to support the inclusion of Jewishness into feminist understandings of difference.

CRITICAL COMMUNICATION PEDAGOGY

According to Allen, critical communication pedagogy "depicts teachers as agents of change, and it portrays the classroom as a significant site of social influence" (2011, 191). It is within this pedagogical philosophy that I actively incorporate my identity into the courses I teach. In the context of my Speech classroom, I am white, a woman, and a Jew. I have the privilege of choosing to allow my sexuality to remain unseen and unincorporated into my pedagogy. I am aware that self-harm comes with passing and denial of my queer identity and yet I do it. My Jewishness, which too can pass and go unseen, is something I consciously use in my Speech classroom to support my agenda of including Jewishness as a site of difference in feminist theory, in this case, feminist pedagogy. My gender, which is always already present, is a marked difference, particularly on my campus, and also a key aspect of my pedagogy. My whiteness, which privileges from the invisibility of whiteness in the United States is not something I regularly bring into my teaching and I acknowledge it is a privilege of whiteness that I can make the choice to ignore my race.

The negotiation of my classroom identity is a burden, a vulnerability, and, hopefully, a way to better understand identity, privilege, and oppression. It is through my identity in the classroom that I situate my pedagogy, myself within my pedagogical practices, and the navigation of space in my classroom. In the following pages, I offer autoethnographic, narrative accounts of my intersectional identity within the Speech classroom.

A QUEER JEWESS TEACHING SPEECH

The majority of classes I teach are Speech. Speech is a 200-level course required of all students on my campus. It is generally taken in the spring of freshman year or fall of sophomore year, but there are always the stragglers who wait until senior year and the over-achievers whose AP credits allowed them to move ahead early. Speech is a blend of Public Speaking and Introduction to Communication, and when I teach it, I have three primary pedagogical goals: enhancing speaking skills, advocating for the importance of humanities in STEM education, and understanding and practicing communication competency. Speaking skills come from practice, organization, research, etc., and, in my class, are unrelated to the negotiation of my identity—this is not to say identity is not a factor in public speaking, just not the incorporation of my gender or Jewish identity into the classroom. I use the topics of humanities in STEM and communication competency to bring in my gender and Jewishness, respectively.

Advocating for the importance of humanities in STEM education is important for its own sake as well as a means of minimizing my gendered and resulting professional marginalization. Of the thirty-four faculty teaching general education courses in the HU/COM department, only ten are men. Comparatively, in the Physical Sciences department, which is also housed in the College of Arts and Sciences and responsible for teaching general education courses, of the thirty-eight faculty, seven are women. The two most popular majors on campus, Aeronautical Science and Aerospace Engineering have faculty ratios 39:7 and 36:1 male to female, respectively.[2] I absolutely believe teaching students the importance of humanities education in STEM is synonymous with teaching students to take female faculty seriously.

In my speech class, we focus on science communication, the importance and difficulty of appropriately conveying technical information to a lay audience. We discuss both the "how to" and the "why" of good science communication. The "why" is a popular topic for today's STEM classrooms. STEM students need the humanities because they need to: write clearly, engage an audience, organize ideas, ask questions, challenge answers, form opinions, synthesize meaning, and think critically about the effects of new STEM advancements (Glaser 2015; Horgan 2018; Mitcham 2014; Nisbet and Mooney 2007). Grounding the importance of the humanities' impact on STEM in science and engineering journals provides students the initial credibility they seek. Yet this does nothing to shift their sexist views of humanities education and humanities professors. Watching each other improve as the semester advances by incorporating key elements of good communication— the use of storytelling, analogies, personal connections, and understandable language—does.

Unlike writing courses where students don't necessarily see each other's work, in speech, students watch each other's speeches and clearly see which speeches work and which don't. Students know when they have been engaged, informed, and persuaded, and also when they haven't. Through discussions about the incorporation of communication strategies into their speeches and the positive effects those strategies have, students come to value the humanities. By valuing the humanities, students inadvertently value a topic they've consciously or unconsciously feminized. This is a step toward gender equality; this is feminist pedagogy and feminism in action.

Teaching communication competency is also feminism in action and it is where I negotiate the invisibility of my Jewish identity. In Speech, I specifically use the term communication competency as opposed to cultural competency because of the conservative student body. Over the years, I've noted marked contrast between the receptions of the two terms. According to my students, cultural competency reeks of "PC" language and oversensitive people who need to "get over themselves." Using the term "cultural competency" rather than "communication competency" results in comments such as "a feminist with an agenda" or "pushing her liberal agenda" written on my teaching evaluations. Communication competency, what I argue has a more professional and neutral tone, resonates better with the students and creates less resistance. The terminology of cultural vs. communication competency is of no importance to me; it's the underlying meaning that matters.

Communication competency is imperative to public speaking as well as everyday interactions; it primarily includes nonverbal cues (looking and smelling our best, eye contact, a firm handshake, etc.), written communication, and word choice, specifically how language and identity interact. When we discuss audience/demographic analysis, I remind them we can't always see people's identities; class, ability, religion, and sexuality are not necessarily visible and so we need to be aware of our language at all times. I reiterate that this isn't just for speeches, but also general communication, like job interviews—you never know what you cannot see about someone and if or when you may be ruining your chance at an opportunity. When we discuss written communication, such as emails and cover letters, I insist they use people's correct titles. This is often a good time to remind them I am a Dr. and not a Mrs. and they have no right to assume my marital status—nor does my marital status matter when emailing me about their academics. The gendered nature of titles often receives push-back from the students who insist they are "just being polite" or they "were raised that way." This is where I remind them that titles and general communication competency aren't some silly need for politically correct language but strategic avoidance of offending people you do not know. Connecting language to career development as opposed to people's feelings makes sense and provides value.

Career development begins with good grades; good grades begin with respectful classroom spaces. According to Schrodt (2013) students positively associate a professor's appropriate disclosure with content relevance. I come out as Jewish to demonstrate invisible identities. I ask if any students knew

I was Jewish because of my name, and at times some can. Most cannot and they see the concept of invisible identities in action. I also come out to explain cancelled classes in the fall due to the High Holidays. Each time I come out, I am scared. But I do it anyway. When that look of surprise and confusion washes across some faces, I know they are thinking "she doesn't look Jewish" or "I've never met a Jew before" because at times they have said this aloud. They have also asked about the holidays, curious about unknown traditions, wanting to learn more and understand something new. Sometimes, there is also that one student, whose name makes me think they are Jewish, that visibly relaxes knowing they are not alone.

Just this past semester, on the last day of class, after saying my goodbyes and wishing them a wonderful winter break, one student happily responded "Merry Christmas!" To which another jumped in, "Dude, she's Jewish." His sense of satisfaction was noticeable. And when another student followed with, "Happy Holidays"; I genuinely felt a shift took place. Students who may have thought "Happy Holidays" was some sort of leftist, liberal attack on Christmas suddenly had a tangible situational construct of why language matters and how professionalism truly means inclusivity of diverse identities.

CONCLUSION: ON (NOT) COMING AS QUEER

I've never come out as queer to my Speech students. The Speech classroom does not feel like a safe space. I'm out on campus, I'm the advisor of PRIDE, and I would never hide or deny my identity if asked, but I don't announce it. I wonder if my fear is unfounded. Maybe I am assuming the worst of my students. Perhaps I am projecting my own stereotypes about white conservative men onto the room in front of me. Or, perhaps under the Trump administration my fears are justified.

By keeping my sexuality hidden, I realize I am "becoming complicit with respectability hierarchies that undermine [my] own *pedagogical* goals" (Branfman 2015, 73). I am, according to Goffman "covering" my stigmatized identity as opposed to passing. I do not claim membership in another social category to avoid stigma, rather I "keep the stigma from looming large... to withdraw overt attention" (1963, 102). Further, I am adhering to queer "respectability politics" by clinging to cis-hetero conventions of identity performance as a means of avoiding any stereotypes that might discredit me and/ or my teaching (Higginbotham 1993). These sorts of assimilation strategies inevitably create a gap between members of my queer community who come out and do the work of social acceptance and I, who covers my identity and privileges from its invisibility. By covering, I am "complicit in cultural... systems of oppression" (Branfman 2015, 76).

As I write this, my accounts of classroom identity management provide me with new perspectives on my pedagogy and a life committed to social justice. I spend much of my time concerned with how students may "attribute anything I do that offends or frightens them to the fact" of me being queer (Cummings 1999, 76). I wonder: How might my course evaluations further denounce my gender by adding my sexuality? Will I increase the number of students who comment on my "liberal agenda"? And how do I negoti- ate these low scores with an annual performance evaluation that determines merit-based raises? Knowing the bias always already present in course evalu- ations against marginalized bodies,[3] and seeing firsthand peers denied tenure and promotion for poor evaluations, I take seriously the words of Branfman: "survival takes priority over pedagogy" (2015, 81). Conversely, Cummings' work also reminds me that I may be the first queer adult role model or ally an LGBTQ student comes across. More so, I have the ability to dismantle stereo- types and taboos for the straight students. As such, I wonder how my students and my community are suffering because of my fears, and what opportunities might students be missing because of my assumptions about their beliefs.

Writing this chapter inspires me to change and forces me to question my assumptions. I want to come out to my students and yet, I am scared. I regularly come out in my communication courses, but those students are different. I feel safe with them. I don't feel safe in the Speech classroom and I admire my Speech students who do come out. When I look at them, I feel ashamed for not coming out. I know students see the teacher as the arbiter of power in the classroom, but in the Speech classroom, I feel powerless. The room of mostly white men intimidates me. As I write these words, I realize it all comes down to those damn course evaluations and a fear of the low scores those men will give me. Those men and their socially justified hatred of marginalized bodies, which for me materializes as annual scores about my teaching capabilities, have hindered my pedagogy and my propensity toward social justice.

And for what? I have tenure and I am economically stable enough that the fraction of a percentage point I won't get as a raise is fine. I'll survive. Those scores, regularly proven to be racist, misogynistic, and homophobic, prevent me from being an ally to my students and a role model in my classroom. There are other marginalized bodies in my classroom, and I am not doing the work of protecting them when I hide myself. As I write this, I am embar- rassed of my silence. I know what "[I] allow, [I] encourage,"[4] that "silence in the face of injustice is complicity with the oppressor"[5] and that if I am "neutral in situations of injustice, [I] have chosen the side of the oppressor."[6] I hear my favorite and probably the most cliché social justice mantra running through my brain: "Be the change you want to see in the world."[7] I want to be that change. I need to be that change. I have prided myself on being that change in the past. And now, when being that change is as important as ever, it's time I am the change again.

NOTES

1. In 2016, the International Holocaust Remembrance Alliance...officially addressed the spelling of antisemitism..."Antisemitism should be read as a unified term so that the meaning of the generic term for modern Jew-hatred is clear." (https://www.holocaustremembrance.com/spelling-antisemitism).

2. In comparison, Purdue University, with the top ranked aviation program in the U.S. has a ratio of 43:6 in their Aviation and Transport technology program, and the University of North Dakota, ranked number two has a ratio of 33:5. Purdue's School of Aeronautics and Astronautics has a ratio of 35:6 and MIT's Aeroastro Department a ratio of 40:10.

3. For research and editorials on this subject, see:

> Falkoff, Michelle. 2018. "Why We Must Stop Relying on Student Ratings of Teaching." *Chronicle of Higher Education*. April 25, 2018. https://www.chronicle.com/article/Why-We-Must-Stop-Relying-on/243213.
>
> Flaherty, Colleen. 2019. "Busting Student Eval Myth?" *Inside Higher Ed*. December 9, 2019. https://www.insidehighered.com/news/2019/12/09/study-attempts-debunk-criticisms-student-evaluations-teaching.
>
> Flaherty, Colleen. 2020. "Even 'Valid' Student Evaluations are "Unfair.'" *Inside Higher Ed*. February 27, 2020. https://www.insidehighered.com/news/2020/02/27/study-student-evaluations-teaching-are-deeply-flawed.
>
> McMurtrie, Beth. 2019. "'Brilliant' Philosophers and 'Funny' Psychology Instructors: What a data-Visualization Tool Tells Us About How Students See Their Professors." *The Chronicle of Higher Education*. November 14, 2019. https://www.chronicle.com/article/Brilliant-Philosophers/247523.

4. Carrie Heinze-Musgrove
5. Ginette Sagan
6. Desmond Tutu
7. Mahatma Ghandi

REFERENCES

Antler, Joyce. 2018. *Jewish Radical Feminism: Voices from the Women's Liberation Movement*. New York: New York University Press.

Beck, Evelyn Torton. 1988. "The Politics of Jewish Invisibility." *NWSA Journal*, 1, no. 1: 93–102.

Branfman, Jonathan. 2015. "'(Un)Covering in the Classroom: Managing Stigma Beyond the Closet." *Feminist Teacher*, 26, no. 1: 72–82.

Branfman, Jonathan. 2019. "'Plow Him Like a Queen': Jewish Female Masculinity, Queer Glamor, and Racial Commentary in *Broad City*." *Television and New Media* (June, 2019). https://doi.org/10.1177/1527476419855688.

Brettschneider, Marla. 2016. *Jewish Feminism and Intersectionality*. Albany: State University of New York Press.

Brodkin, Karen. 1998. *How Jews Became White Folks and What That Says About Race in America*. New Brunswick: Rutgers University Press.

Crenshaw, Kimberlé. 1989. "Demarginalizing the Intersection of Race and Sex: A Black Feminist Critique of Antidiscrimination Doctrine, Feminist Theory and Antiracist Politics." *The University of Chicago Legal Forum,* 1989, no. 1: 139–168.

Cummings, Martha. 2009. "Someday This Pain Will Be Useful For You: Self-Disclosure and Lesbian and Gay Identity in the Classroom." *Journal of Basic Writing,* 28, no. 1: 71–89.

Dyer, Richard. 1997. *White: Essays on Race and Culture*. New York: Routledge.

Ferber, Abby. 2012. "The Culture of Privilege: Color-Blindness, Postfeminism, and Christonormativity." *Journal of Social Issues,* 68, no. 1: 63–77.

Ferguson, Roderick. 2004. *Aberrations in Black: Toward a Queer of Color Critique*. Minneapolis: University of Minnesota Press.

Gay, Roxanne. 2014. *Bad Feminist*. New York: Harper Perennial.

Gilman, Sander. 1991. *The Jew's Body*. New York: Routledge.

Glaser, Dan. 2015. "The Risky English Major? Not So Fast." *US News and World Report* (August 22, 2015). https://www.usnews.com/opinion/knowledge-bank/2015/05/11/stem-fields benefit-from-liberal-arts-skills.

Goffman, Erving. 1963. *Stigma: Notes on the Management of Spoiled Identity*. New York: Simon & Schuster.

Higginbotham, Evelyn Brooks. 1993. *Righteous Discontent: The Women's Movement in the Black Baptist Church, 1880–1920*. Cambridge: Harvard University Press.

Horgan, John. 2018. "Why STEM Students needs Humanities Courses." *Scientific American* (August 16, 2018). https://blogs.scientificamerican.com/cross-check/why-stem-students need-humanities-courses/.

Kaye/Kantrowitz, Melanie. 2007. *The Colors of the Jews: Racial Politics and Radical Diasporism*. Bloomington: Indiana University Press.

Mitcham, Carl. 2014. "The True Grand Challenge for Engineering: Self-Knowledge." *Issues in Science and Technology,* 31, no. 1 (Fall): 19–22.

Morgensen, Scott. 2011. *Spaces Between Us: Queer Settler Colonialism and Indigenous Decolonization*. Minneapolis: University of Minnesota Press.

Muñoz, Jose Esteban. 1999. *Disidentifications: Queers of Color and the Performance of Politics*. Minneapolis: University of Minnesota Press.

Nguyen, Tan Hoang. 2014. *A View from the Bottom: Asian American Masculinity and Sexual Representation*. Durham: Duke University Press.

Nirenberg, David. 2007. "Deviant Politics and Jewish Love: Alfonso VIII and the Jewess of Toledo." *Jewish History,* 21: 15–41.

Nisbit, Matthew, and Chris Mooney. 2007. "Framing Science." *Science Magazine,* 316, no. 5821: 56.

Pegueros, Rosa Maria. 2004. "Radical Feminists—No Jews Need Apply." *Nashim: A Journal of Jewish Women's Studies & Gender Issues,* 8 (Fall): 174–180.

Prell, Riv Ellen. 1999. *Fighting to Become Americans: Jews, Gender, & The Anxiety of Assimilation.* Boston: Beacon Press.

Rowe, Kathleen. 1995. *The Unruly Woman: Gender and the Genres of Laughter.* Austin: University of Texas Press.

Schrodt, Paul. 2013. "Content Relevance and Students' Comfort with Disclosure as Moderators of Instructor Disclosures and Credibility in the College Classroom." *Communication Education,* 62, no. 4: 352–375.

Sedgwick, Eve. 1980. *Epistemology of the Closet.* Los Angeles: University of California Press.

Silverman, Rachel E. 2016. "Jewish Lesbian Identity, Feminist Antisemitism, and *The L Word* as a Site for Activism." *Journal of Jewish Identities,* 9, no. 1: 1–18.

Part II

PERSONAL NARRATIVES AND REFLECTIONS ON CRITICAL, INTERSECTIONAL PEDAGOGY

Chapter 9

Sawubona—We See, Value, and Respect You

A Critical Pedagogical Invitation to Communicate

Eddah M. Mutua

Communication in diverse contexts is considered successful when shared meaning is created among participants. The invitation to *see*, *value*, and *respect* addresses the imperative for acknowledgment of all in communication. In a classroom setting, educators may consider a more reflective approach to enrich students' learning by adopting pedagogical practices that integrate diverse perspectives of marginalized groups. This chapter discusses my experiences as a foreign-born faculty in the United States. I contend that these experiences cannot be dismissed or underestimated, as they impact the classroom in numerous ways, for better or worse. Often, the impact of differences that foreign-born faculty encounter in the classroom evoke critical interrogation of the many layers of experience that make us the teachers we aspire to be. This interrogation elucidates the differences between a teacher's experiences and those of their students and what is needed to create a shared meaning in the classroom. In this chapter, I reflect on ways that my African cultural upbringing and experiences as a foreign-born faculty member in the United States inform conceptualization of intersectional and transnational communication praxis in communication studies. It matters that experiences of foreign-born faculty are acknowledged as a relevant contribution to theorizing about communication pedagogy in increasingly diverse classrooms (Atay 2018; Pindi 2018; Toyosaki 2018). These experiences are not to be perceived as atheoretical, petty, outrageous, angry utterances, or simply hearsay. The lessons learned from my subjugated position in the US academy allow me the opportunity to consider varied ways to engage communication scholars to think and act interculturally. Such engagements include intellectual exchanges that privilege diverse historical, cultural, and philosophical perspectives to inform how we create inclusive communication pedagogies in an increasingly diverse world. I discuss selected lived experiences that represent a confluence of intersectional and transnational perspectives relevant to critical communication pedagogy. By so doing, I extend an invitation to critical communication scholars to engage in intersectional and transnational communication praxis to privilege a mutual appreciation of our epistemological and other forms of diversity.

I introduce a Zulu greeting *Sawubona* (We see, value, and respect you) to extend theoretical and pedagogical understanding of intersectional and transnational experiences. Specifically, I respond to Francis Nyamnjoh's scholarly call to fellow African scholars engaging with Western theories to try finding ways to "extend the theoretical cloth to make room for African experiences" (Wesserman 2009). With this in mind, I introduce *Sawubona* to extend theorizing about intersectional and transnational perspectives to include African experiences. The larger context of the lens of analysis relevant to understanding *Sawubona* is grounded in the critical call to privilege non-Western knowledge. Jean Comaroff and John Comaroff (2012), in the seminal essay "Theory from the South" urge academics to deconstruct the way

> Western enlightenment thought has, from the first, posited itself as the wellspring of universal learning, . . . it has regarded the non-West—variously known as the ancient world, the orient, the primitive world, the third world, the underdeveloped world, the developing world, and now the global south—primarily as a place of parochial wisdom, of antiquarian traditions, of exotic ways and means. (113)

This critique of Western knowledge offers insights into teaching intersectional perspectives that center other knowledges including knowledge from the Global South. It is an invitation to engage in critical equitable and reflexive actions to reverse trends that privilege Western knowledge.

As narrated in this chapter, my lived experiences form the basis of the resolve to be a *teacher-scholar* who endeavors to be self- reflective, theoretically critical, interculturally oriented, and global-minded. I will focus on the paradigmatic and influential case of Sawubona in ways it forms the context for theorizing intersectional and transnational communication praxis. In addition, I briefly, explain how Ubuntu philosophy helps to give deeper meaning to *Sawubona* and its role in communication and pedagogy. *Sawubona* as a pedagogical practice acknowledges the presence of self and others and stands to inform critical communication pedagogy as our classrooms become increasingly diverse. I discuss how my lived experiences in Kenya and in the United States shape how I conceive the concept of *Sawubona*. These experiences reveal reverence for spirituality, community, interdependence, empathy, respect, and concern in African culture. I recognize that my African cultural experiences may be different from what I encounter in my culturally heterogeneous class-room in the United States. For this reason, I acknowledge the presence of others who are different from me by educating myself about the world in general and especially US marginalized and hidden cultural, social, and political histories. As a nonwhite foreign-born faculty, I endeavor to understand the indications of cultural differences in a world demarcated as West/Western and Non-Western in order to challenge the attempt to make Non-Western cultures invisible or alien in a diverse world. Appiah (2018) urges us to "untangle some of our confusions about the culture . . . of what we've come to call the West . . . . "Western" here can look simply like a euphemism for white" (190–91).

It is my hope that communication scholars seeking to promote emancipa-tory aims of critical pedagogy in order to decolonize the field are motivated to welcome other forms of knowing. Accordingly, my invitation is for scholars to examine the relevance of *Sawubona* as an acknowledgment of presence of *self* and the *other* and a decolonizing practice in the classroom.

SAWUBONA

Sawubona is a greeting of the Zulu people in South Africa. It translates as "We see you, value you, and respect you." *Sawubona* acknowledges that presence is multidimensional. It involves seeing, feeling, connecting, and acknowledging the ancestors, elders, and everyone in real sight and out of sight. Even when it is one person greeting another, the presence is plural. The greeter says *Sawubona* and the response is *Sawubona.* Mhalangabezi ka Vundla (2020), describes the exchange as follows:

> Firstly, Sawubona is in the plural. We SEE YOU-meaning we acknowledge you. We see that you have been favored with another day. The greeting is accompanied with soundless clapping of hands and a humble slight bow of head and upper body. The response is the same. All this is slow and deliberate. Then enquiries about the well-being of your homestead also in the plural. KUNJANI... How is it with you. To which the reply is SIYAPILA- we are ALIVE we are well. Both sides exchange these words. The underlying understanding is that we are ALIVE because we are protected / favored by those who went before us. The exchange is concluded with SIYABONGA- we give thanks by both sides. (Mhalangabezi ka Vundla, SMS message to author, June 10, 2020)

The greeting affirms that the encounter of two or more people is an acknowl-edgment that "we see each other" including those who are not physically present. It also reveals that the exchange of pleasantries that takes place during the encounter is deliberate and serves as an invitation to connect with others not present, for example, asking about the well-being of the family. Orlando Bishop (2007) explains the ancestral and spiritual meaning of *Sawubona* as an acknowledgment of the interconnectedness of those in contact and seeing as a dialogue and witness to one's presence, agreement, and an invitation to communicate. This is a departure from the US-centric way of greeting. *Sawubona* is not an individualistic greeting (how are you? or hi).

Furthermore, *Sawubona* signifies an experience where community and interconnectedness are prioritized, what the Bantu people of Southern Africa call *Ubuntu*. *Ubuntu* philosophy is community oriented and privileges humanity toward others. Simply stated, *Ubuntu* is *"I am, because we are; and because we are, I am"* (Mbiti 1969; Moemeka 1998). In other words, *Ubuntu* helps us to understand how *Sawubona* is an affirmation of the urgency to connect and sustain community across differences. I believe that *Sawubona* and *Ubuntu* are relevant in contexts outside of the African cultural setting. The emphasis laid on acknowledgment of presence (self and other), creating shared meaning, and finding common ground is relevant in the US classroom.

The question for critical communication scholars is what is underneath *Sawubona* that motivates us to dig deeper into embracing *Sawubona moments* in our teaching? A *Sawubona moment* is the urge to reflect or act on creating a space to recognize an impassioned desire to purposefully *see*, *value*, and *respect* experience emanating from an encounter with differences. The pragmatic case of *Sawubona* (see, value, and respect) can be integrated into communication and pedagogy by developing inclusive curriculum and learning resources and employing critical analytical frameworks that center intersectional and transnational perspectives in communication. Sawubona calls for engagement that acknowledges the presence of everyone in the classroom, and utilizes different forms of knowledge systems to explain diverse lived experiences. By so doing, avenues are open to promote constructive curiosity, critical thinking, intercultural/interracial relationships, conversations, and connections across differences. Theoretically, *Sawubona* represents knowledge from the African continent to showcase orientations which are largely overlooked in Communication Studies.

I learned about *Sawubona* from an African scholar attending the 2017 National Communication Association Conference. Upon learning about the greeting, I recall feeling strongly connected to its meaning at different levels. At a personal level, I wanted to reflect on my own life in order to capture moments that would help me understand its relevance in a classroom setting. As a teacher, I wanted to enrich my pedagogy from a perspective that resonates with me at a deeper level of acknowledgment of presence, existence, and humanity of others. I did not want to respond to differences in my classroom using a generic approach that treats differences as a checklist. I had an opportunity to engage colleagues in a conversation about *Sawubona* as a pedagogical practice at the 2019 Central States Communication Association Preconference on "Teaching with a Global Mindfulness." I believe that intellectual exchanges about this topic provide a relevant context to apply the principles of *Sawubona* in the classroom. Teaching with a global mindfulness calls for pedagogical practices that place emphasis on acknowledging diverse knowledge systems and life experiences. Doing so, learning experiences are created as an acknowledgment of diverse perspectives that help us to make connections needed in a global world. *Sawubona* offers these connections as a paradigm shift to center African ways of knowing as relevant in communication pedagogy. Tomaselli (2019) observes that "In our increasingly conflicted multicultural world it is imperative that joint talks between the different approaches be placed on the academic agenda" (30–31). Communication scholar Amy Aldridge Sanford has adopted *Sawubona* in her scholarship in social justice. Sanford advocates for the use of new cultural approaches and calls on individuals and communities to embrace *Sawubona* as an invitation to engage dialogue or deal with challenges of power imbalances and cynicism (Sanford 2020, 131).

So far, I have explained the meaning of *Sawubona* as a framework for considerations about promoting intersectional and transnational communication praxis in our classroom. How we go about concretizing *Sawubona* in our classrooms is spoken for in the title of this chapter. *Sawubona* as an "invitation to communicate" signals an invitation to co-create a learning space where the presence and diverse experiences of students and their professors and especially foreign-born faculty are acknowledged.

In the following section, I will share my own story to illustrate how I respond to the impassioned desire to embody *Sawubona*. I reflect on my cultural upbringing and teaching experiences in the United States to illustrate how *Sawubona* can help us make sense of othered experiences. Through these reflections, I wish to return to the source of my motivation and urgency to develop a new understanding of the cultural, historical, and political divergences that must be negotiated in today's challenging teaching environment. These various experiences have provided me with a feeling of groundedness, while also inspiring me to interact with others different from me with greater understanding and empathy.

MY CULTURAL BACKGROUND

I was raised by my grandparents who had little to no formal education, but had abundant wisdom engrained in local ways of knowing. They were raised in households that practiced African traditional values until they converted to

Christianity in the mid-1930s. My grandfather's "new" identity as a Christian allowed him the opportunity to attend school where he was able to attain a colonial education equivalent of eighth grade. He became a public health worker in the village. He inspected slaughterhouses, butcheries, eateries, dispensaries, schools and other public facilities. I recall him telling me that his job entailed maintaining high standards of hygiene and always staying deferential to those he came into contact with. It is important to note that the British colonial education system was not necessarily set to meet the interests of the colonized. It was to serve the interest of the colonial administration.

On the other hand, my grandmother did not have formal education even though she had converted to Christianity. In most part, she lived her life and performed her responsibilities based on the perspectives of African traditional values of community, empathy, respect, and harmony. As a Christian she was an active member of the church. She had memorized bible verses and gospel hymns translated into our local language *Kikamba.* Generally speaking, she was attuned to cultural traditions of the *Akamba* people (our ethnic group) as well as the Christian traditions. *Nyanya,* "grandmother" in *Kiswahili* as we fondly called her, did not seem bothered by the fact that she did not know how to read or write in *Kikamba* (our language), *Kiswahili* (Kenya's national language) or English. All her grandchildren knew was her kindness, love, and discipline. We also knew that she was wise because she kept records of everything in the home including livestock, harvest, and chores to be undertaken inside and outside of her home. She knew how to run a home, grow food for the family, maintain the fields, heal minor ailments with local herbs or foods, give good advice, pray, sing, dance, tell stories, and many other things. Like my grandfather, I believe that she was very wise in practical and cultural knowledge. This brief introduction of my grandparents leads me to recount a conversation with my grandfather about my educational endeavors. The purpose of sharing this story is to expand the understanding of *Sawubona* as a pedagogical practice that embodies diverse lived experiences, community involvement, and invitation to communicate across differences.

In the mid-1990s, I traveled back to Kenya from the University of Wales, Aberystwyth, to collect data for my Ph.D. research. I visited my grandparents in the village. My grandfather wanted to know what I was doing "in that far land." I told him that I was working on a Ph.D. "What is that?", he asked. This question reveals that perhaps, I should have considered a different way to explain what I was doing in Wales. To be honest, I did not know how to explain what a Ph.D. is. Instead, I responded by saying I was training to be a university teacher. I knew he would at least understand what I was doing in Wales if I connected it to teaching. For my undergraduate studies, my grandfather had wanted me to attend a local university in the outskirts of Nairobi that specialized in training teachers. I turned down his wish to be a teacher.

As I reflect on this conversation, I realize the need to pay attention to my grandfather's response to the claim that I was "training" to be a university teacher. The response is narrated in *Kikamba* and translated into English as follows: *Uu nuseo muno. Ninesii wikinengo kya walimu kuma wimunini.* "That is very good. I always knew you had a gift of the art of teaching from a young age." I was curious to know what formed his views about teaching given that he had little formal education and had not encountered many teachers in his life. I asked him how he knew I would be a teacher and the response was as follows: *Ndyeesi. Undu usiasya andu na undu unenaa na kwithuukiasya andu maineena nundu useo. Ndusembeaa maundu.* "I knew. The way you look at people, talk or listen is a good thing. You do not rush into things."

This conversation reveals my grandfather's view on being a teacher and teaching. Being a teacher is not simply having the gift of teaching (*kinengo kya usomethya*) but mainly embodying the art of teaching *(kinengo kya walimu).* It is the awareness of others (how you look at people, talk and listen to them) and one's involvement with what you see, hear, or say that makes teaching intentional and community-oriented. It matters how you look at people (with disgust, gratitude, empathy, or sneer, etc.), what you see (good or bad, open or masked), how you listen (well, kindly, pseudo-listening, or don't listen), how you talk (carefully or dismissively), and how you respond (verbally or silently). Thus, attentiveness and connecting with others reflects the *we/us* value emphasized in communalistic society. According to Andrew Moemaka (1998), "communalism is the principle or system of social order in which . . . each one is an integral part of the whole, and derives his or her place in the context of the community" (124). I recognize the relevance of cultural meanings assigned to teaching to the African cultural context. However, the question for me is whether these values can be relevant in a different cultural context. In other words, what does this theorizing about the art of teaching, the role of the individual in the community, and community expectations of an individual mean to me as a foreign-born faculty member in the United States? Indeed, the African experiences shape who I am today and serve as the foundation of my will and ability to navigate and negotiate the US academy. It has not been an easy road but what I cherish is the good that has come from a place of pain, despair, and confusion. In the next section, I will share the challenges encountered and how I continue to find ways to enrich my understanding of the new cultural environment so that my role as a teacher can be an invitation to see, value, and respect others.

EXPERIENCES IN THE UNITED STATES

I came to the United States in November 1999. Since then, I have encountered a number of problems that obstruct the realization of ideals embedded in *Sawubona*, *Ubuntu*, and communalism. Such problems include prejudice, a systematic bias against non-Western knowledge, structural racism, sexism, and micro-aggression. When I started teaching in 2001, about the same time I started interacting with more people who are different from me, I found that my "foreignness" was often received with mixed reactions. For example, my accent and "Africanness" became the "new" identity markers. Some comments about my accent such as "where is that accent from," "your accent is cool," or "you have a thick accent" bothered me because I felt so "othered." Similarly, my dressing style seemed to draw almost similar comments such as "your style is so ethnic," "that is exotic," or "do you feel out of place when you wear your African outfits in public?". Other examples of my experiences are discussed in a short essay titled 'You were not born here' (Mutua 2012). In response to these new experiences, I was angry and sometimes in despair about ever being able to learn to do things the "American way." The other fact that troubled me is how my education qualifications were othered. I did not attain my education in the United States and, often I felt some people were insinuating that I would not succeed in the US academy. For example, several faculty members I met at conferences would tell me it will be difficult to find a tenure track (full-time) teaching position as foreign-trained. This made me feel as if I was not good enough. I was angry. Despite this, I did not give up on the commitment to educate myself about this new place which seemed somewhat hostile, belittling, and bewildering.

Anger is inevitable when "othering" continues to be directed at a "foreign" body. Over the years, I continue to learn about anger because I realize that I am not the only one angry in the United States. The anger felt by minority groups is manifested in unequal power relations, historical, political, and economic factors which must be understood by foreign-born individuals like me. As such, I find it comforting to learn about the different meanings about "anger" by Audre Lorde, "rage" by James Baldwin, or "eloquent rage" by Brittney Cooper. These scholars give me a new understanding of "anger" as freedom, resistance, and acknowledgment of injustices against marginalized groups in the United States. In addition to knowing that anger is destructive to the body, mind, and soul, I now know something more about constructive anger. Brittney Cooper asserts that "rage can help us build things, too. The clarity that comes from rage should also tell us what kind of world we want to see, not just what kind of things we want to get rid of" (2018, 274). Where do I go from here with this understanding to enable me negotiate my interactions in the US academy? These conflicted interactions and new understandings are moments to reflect on *Sawubona* in order to create community.

I am aware of the historical, political, and cultural differences between where I was born and raised, and where I now work and live. Nonetheless, in the era of globalization, I am also able to find some common ground between them. For example, I have interacted with members of US-born minority groups and people from different parts of the world and found connections between us through shared history and culture. These connections are helpful but are not very frequent in the academy which is predominantly white. As a matter of fact, I must attend all the time to negotiating an academic environment where perceptions about me are overwhelming: outsider, insider/outsider, foreigner, culturally different, Black African female, angry, "example of affirmative action gone wrong," and/or token. On the other hand, I am comforted by the goodwill of the people who positively perceive and are happy to call me their friend and colleague and so do I. Nonetheless, whatever negative label is put on me, I know it matters because it allows my teaching and interactions with other academics to go beyond the superficial in addressing such misconceptions. I must build on and modify structures of knowledge construction that privilege the West as the center of how we make sense of the world. To a large degree, this academic environment challenges my African cultural ideals of community, respect, and harmony. For example, it is exhausting to build meaningful relationships when students' focus is on grades-oriented learning, self-promotion, competition, self-indulgence, assertiveness, or overly verbalized confidence. Likewise, faculty members have pretty much the same focus in tying teaching and learning to likeability and course evaluations.

In the academy, horrendous acts of favoritism, narcissism, misogyny, racism, and bullying often go unchecked. I have experienced occasions where my white colleagues get defensive when I challenge them. For example, I had a white male ask me if I thought he did not know his job when I offered a suggestion about working with minority students. I have learned that when I demand an answer or accountability, the response is dismissive. Here are some responses I have received: "you seem to have an angry tone whenever you talk," "your tone is bad," "she yells at people," "she is mean," and "she is not as good as she pretends to be." I can go on and on, but at the end of the day, I know that I have to find a way out for me. This way out is not scripted for me in the United States. I have to script it myself. What I mean is that the way for me to go is to see the enactment of *Sawubona* in a new cultural environment.

Thus, as part of the pathway to sustain my commitment to inviting and welcoming educators to privilege other perspectives in the academy in general, and communication studies in particular, there are questions to be asked and answered. These are questions that have become part of my academic life while dealing with what Stuart Hall and Bill Schwartz (2017) call "the awkward presence of difference" (p. 158). Some of the questions I contemplate from time to time include the following: Should I just accept that it is awkward to be the only Black person in a room? When do I push back or remain silent? How do I push back? When is it worth my time and well-being? Do I let myself get to the point "fake it until you make it" in pursuing fairness and contentment, or do I dare face the consequences for talking back? These questions capture emotions emanating from othering directed at faculty of color and more so nonwhite foreign-born faculty members who are not US trained. As I have come to learn more about the US academy, I know I am not alone among those "presumed incompetent" (Muhs et al. 2012). In view of this, I continue to fight to deconstruct this delusional thinking about faculty of color or foreign-born non-US-trained faculty as incompetent. It is therefore imperative to critically examine ways that the academy deals with difference matters (Allen et al. 1999).

Stuart Hall and Bill Schwartz offer an insightful perspective about how to make sense of "new problem spaces" (2017, 172) to avoid getting fixated by the harm caused. I am encouraged by the prospect that these spaces "provide not only home from home but a new site of knowledge and allow one to put these issues in a wider historical and personal context" (2017, 172). Exploring ways to reach a wider context to understand our experiences solidifies the exigency essential to our reckoning of intersectional and transnational perspectives. For instance, I have had to educate myself about histories of US minority groups, attend intercultural events, and interact with people from different backgrounds in the United States in order to expand my intercultural knowledge. In Kenya, the British education system did not focus much on experiences of minority groups including the Black experience (Mutua 2016). This intentional learning acknowledges the presence of others regardless of the presumptions about my identities and experiences. I believe educators including white educators can commit to learning about what they do not know as well.

EXTENDING THE THEORETICAL UNDERSTANDING OF INTERSECTIONAL AND TRANSNATIONAL PERSPECTIVES

I introduced *Sawubona* to extend theoretical and pedagogical understanding of intersectional and transnational experiences. Specifically, I wanted to contribute to Francis Nyamnjoh's (2009) call to African scholars to extend the theoretical cloth to make room for African experiences. Now, I can illustrate ways that *Sawubona* can enrich the understanding of ways to integrate African experiences in teaching about intersectional and transnational perspectives as well as how to understand othered experiences.

Lesson #1

Sawubona extends theoretical understandings that make room for African perspectives in scholarly work in the classroom and the US academia at large. The conceptual modelling for *Sawubona* places emphasis on acknowledging physical and spiritual presence as well as diversity in thought and practice. Given the diversity of African culture(s), *Sawubona* still presents universal values relevant to many cultural groups besides the Zulu people of South Africa. *Sawubona* takes a wholistic approach which emphasizes on the interconnectedness of people to the living and non-living, the past, the present, and the future. To connect with people is to inquire about their well-being including that of the family, and the community in general. The meaning of *Sawubona* in its larger cultural context as shown through my cultural upbringing and professional life contextualizes its relevance as a pedagogical practice to promote intersectional and transnational perspectives in communication studies. *Sawubona* seeks to go deeper because it is not fixated on categories namely, the "race, class, gender and sexuality mantra" which produces a flat, formulaic, superficial and "roster-like approach" to intersectionality (Yep 2014, 87). Gust Yep's (2014) work on thick(er) intersectionality (TI) sets an example of how we can expand the understanding of intersectionality by acknowledging i) struggles about premature closure of identity, ii) the messiness of the everyday, iii) affective investments, and identities embodied, and iv) lived in specific geopolitical and historical contexts (87). I believe that we can learn about these four defining characteristics of TI by using *Sawubona* as an invitation to communicate.

Lesson #2

Sawubona helps us understand intersectionality by its pragmatic approach which involves taking deliberate action to impart knowledge about diverse perspectives in communication studies. I have resisted the "push" to see myself as a victim of my identities and experiences by using my research, teaching, and service as an avenue to impart new perspectives about African experiences. Nyamnjoh (2009) urges us to allow a given situation or context of our work to tell the story rather than say this is the story or this is my story. As a member of Central States Communication Association (CSCA) and National Communication Association (NCA), I have organized and presented in panels that provide spaces to interrogate marginalized experiences and ways to foster appreciation of our epistemological and other forms of diversity. Additionally, my service in several CSCA and NCA committees and taskforce groups has provided opportunities for me to engage with colleagues in critical conversations about diversity, equity, and inclusion. These are opportunities that tell our stories, reveal our experiences and invite others to communicate.

Lesson #3

Sawubona welcomes diversity of knowledge and invites educators and students to embrace the readiness to learn, un/learn, or re/learn about different experiences. *I/we see you* is an invitation to communicate and exchange knowledge. *Sawubona* as a pedagogical practice offers an opportunity to present the classroom as a community of diverse presence. It is this acknowledgment of presence that helps me to move through the difficulties of teaching while different. bell hooks (2003) asserts that it is possible to "learn liberating ideas in a context that was established to socialize us to accept domination, to accept one's place within race, sex, and hierarchy" (2). While it is the case that the US classroom and the academy in general exhibit these hierarchical trends, "a context for a counter-narrative, one in which learning could take place that did not reinforce white supremacy (3)" must be created. My involvement to create connections that make the classroom a community of diverse presence focuses on how we all relate to each other as a community of learners. Each student is assured that they are welcome to share their stories throughout the semester as applicable. They are encouraged to embrace their gut and know that it is okay to be curious, ask questions, make mistakes, and fix them.

On my part, I consider specific historical, political, and/or cultural context relevant to the topic or experience to be shared. For example, it is important to start talking about Africa's colonial experiences as the entry point to dispelling the myth created by the colonizers about the need to "civilize" Africans. Colonialism did not civilize Africans; it robbed Africa of her resources. A conversation that is always well received is about diversity of African languages and colonialists' push for Africans to learn European languages. It helps students to understand why I have an "accent" when I speak US-American English. Explaining difficulties of learning foreign languages resonates with the students. I explain why some English words are difficult for me to pronounce and prefer to write them on the chalkboard. For example, my first language *Kikamba* does not have "r" and as such, it is difficult to pronounce "r" and "l" in one word like pluralism. I have to pause and think about how to say it. As these conversations about language continue, students learn that *Kikamba* or *Kiswahili* words are difficult for them to pronounce too. On African epistemologies, I use proverbs or assign stories that teach about how Africans interpret their social world. These are just few of the examples of what can be done to present the classroom as a community of people interested in sharing their experiences. From bell hooks, I deduce a deep wisdom that education is an act of freedom, hope that creates life-sustaining communities of resistance (2003, 12) and advancement of "transnational literacy" (advocated by Gayatri Spivak's in *Outside in the Teaching Machine*, as cited in hooks 2003, 7).

As illustrated through my lived experiences in Kenya and the US academia, it is imperative to bring into conversation different approaches needed to enrich communication pedagogy in our classrooms. Certainly, *Sawubona* is an approach to "universalizes" values that we all yearn for—to be seen, valued, and respected.

CONCLUSION

As I contemplate my concluding remarks, a thought that comes to mind is what idea or occasion stands out for me in this chapter. Some readers may have a different opinion from mine as to what stands out for them. For me, the occasion is the 2017 NCA panel when I learned about *Sawubona*. The moment reveals that different contexts of our work—research, teaching, and service—are opportunities to practice self-reflection and learn about other experiences. Thus, this chapter is a result of a commitment to adhere to the invitation to communicate as exemplified in *Sawubona*. The symbolic meaning of *Sawubona* embodies values that educators and students desire—to be seen, valued, and respected, to be inclusive in our teaching and learning, and to be respectful in ways wc interact with those who are different. The invitation to communicate, create community, connect, and learn motivated me to reflect on my own cultural upbringing in view of my experiences in the United States as a foreign-born faculty member and ways to extend our understanding of intersectional and transnational perspectives in communication studies. I have learned that our pedagogies should open opportunities for students and faculty alike to see such experiences like mine and others from marginalized groups as embodiments of history, "globalness," cultural and spiritual values, epistemic consciousness, humility, pain, and joy. In the frequently oppressive academic milieu, we can find opportunities that are liberating. I wish for my colleagues in the academy who have presumptions about people like me can find motivation to practice self-reflection and learn about others. We all have work to do in making the classroom and the academy an even playing ground.

I remain optimistic about the opportunity to acknowledge our diverse presence when we allow the heart, mind, and soul to be at the right place. It is the eagerness and flexibility to seek new approaches to teaching and assisting students that will allow us to acknowledge other experiences and their presence in our classrooms.

In acknowledgment of the work we have to do as critical pedagogues in settings that could easily tear us apart, finding a source of self-regard, self-love, and joy can serve as the ingredients to embody our critical selves as teachers. I conclude this chapter by acknowledging, as Toni Morrison (2019) posits, that in "all our education, whether it's in institutions or not, in homes or streets or wherever, whether it's scholarly or whether it's experiential, there is a kind of progression, . . . knowing the limitations and the danger of exercising one without the others, while respecting each category of intelligence, is generally what serious education is about" (p. 307). My hope for critical communication scholars to act is now. We all may have different paths to realizing *Sawubona* moments. Regardless, let's find these paths and celebrate the indivisible act to see, value, and respect others.

REFERENCES

Allen, Brenda J., Mark Orbe, and Margarita Olivas. 1999. "The Complexity of Our Tears: Dis/Enchantment and (In)Difference in the Academy." *Communication Theory*, 9, no. 44: 402–429. https://doi.org/10.1111/j.1468-2885.1999.tb00206.x.

Appiah, Kwame Appiah. 2018. *The Lies that Bind US: Rethinking Identity*. New York, NY: Liveright Publishing Corporation.

Bishop, Orlando. 2007. *Sawubona*. Retrieved from 2007. https://www.youtube.com/watch?v=2IjUkVZRPK8.

Cooper, Brittany. 2018. *Eloquent Rage. A Black Feminist Discovers Her Superpower.* New York, New York: Picado St. Martini's Press.

Hall, Stuart, and Bill Schwarz. 2017. *Familiar Stranger: A Life Between Two Islands.* Durham, NC: Duke University Press.

hooks, bell. 2003. *Teaching Community: A Pedagogy of Hope.* New York: Routledge.

Mbiti, John. S. 1969. *African Religions and Philosophy.* London: Heineman.

Moemeka, Andrew. 1998. "Communalism as a Fundamental Dimension of Culture." *Journal of Communication*, 49, no. 4 (Autumn): 118–141. http://eprints.coven antuniversity.edu.ng/1080/1/Communalism%20As%20A%20fundamental%20 Dimension%20Of%20Culture.pdf.

Morrison, Toni. 2019. *The Source of Self-Regard: Selected Essays, Speeches, and Meditations.* New York, NY: Alfred A. Knopf.

Muhs, Gabriella Gutierrez, Yolanda F. Niemann, Carmen G. Gonzalez, and Angela A. Harris. 2012. *Presumed Incompetent: The Intersections of Race and Class for Women in Academia.* Logan, UT: Utah State University Press.

Mutua, Eddah. 2012. "You Were Not Born Here." *Women & Language*, 35, no. 2 (Fall): 91–94.

Mutua, Eddah. 2016. "How I Came to Know: Moving Through Spaces of Post/ Colonial Encounters." In *Globalizing Intercultural Communication: A Reader*, edited by Kathryn Sorrells and Sachi Sekimoto, 95–102. Thousand Oaks: Sage Publication.

Nyamnjoh, Francis. 2009. "Extending the Theoretical Cloth to Make Room for African Experience: An Interview with Francis Nyamnjoh." Interview by Hermann Wesserman. *Journalism Studies*, 10, no. 2: 281–293. https://www.nyamnjoh.com/2009/04/extendingthe-theoretical-cloth-to-make-room-for african-experience-an -interview-with-francis-nyamnj.html.

Pindi, Gloria N. 2018. "Hybridity and Identity Performance in Diasporic Context: An Autoethnographic Journey of the Self Across Cultures." *Cultural Studies ↔ Critical Methodologies*, 18, no. 1: 23–31. https://doi.org/10.1177/153270861773563.

Sanford, Amy Aldridge. 2020. *From Thought to Action. Developing a Social Justice Orientation*. San Diego, CA: Cognella.

Tomaselli, Keyan. (2019). "Intercultural Communication: A Southern View on the Way Ahead: Culture, Terrorism and Spirituality." *Annals of International Communication Association*, 44, no. 1: 19–33. https://doi.org/10.1080/23808985 .2019.1595696.

Toyosaki, Satoshi. 2018. "De/Postcolonial Autoethnography: Critical Relationality With the Academic Second Persona." *Cultural Studies ↔ Critical Methodologies*, 18, no. 1: 32–42. https://doi.org/10.1177/1532708617735133.

Yep, A. Gust. 2016. "Toward Thick(er) Intersectionalities: Theorizing, Researching, and Activating the Complexities of Communication and Identities." In *Globalizing Intercultural Communication: A Reader*, edited by Kathryn Sorrells and Sachi Sekimoto, 86–94. Thousand Oaks, CA: Sage.

Chapter 10

Family Stories, Pedagogy, Inclusive Practices, and *Autohistoria*

Sergio Fernando Juárez

INTRODUCTION

It starts with a story; I begin my classes each semester by introducing myself and telling my students a family story. The first day of the class is filled with nerves, but today I'm feeling more nervous. In class earlier than usual, I tidy up the room, organize the chairs, and stand in front of an empty class rehearsing my introduction. Some of my nerves ease as students walk in; I see there are a lot of Latinx students in the room, and my nerves dissipate. This is the right choice; I tell them my mom's story of coming to the United States,

> Me vine sin nada, del ejido me vine en bas a Tijuana. Luego que viene un primo por mi y que me lleva con tu tio. Yo queria trabajar, me espere un dia y que me voy sola a buscar un trabajo. Sin saber ingles que me tomo el bas ni sabia a donde iba. Que sigo a gente, hay que se bajaron me baje tambien. Ahi estuve caminando parriba y pabajo haste que sale un hombre de una oficina y me habla pero no le entiendo. Que me lleva a una oficina y una muchacha me traduce. Me dieron trabajo ese dia, trabaje, y luego que el mismo señor me lleva patras pa la casa.

The way my mom told me this story was in a very matter-of-fact tone and she was proud of her courage to travel alone, to take a bus from her hometown to the border and that she took it upon herself to find work rather than sit and wait for someone to get her job. That despite the language barrier she was able to find work. I was and still am proud of this story.

I share this story for several reasons. First, I am proud of my mother who left home by herself; at seventeen years old she left her family in Mexico, with little money and mostly hope. Second, it is a message that resonates with many students in the room whose families have similar experiences. Lastly, I hope that by telling my story I can increase a sense of belonging for students and myself. In this chapter I utilize Anzalduá's *Autohistoria-teoria* as a methodology to interrogate the pedagogical choice of telling of my family story. Through a lens of Aztec mythos, I explore my attempt to identify with Latinx students and in pursuit of creating a home space for both students and myself. [1]

While my Mexican American identity to some may be inconsequential, to others, my story *is* their story, my family story is *their* family story. My body standing at the front of the room is a rarity and more so is my mother's story. Stories like my mother's are rarely heard because bodies like mine have been historically excluded from university classroom spaces. One reason is that my body is deemed illegitimate in spaces like these. Gloria Anzaldúa (2007) posits the only "legitimate" inhabitants within the borderlands are those in power: whites and those who align themselves ideologically with whites. Anzaldúa (2007) makes this argument because in general it is white bodies that are normalized and therefore deemed legitimate inhabitants. Meanwhile brown bodies are deemed illegitimate; our bodies are rarely seen, much less accepted, but furthermore systematically excluded from roles as students and professors. My body in the role of professor is not immediately read as legitimate in this space. Moreover, stories like my mother's that resonate with many students like myself are rarely heard. Therefore, the telling of my mother's migration story becomes a part of my family story of migration. I put my body into action by telling the class that my body in this space is not a haphazard accident. I am not a haphazard accident. I tell them the "how" and the "why" of my family's migration to the Central Coast of California. Every semester now I tell a version of this story to do what Alexander (2010) calls a critical performative pedagogy, putting my body into action as a purposeful act (319). As Alexander (2010) puts it, "[c]ritical performative pedagogy must acknowledge that inequities in power and privilege have a physical impact on our bodies and consequently must be struggled against bodily, through physical action and activism" (319). Purposeful actions that interrupt norms shed light on body politics that often go uninterrogated; practices and policies exercise power that marks, regulates, and negotiates on/through bodies (Sorrells 2016, 54).

My body in this space interrupts the "traditional" classroom, and traditional notions of who belongs in a classroom are disrupted when students hear my story. I call attention to the politics of bodies, interrupting norms not only by being in this space but by the purposeful action in adding my family's narrative. I do this to identify with students who might otherwise not have someone to identify with. Through this in-class performance I hope migrant Latinx and more students can resonate with my experiences and see themselves as belonging in the physical classroom spaces (Alexander 2010, 319). I identify as unapologetically both Mexican and American and purposely disclose my ethnicity to my students because I hope to inoculate imposter syndrome that might arise in students sitting in my classroom.

Imposter syndrome, as defined by Cokley et al., "is the belief in oneself as an intellectual fraud and involves an individual finding it difficult to internalize [their] achievements"; this may also include feelings of not belonging at an institution (2017, 141). Unfortunately, imposter syndrome is common among Latinx students; a widely experienced feeling of not belonging or a lack of belonging (Bravata et al. 2020, 1272). Like many students of color, I experience imposter syndrome myself, we both struggle to find a home in the academy (Calafell 2007, 428). But it also manifests in a feeling of "cheating the system."

There are moments I believe I have cheated my way in, that I do not belong. I question my belonging because I do not share the same interests as my colleagues, have similar experiences, or identify with canonical scholars. Or I do not quite understand concepts that have little in common with my background experiences. Further, I question my success in the field, my scholarship, and whether my scholarship interests in Latinx contexts and social justice are valid, or whether I am just confused. I question my efforts to merge communication theory with social justice. I feel like an imposter and I recognize why scholars consciously or unconsciously avoid addressing social justice in their scholarship. It is a feeling of exclusion and a lack of a physical or ideological home.

Teaching is a process of social and self-discovery and *autohistoria-teoria* is a useful methodological tool because its scope is turned inward, where I can interrogate my own communicative practices of pedagogy. At a microlevel of communicative practices, these are individual or interpersonal dynamics that occur at smaller scale (Sorrells 2016, 135). Anzaldúan theories such as the *Coatlicue* state, *Nepantla*, and the *Coyolxauhqui* imperative help me illuminate the everyday practices of my pedagogy. Through the exploration of Aztec mythos and in the telling of my family story, I interrogate my Latinx identity and pedagogical choices in the pursuit of creating home spaces for both students and myself (Nuñez 2014, 138). In this process of discovery, I invite the reader to experience my path of *conocimiento* (Conley 2019, 231).

AUTOHISTORIA-TEORIA AS METHOD

Autohistoria is the fusing of personal narrative with theoretical discourse, and on the page it may look like vignettes merged with autobiographical prose (Anzaldúa 2015, 6). Anzaldúa describes it best in Spanish "conectando experienceias personales con realidades sociales," meaning that *autohistoria* is connecting personal experiences with social realities (Anzaldúa 2015, 6). *Autohistoria-teoria* makes personal experience the subject of study, and interrogates and intervenes while constructing/building knowledge. This is a discovery process that Anzaldúa (2015) describes as "inventing and making knowledge, meaning, and identity, through self-inscriptions, by placing our experiences as the subject of study in relation to social realities" (3). In the writing of my *auto-historia* I am inventing and making knowledge from my particular social position. Through a storytelling format I theorize about "my own and other struggles, for representation, identity, self-inscription, and creative expression" (Anzaldúa 2015, 3), and I write to invent/make knowledge, construct meaning, and disrupt the normalization of bodies in university classroom. *Autohistoria-teoria* provides a methodology that allows me to illuminate my own experiences as I unpack the struggles of marginalized bodies. *Autohistoria-teoria* offers an opportunity to build knowledge from historically underrepresented voices, but also to build new bridges and new understandings of developing academic theories.

Anzaldúa, utilizes *autohistoria-teoria* to imagine a new literary world. She theorizes about the act of writing itself. *Autohistoria-teoria* is both a method and an embodied process; a process of self-discovery through constructing knowledge while engaging new information. Writing and pedagogy, like research, is also a performance. The new information gained as we perform in writing is not inconsequential, the knowledge gained through writing illuminates theory and changes us (Madison 2006, 245). There are physical, psychological, and even spiritual effects of these processes. Anzaldúa (2015) used *autohistoria-teoria* as a way to weave in theory with her life story for the goal of intervening, disrupting, and challenging existing power structures that have primarily constrained women (7). I argue these same constraining structures have also systematically limited marginalized communities in education.

A form of critical ethnography, I utilize *auto-historia* to weave together my life story, reflect upon my pedagogy and culture, while telling a story about history, myth, and theorizing about new realities (Anzaldúa 2000). As we engage in theoretical development and discover new knowledge, going through the research process also changes us, it illuminates us. The new knowledge impacts not only our students but impacts ourselves. Gaining knowledge is a process, an embodied journey of *conocimiento,* including the knowledge gained when engaged in institutional change (Anzaldúa 2015, 7). In the classroom, an embodied space, we learn to perform the role of professor, we learn the performance of effective professor, for ourselves and our students.

TELLING MY FAMILY STORY OF
MIGRATION FOR THE FIRST TIME

I began my pedagogical journey at California State University Channel Islands (CI), a Hispanic Serving Institution (HSI), as defined by Title V of the Higher Education Act. The university's total undergraduate student enrollment population (of the university or college) is at least 25% Latinx (Hispanic Association of Colleges and Universities, n.d.). The school is located just north of Los Angeles in Camarillo, California, and surrounded by agriculture. Although situated near a large pocket of Latinx community, I did not always tell my family story of migration during the introduction to my classes. Uncomfortable revealing the history of migration, I believed that this revelation would negatively impact students' perceptions of me as well as signify to students possible political perspectives. Feeling the need to justify my competence to the class, my introduction consisted of my academic credentials and not much else.

I had taught at CI for a couple semesters and I did not make many connections with Latinx students and I did not understand why. It was not until having been a co-director for the Migrant Summer Leadership Institute (MSLI), a program designed to "expose current high school migrant students to STEM (Science, Technology, Engineering, and Math) education through intensive curricular and co-curricular experiences in a 4-year university setting" (CI, nd), that I discovered that my story resonated with migrant parents and students. As a part of this program we hosted 20 parents for a weekend. During that weekend a panel of past program student participants described their relationships with their parents and their struggle to communicate why their education was important to them. Prior to the panel, I was introduced to the parents and I told my mother's story of migration knowing that they are parents of migrant families themselves. In that moment I was hoping to connect with them.

Unplanned and unscripted I began to tell our program's migrant parents how my parents migrated here to the Central Coast in order to create a common ground.

> I wasn't sure what to expect, I am standing alone behind a podium, in a hall that seats about seventy-five students and I look out into the room. In front of me, half the room is filled with migrant parents. The other half with our staff of undergraduate students and administrators. My goal was to introduce myself and my mom's story pops in my head. I don't tell them that story they've heard that one, they've likely lived that one. Instead I tell them about myself, the son of immigrants. In Spanish I tell them:

Me llamo Sergio Fernando Juárez, I am purposeful about pronouncing my name in Spanish. I continue, mis padres vinieron de Durango y Jalisco (estados de Mexico). Mis padres vinieron sin papeles, pero en esos tiempos era diferente. Ellos llegaron aqui por una vida major, para trabajar. Antes aqui habia muchas granjas de limon, naranjas, y aguacate. Soy nacido en Santa Barbara pero mi primer idioma fue Español, pero del rancho. Yo estoy aqui por ellos, todas las oportunidades son por ellos. Yen poco tiempo tendre my doctorado por ellos.

My parents had migrated here as well to find work and give my siblings and I a better future, "un mejor futuro" which they told me they wanted to give their children. I did not know what kind of response to expect. But once the panel session ended, a parent walked up to me, she had tears in her eyes but I didn't know how to respond. She tells me in Spanish, "por eso sacrifice por mis hijos, para que salgan adelante." For a moment she reminded me of my mom. Her affirming words washed over me with a sense of peace. I felt validation, for a brief moment I felt like this is where I belong. Throughout the day and the following day several parents would stop and talk. A father told me he would like his son to be a professor, saying "nomas que se ponga las pilas" to which I responded "si se pone las pilas no hay razon por que no." While they did not directly say they were proud of me I could sense empowerment, in them and in myself. For the first time, I feel it, a sense of belonging, I don't feel like a stranger. I say to myself, "this is where I'm supposed to be." This feeling comes with pride but also that I'm on to something. I don't know quite what it is yet. Fueled by the parents' curiosity that someone like me, that spoke Spanish like them, would be in leading a program at a university, a parent asks me what my role is and I respond, "soy professor." They smile and I can see it, a sense of pride. I had never met them but my mother's story had inspired them. They had migrated here to the U.S. and my family's story had resonated with them.

The telling of my family's migration story was a pivot to the beginning stages of developing culturally sustaining pedagogical practices or what Alim and Paris have named identified as a culturally sustaining pedagogy (Alim and Paris 2017, 1). The concept of culturally sustaining pedagogy (CSP), is one that "seeks to perpetuate and foster-to sustain-linguistic, literate, and cultural pluralism as part of schooling for positive social transformation" (Alim and Paris 2017, 1). Offering my mother's story affirms my family history, a history that resonates with others with similar experiences. It is a practice that fosters a cultural pluralism in academic spaces, that multiple bodies belong in these spaces. From this experience I witnessed that having professors and educational leaders that identify with students is a significant benefit. I began connecting inclusive concepts like CSP with my pedagogy by developing programming that centers on the experiences of students. Building culturally sustaining programming is effective because of a commitment to social justice. This commitment to social justice parallels the commitments of CSP Fassett and Warren identify ten commitments of Critical Communication Pedagogy (CCP) that are oriented around social justice. For example, CCP is committed to centering culture, in that "Culture is central to critical communication pedagogy, not additive" (Fassett and Warren 2007, 42). Telling my story in the classroom is influenced by the commitments of CCP, narratives like my mother's story of migration engage students in dialogue as a metaphor but also as a framing for our relationship with others (Fassett and Warren 2007, 54).

EMBODYING NEPANTLA

After my summer experience I decided that I would tell my family story once again, this time at the beginning of the semester. The concept of *nepantla, a Nahuatl*, whose direct translation means "in between space," was first introduced by Anzaldúa (2015) as a new iteration of the borderlands, a description of the experiences of people who live in the margins, border spaces, or as understood by some, liminal spaces (245). It is a way of explaining transitional moments of crisis when we have issues of identity, epistemology, or possibly ontology (Anzaldúa 2015, 245).

I decided that revealing my family's story to my students would be a good practice because "*Nepantleras* both affirm ethnic/national identities and align with wider social movements," and so I share my mother's story to affirm ethnic and national identities associated with Mexican-American and to a lesser extent other Latinxs who might identify with this story (Anzaldúa 2015, 244).

> I look around the room and I can see smiles on their faces. Although I had rehearsed my story, I was nervous. It is the first day of school, the room is bright and I feel the heat of the lights. The room is tight barely fitting thirty seats and luckily my class is a max of twenty-five. I scan the room, I see a lot of students of color, the class is a bridge course designed to support incoming transfer students. They are staring intently looking to me waiting to begin, I see smiles and decide it's a good space to tell my family story. I think it will resonate with this crowd of students.
>
> I feel good about sharing my story, I could feel myself standing tall. I did it and it felt good. A student after class walks up to me and asks "did you say that your family is from Jalisco?" I respond, "Yeah they are." She says, "Mine too, I've never had a professor from Jalisco, which part?" I respond, "Near Chapala." She says "Mine too, that's awesome." I felt positive we could identify with one another with few words.

I immediately noticed effects in communicating with students; students of Latinx descent were more likely to communicate with me. Some felt safe enough to reveal to me their status as undocumented residents, and would reveal their struggles as first-generation students whose parents didn't quite understand their goals of achieving a college degree. Having the courage to share my story offered an opening to not only connect with these students, but to mentor students who would institutionally and interpersonally otherwise find it difficult to identify a mentor.

Students would come to my office hours, they would talk to me about their family struggles, but also share their aspirations with me. Students reached out to me and asked to meet with me; they were looking for some guidance about financial aid, scholarships, most of all, opportunities. Some needed help with letters of recommendation to programs they were hesitant to apply for because they didn't want to be a bother. Those words resonate with me for the wrong reasons. I know what they are feeling and I struggle internally when I hear those words, because I know the feeling of being a burden is internalized. Our requests to be recognized in a system that has excluded brown bodies are a bother. Our struggle to be included and finding a home in education in general is an experience of being a bother to someone who is not interested in creating equitable spaces. These words also eat at me because I still do this; at times the words "I don't want to be a bother" are common in my vocabulary.

COATLICUE: FALLING APART

In the California State University System, a large discrepancy exists. Here, the ratio for Latinx student per professor is 200+ students per professor, whether they are tenured or not (Campaign for College 2018, 22). Yet, there is a struggle to create and develop culturally sustaining practices because university institutional structures are resistant to such practices. Generally, institutions make the argument they are lacking in funding, or because faculty do not want to change. This was a struggle for me, what Anzaldúa (2015) called an *arrebato*, a personal rupture in my life. This rupture stemmed from experiencing systemic racism, to know that there are effective practices, support, and programming, yet well-intentioned institutions, including those designated as HSIs, are resistant to such changes. They are only willing or able to support such projects in a limited capacity such as a two-week summer program.

Further, after suffering this arrebatamiento I felt a *susto*, a shock, that shook my foundational understanding of university education, and I felt doubts in being a professor (Anzaldúa 2015, 124). At the time I did not quite understand how this shock was affecting me. I could see why the telling of my mother's story of migration was important to people like the parents of migrant students and the students themselves. I knew statistics like graduation rates and first-hand knowledge of the struggles of being a first-generation student yet I did not fully grasp the power of my body in this space and the telling of how I came to be here. Parents saw someone who came from similar struggles, whose parents, like themselves, had sacrificed their lives in their native lands and migrated here in this anti-immigrant political climate, without any guarantees, and achieved academic success. Yet, there is resistance to the adoption of inclusive practices which makes the project of reforming academic spaces extremely difficult.

Making space is not easy, the telling of my story allowed students who identified as Latinx, or migrants, or first-generation students to identify with me but also came at a price. Students who might not otherwise have a professor to identify with now had someone they could go to. Being the only outlet for so many is not always easy. I quickly learned the difficulty of being one of the few Latinx professors on campus. Although I was in a non-tenure track position at the time, telling my story made me someone who students sought out. Even students from different disciplines came to me for guidance, letters of recommendation, as a reference, and more. This quickly became a difficulty. I was learning of the difficulties of what it meant to be a faculty of color in general. Harris and Lee (2019) document the disparity between the amount of faculty of color and graduate students, and this dynamic is a cause of additional labor. I felt the pressure of being a limited resource at a HSI that had a limited number of professors of color, specifically Latinx professors, as I was mentoring Latinx students (Harris and Lee 2019, 103). Like emotional labor, yet very different, there is an additional labor faculty of color take on when mentoring students of color and trying to create a home space (Calafell 2007, 432).

One such case was one that I will not soon forget. I had a student come to me, a young Latinx male who at times expressed to me that for several reasons he should not be "here." The following semester Antonio sent a message.[2] The email itself did not hint at an urgent matter. I followed up the email a couple days later and gave him some time to schedule a meeting. Antonio didn't respond.

Sometime in the middle of the semester I ran into Antonio, who was hoping to meet with me before he left. He said he wanted to talk with me and with luck we ran into one another. He tells me that out of respect he wanted to explain to me why he was dropping his classes to return home. On my way out to lecture on another campus,, I run into him on the steps of the our building. He sounds serious but then again in the short time I've known him he's had a serious demeanor

and it seemed hard for him to tell me "I've got to go back home, you know…
some family stuff happened, and I've gotta be there." I'm usually in a hurry to
get to my next class but this news stops me. My mind races because I don't want
to see him leave, I feel an urgency but he does not. I ask him if he's sure this is
what he wants to do. I hear guilt in his voice. He's telling me he's going home
to be there for his family as if he's done something wrong, like he's been selfish
for thinking he could pull this off. I sense that specific guilt but I don't have a
response. I couldn't find the words to tell him he shouldn't feel guilty, that I can
help. I ask if he's sure. I ask him for his phone number so that I can help him. I
want to keep in touch with him, but he talks about something else. I follow up
by asking him to email me. He says he'll do that.

   I was shocked, I didn't know how to respond. I asked if he was sure and that
I might be able to find other resources to him. But I sensed in him that he had
made up his mind. I asked him for his phone number in order to keep in touch
but didn't follow up. I never actually got his phone number and it haunts me.
Possibly because we both identify as Mexican, or that we were the eldest brother
of a mixed status household. I saw myself in him, and if it was not for couple
mentors that could have been me. I tell myself over and over I could have helped
him. I could have done more to keep in contact. I did not quite understand that
Antonio needed more than my support. But I also did not understand how a
student who was doing well could all of a sudden just disappear. I didn't understand that I wouldn't hear from him again.

This situation put me in what Anzaldúa describes as *coatlicue state*.
Coatlicue is an Aztec goddess, described as mother of the gods and ruler of
life and death; it is a state that describes the inner struggle. It is a state that
people in *nepantla* experience, it is those moments when people who live in
liminal spaces struggle because their multiple worldviews clash, for example,
when a Chicana experiences "opposing Mexican, Indian, and Anglo worldviews" (Anzalúa 2015, 242). This moment placed me in a place of struggle.
For me education is the ultimate goal and on the one hand, family should
understand, but on the other, family comes first. I did not understand where
the cracks were for him, for me, and in the system. I did not understand that
systems exist that allow students to be forgotten. Still, there was a moment I
did not want to be a mentor anymore. The additional emotional labor is difficult but the feeling of hopelessness is worse. I am reminded that mentoring,
advocating, for students of color, and pushing for social change in our institutions is taxing (Harris and Lee 2019, 106).
Antonio struggled with his situation because he came from a single-
parent household, had both younger and older siblings, and was relied on
by his family financially. He struggled. He felt he was betraying his familial
duties by choosing school over family responsibilities (Ojeda et al. 2011,

243). Yet he really enjoyed reading; he enjoyed the class discussions. He appreciated our discussion of toxic masculinity and wanted to learn more about how he could be more supportive of feminism. He had an accent and revealed to me how he felt when he wouldn't be taken serious because of his accent and how he would hope to be a professor like me. He was a junior college transfer and had moved away from his family to come to school. It was a financial struggle to afford on-campus housing, to afford semester tuition, but what weighed on him more heavily, what he revealed to me, were his family obligations. He said that hopefully he won't have to leave school to support his family. At the time my suggestion was to think of how he can help his family in the future with a degree and possibly a career in education. I didn't understand what he was communicating at the time, I didn't understand he was asking for help, I had offered a superficial response and asked few questions, and I much less understood that this was an important hint of what was to come.

COYOLXAUHQUI: A PROCESS OF
HEALING FROM THE WOUNDS

I needed to move on from this moment, he left during the Spring semester and this gave me all summer to consider what happened. I was hesitant to tell my story again to a new set of students. Being in a *Coatlicue state* is difficult; I was angry at the system, at myself. I was less involved on campus; I had stopped attending our Latinx faculty and staff meetings. I did not want anyone to experience this again; in a state Anzaldúa (2015) would describe as *Coyolxauhqui*, developed from the Aztec goddess of the moon (243). La diosa de la luna, the mood goddess, was the daughter *Coatlicue;* she became the moon after being killed by her brother Huitzilopochtli, the god of war and the sun. *Coyolxauhqui* had attempted to attack her impregnated mother, when out of the womb sprang *Huitzilopochtli*. He killed *Coyolxauhqui* and dismembered her into a thousand pieces, then tossing her into the sky to become the moon. Anzaldúa (2015) developed the Coyolxauhqui imperative from this story to describe a complex healing process. A process of having to pull yourself together to make yourself whole to find a path forward. I was broken into pieces like Coyolxauhqui. I did not understand it but I needed healing for this wound. Although I had lost a student, I had to pull myself together to help other students. The healing came over time, through the guidance of students, helping students of color on a research project, applications to scholarships, internships, and to graduate school.

The healing came when I understood that I am one person in a system of inequality. That I alone will not be able to change the system, I will need help; I will need to be a bridge to build pathways. This knowledge or *cono-cimiento*, can only be understood when engaging systems of inequality, there is an embodied knowledge that is developed when pushing back against these systems. Building culturally inclusive pathways will not be easy. As people of color we want to help others like ourselves but pushing back against inequitable systems is difficult. Often, they push back and it hurts. It hurts professors and it certainly hurts students. While my goal remains to design culturally sustaining pedagogy that values Latinx students, their experiences, and worldviews, that privileges their complex linguistic repertoire, it will hurt (Irizarry 2017).

CONCLUSION

Developing inclusive pedagogical spaces is a journey both collectively and individually. Making space for students regardless of identity is a process, sometimes it is painful because there is pushback that can send you into a *Coatlicue* state. Still, the knowledge of challenging the status quo is in and of itself knowledge, or conocimiento. As we take on this process we must heal ourselves and experience the Coyolxauhqui imperative. This means that for making space and creating pathways, it takes a risk. Taking a risk to tell your family story can be daunting for fear of appearing biased or unobjective. Yet leaving our stories and bodies outside our teaching can have detrimental consequences. Being vulnerable and open to share our stories in pedagogical practices can offer opportunities to create inclusive spaces.

The telling of my mother's story of migration, like my body in the classroom on the first day of class, is not a haphazard accident. It is a purposeful attempt to identify with students to create a home space for them and myself. Yet, taking this risk in the classroom, like migrating away from home, there is risk that comes with moving away from our comfortable spaces in hopes of a better tomorrow. We risk facing disappointment and I believe ultimately it is a risk worth trying in order to build a better future for those that come after us. Anzaldúa helps us understand these ongoing processes, moments where we fall apart and how we can pull ourselves back together.

The development of inclusive communication pedagogical practices and spaces encourage paths that require self-exploration and social-exploration. *The scope of* Anzaldúa's a*utohistoria-teoria* method encompasses this specific area. These pathways and bridges of vulnerability and inclusivity will not only be built through the voices on marginalized communities, like mine, but in conjunction with others. Many of us occupy both marginalized and privileged positions and through these positions can offer invaluable, embodied insight into our pedagogical spaces. This is not to discount or diminish the very real systematic oppression that privileges specific communities but to point to the need to build bridges together. Most importantly, those in privileged positions must become aware of their position and be willing to cede power they have being in that position.

The process of self-discovery and disseminating through personal story will lead to social-discovery and new social knowledge. This pivot through critical communication pedagogy and culturally sustainable pedagogy will lead to knowledge that Yosso calls community cultural wealth (Yosso 2005, 75). It is a transition from building knowledge or pedagogical practices that essentialize marginalized communities and frame them from a deficit perspective to imagining and creating liberatory pedagogical practices. Practices that center on the material realities of marginalized bodies, aware of a history of inequitable educational practices, committed to not reproducing those practices, and grounded in a caring or social justice that privilege historically marginalized communities (Mendoza Aviña 2016, 470).

NOTES

1. The term Latinx is utilized throughout the text; it is a recently developed term that promotes gender-inclusive language because it disrupts the gendering that comes with the term Latina/o. Also, like Latina/o, the term Latinx is a unifying term that evokes the similar experiences of migrant families from throughout Latin America in the United States, Salinas, Cristobal, and Adele Lozano. 2019. "Mapping and Recontextualizing the Evolution of the Term Latinx: An Environmental Scanning in Higher Education." *Journal of Latinos & Education*, 18, no. 4: 302–315. doi:10.108 0/15348431.2017.1390464.

2. The name Antonio is a pseudonym to protect the student's identity.

REFERENCES

Alexander, Bryant Keith. "Critical/Performative/Pedagogy: Performing Possibility as a Rehearsal for Social Justice." In *The SAGE Handbook of Communication and Instruction*, edited by Deanna L. Fassett and John T. Warren, 315–342. Thousand Oaks, CA: Sage.

Alim, Samy H., and Django Paris. 2017. "What Is Culturally Sustaining Pedagogy and Why Does it Matter?" In *Culturally Sustaining Pedagogies: Teaching and Learning for Justice in a Changing World*, edited by Samy H. Alim and Django Paris, 1–21. New York, NY: Teachers College Press.

Anzaldúa, Gloria. 2000. *Interviews = Entrevistas.* Edited by AnaLouise Keating. New York, NY: Routledge.

———. 2015. *Light in the Dark, Luz en lo Oscuro: Rewriting Identity, Spirituality, and Reality*. Edited by Analouise Keating. Durham, NC: Duke University Press.

Bravata, Dena M., Sharon A. Watts, Autumn L. Keefer, Divya K. Madhusudhan, Katie T. Taylor, Dani M. Clark, Ross S. Nelson, Kevin O. Cokley, and Heather K. Hagg. 2020. "Prevalence, Predictors, and Treatment of Impostor Syndrome: A Systematic Review." *Journal of General Internal Medicine*, 35: 1252–1275. https ://doi.org/10.1007/s11606-019-05364-1.

Calafell, Bernadette Marie. 2007. "Mentoring and Love: An Open Letter." *Cultural Studies* ↔ *Critical Methodologies*, 7, no. 4: 425–441. doi:10.1177/1532708607305123.

Cokley, Kevin, Leann Smith, Donte Bernard, Ashley Hurst, Stacey Jackson, Steven Stone, Olufunke Awosogba, Chastity Saucer, Marlon Bailey, and Davia Roberts. 2017. "Impostor Feelings as a Moderator and Mediator of the Relationship Between Perceived Discrimination and Mental Health Among Racial/Ethnic Minority College Students." *Journal of Counseling Psychology*, 64, no. 2: 141–154.

Conley, Tara. 2019. "Black Women and Girls Trending: A New(er) Autohistoria-Teoria." In *This Bridge We Call Communication: Anzaldúan Approaches to Theory, Method, and Praxis*, edited by Leandra Hinojosa Hernández and Robert Gutierrez-Perez, 231–256. Boulder, CO: Lexington Books.

Fassett, Deanna L., and John T. Warren. 2007. *Critical Communication Pedagogy.* Thousand Oaks, CA: Sage.

Harris, Tina M., and Celeste N. Lee. 2019. "Advocate-Mentoring: A Communicative Response to Diversity in Higher Education." *Communication Education*, 68, no. 1: 103–113.

Irizarry, Jason. "For Us, By Us" A Vision for Culturally Sustaining Pedagogies Forwarded by Latinx Youth." In *Culturally Sustaining Pedagogies: Teaching and Learning for Justice in a Changing World*, edited by Samy H. Alim and Django Paris, 83–98. New York, NY: Teachers College Press.

Madison, D. Soyini. 2006. "Performing Theory/Embodied Writing." In *Opening Acts: Performance in/as Communication and Cultural Studies*, edited by Judith Hamera, 243–265. Thousand Oaks, CA: Sage.

Mendoza Aviña, Sylvia. 2016. "That's Ratchet": A Chicana Feminist Rasquache Pedagogy as Entryway to Understanding the Material Realities of Contemporary Latinx Elementary Aged Youth." *Equity & Excellence in Education*, 49, no. 4: 468–479.

Nuñez, Anne-Marie. 2014. "Cultivating Authenticity in the Academy: Becoming a Latina Scholar." In *Cross-Cultural Women Scholars in Academe*, edited by Lorri J. Santamaría, Gaëtane Jean-Marie, and Cosette M. Grant, 134–151. New York, NY: Routledge.

Ojeda, Lizette, Rachel L. Navarro, and Alejandro Morales. 2011. "The Role of La Familia on Mexican American Men's College Persistence Intentions." *Psychology of Men & Masculinities*, 12, no. 3: 216–229.

Sorrells, Kathryn. 2016. *Intercultural Communication: Globalization and Social Justice.* Thousand Oaks: CA, Sage.

Yosso, Tara J. 2005. "Whose Culture Has Capital? A Critical Race Theory Discussion of Community Cultural Wealth." *Race Ethnicity and Education*, 8, no. 1: 69–91.

Chapter 11

Unmasking the Hegemony of English

Exploring English Neo-Imperialism and the Internationalization of Whiteness

Sachiko Tankei-Aminian

I was a minority [in a predominantly non-white, non-English-speaking country] as a White American." In my Interracial/Intercultural Communication class, a number of white students say it, while attempting to suggest that white privilege exists only in societies where white population is the numerical majority. When we engage in critical race pedagogy, we often encounter some students—particularly white students—who try to "find ways to get [themselves] off the hook." (Johnson 2018, 92)

The statement above can be classified as an example of how "white students construct a rhetorical space where whiteness is placed on social margins" (Johnson et al. 2008, 126). Such rhetorical construction of "White outsiders" (Johnson et al. 2008) can be found in statements like "I am 'white,' but at my school 'white' people were the minority" and "I was on the basketball team . . . The majority of the students were black . . . I was treated as an outsider" (126).

However, the problem of the statement is not only their resistance, but their false theorization. First, the students falsely assume that white privilege exists only in a society, like the United States, where whites exist as a dominant group. Consequently, the students incorrectly think that when whites enter the context where a higher number of other racial individuals exist, the former automatically becomes a "powerless" minority in that context.

Another aspect of the false theorization stems from the fact that not just white students, but most US-American students and scholars, especially when they are monolingual English-speakers, are rarely aware of their own English linguistic privilege, let alone English neo-imperialism, which refers to how "'global' English [serves] as a key dimension of the US empire" (Phillipson 2008, 1).

What type of pedagogy is needed to help students to understand how whiteness operates inside and outside the United States and how English neo-imperialism intersects with the internationalization of whiteness?

* * * * *

This personal narrative illustrates how I, as a border-crossing educator/ scholar, commit to offering a deeper understanding of the hegemony of English, Anglo-Americanization, and how English neo-imperialism mediates the expansion of whiteness on a global scale. This piece also problematizes English linguistic imperialism in the Western academic community, where the use of English and its relation to ideologies, unequal power, and injustice rarely have been called into question (Tsuda 2014). I scrutinize the very language—English—I have come to write as well as teach.

I craft this narrative in English—not my mother tongue, Japanese—as a nonwhite, non-native English-speaking sojourner from Japan who has lived in the United States since 1999. In the current Western academic community, the use of English has rarely been called into question, but it has been taken for granted (Tsuda 2014). Yet, I am aware of how proficiency in English serves as a criterion by which to classify people in the context of the dominance of English (Tsuda 2014):

> Native speakers of English reign as a prestigious ruling class of international communication: they can easily express their ideas any time, while non-native speakers and people who do not speak English constitute the "muted" working class of international communication: they are compelled to learn English and have difficulty expressing their ideas. (448)

It is important to note that English was not originally the dominant language in the world. The English language went through a whole transformation in status. English once had been treated as "the inadequate and second-rated tongue of peasants for centuries" (Bryson 1990, 56) before the 16th century. Yet, in the 19th century, in the context of British colonialism and imperialism, English linguistic superiority was propagated along with white and Western superiority (Mizokami 2002, 135).

By the end of the 19th century, in the context of the British Empire's power at its height and the United States' extending military power, "English as the World Language" discourse began to emerge, in which "the apparent discrimination against other languages and races was much less explicitly articulated. Instead, the usefulness of the English language for international communication began to be emphasized" (Mizokami 2002, 140).

Now English has become a hegemonic language and creates "a structure of linguistic and communicative inequality and discrimination between speakers of English and speakers of other languages" (Tsuda 2014, 446). I must acknowledge the paradox of critiquing English linguistic imperialism by using that very language. Yet, I attempt to disrupt the constructed English superiority by using English subversively (Bardhan 2016; Tankei-Aminian forthcoming). I engage in such resistance in my writing as well as in my teaching.

Further, although in the context of English domination, I am a colonial subject as a Japanese speaker. It is crucial to note that the language I speak as a mother tongue—Japanese—is a colonizer's language to others, as well. During the course of Japan's brutal colonial domination, the ethnic Japanese forced people to adopt Japanese language, values, and cultural traditions and, even, Japanese names. Such language invasion was done to the ethnic minority groups in Japan as well as many countries in Asia and the Pacific Islands.

In this sense, I, as an ethnic Japanese, native Japanese-speaking, non-native English speaker, simultaneously position as the oppressor and oppressed in the realm of linguistic imperialism. While intertwining this element, this narrative primarily focuses on my current pedagogy on the hegemony of English, Anglo-Americanization, English neo-imperialism, and "the internationalization of whiteness" (Shome 1999) along with my experiences as a non-native English-speaking educator and writer.

ENGLISH NEO-IMPERIALISM AND THE INTERNATIONALIZATION OF WHITENESS

While critical race communication studies scholarship has extensively explored race and the intersection of other cultural identities, such as gender and class, I rarely find the intersection of race and English linguistic identity. Although some scholars, such as Imahori (2000), Mendoza (2006), Shome (1999, 2006, 2010), and Tsuda (2014), have examined English imperialism and its relation to whiteness on a global scale, in general, there is little discussion among critical race communication studies.

One of the problems is that critical race communication studies is US-centered without connecting issues of power, communication, and culture in the United States to its larger transnational relations (Shome 2010). Another problem is that mostly in the Western academic community, the use of English has been taken for granted and most US-American scholars—even among critical race communication studies—seem to be unaware of the hege-mony of English and their own English-speaking privilege.

Within my critical race communication pedagogy, I teach the issues of race in the US context, including institutional racism, white privilege, oppression, discrimination, and so on, while connecting to how race functions outside the US context. A transnational framework on race strengthens our understanding of whiteness. Examining the internationalization of whiteness helps to recog-nize how whiteness has influenced identities and cultural spaces, where there are few physically white bodies—as well as the contextual nature of privilege.

Furthermore, by examining English neo-imperialism alongside issues of race, my pedagogy deepens our understanding of how English neo-imperial-ism mediates the expansion of whiteness on a global scale. The internation-alization of whiteness strengthens the argument that whiteness is more about discursive practices to "privilege and sustain the global dominance of white imperial subjects and Eurocentric worldview" (Shome 1999, 108), rather than simply about bodies and skin colors.

Exploring and teaching these themes are not only my academic pursuit, but also a personal quest as an Asian non-native English-speaking sojourner/educator in the United States.

Foreign Inferior Other as a Non-native English Speaker

My Asian body "[gets] marked as a site of 'foreign' difference" (Shome 1999, 120). In the United States, Asian Americans have historically been viewed as perpetually foreign no matter how long they have lived there. While white foreign-born non-native English speakers in the United States often can "pass" as white US-Americans no matter how recent they arrive in the United States, my Asian body continues to be marked as foreign Other, even after living in the United States for two decades.

In addition to the perception of foreign Other as Asian, my non-native English-speaking identity gets viewed as a linguistically and, consequently, intellectually, and epistemologically inferior in the United States. In fear of confirming such negative perception, I always go through my life with a heightened attention to communicate in English as flawlessly as possible.

Societal expectations for sojourners/immigrants to pick up English fluency in the United States can be expressed in a seemingly "inclusive" comment like, "Your accent is not too thick. We can understand your English perfectly fine, Professor Sachiko. But that professor in mathematics . . . " At other times, such expectations are expressed as an "instruction," as follows:

A sign was posted on the information board at International Student and Scholars at Southern Illinois University, where I attended graduate school:

"Speak English at all times—even with your friends from home—if you hope to be successful at SIUC!"

(Tankei-Aminian 2016, 203)

Even after completing a doctoral degree in the United States, I did not become as fluent as a native English speaker. I have come to realize that I will never write or speak in English as I do in Japanese, no matter how hard I work at it (Tankei-Aminian, forthcoming). It is one thing for me to come to that realization. Yet, it is another thing when I still face a course evaluation stating something like, "This course was not effective in teaching the required material. I could not understand what the professor was saying most of the time and she could not pronounce half of the English language."

Diangelo (2006) explains this linguistic hierarchical differential in power that nonwhite and non-native English speakers face through our daily interactions:

> When students *[as well as faculty (my own addition)]* of color are also second-language learners, another layer is added to the hierarchical differential in power. Power relations play a crucial role in social interactions between language learners and target language speakers. Language learners have a complex social identity that must be understood with reference to larger, and frequently inequitable, social structures that are reproduced in day-to-day social interaction. (1985)

While feeling the scrutinizing gazes toward me as a foreign inferior Other, I seek for ways in my pedagogy as well as in my writing to combat such perceptions and disrupt English imperialism.

GLOBAL ENGLISH DOMINATION

I have been engaging in critical race communication pedagogy (courses like interracial/intercultural communication and critical race theory in communication) in the predominantly white institutional context in the United States since 2002. The university where I currently teach in the United States has a large percentage of white student population (63% or more). The rest of the student demographics is comprised of Latinx (21%), Black (8.5%), Asian (2.9%), Native American (1%), and International/Non-resident (2%). As I teach issues of race, culture, communication, and identity in a racially mixed classroom setting, I attend simultaneously to the needs of both the majority white students' learning process and the racially and ethnically minority students.

At the beginning of the semester in Interracial/Intercultural Communication class, I start introducing the phenomenon of global English domination. I believe it is helpful to discuss the internationalization of whiteness in class at a later point. First, I share the statistics: English has become the gatekeeper for academic and economic success in the world, although English is just one of approximately 7,097 languages (Lewis et al. 2016). English is "the *de facto* official and working language in most international organizations" (Tsuda 2014, 446). English is the dominant language of scientific communication, the language of more than 80 percent of academic publications (Crystal 2003; Van Weijenm 2012), and being the language of all of the top 50 scientific journals (based on SCImago Journal Rank system) that originate from either the United States or the United Kingdom (Huttner-Koros 2015).

Yet, these numbers do not seem to make students understand deeply enough about English domination. I feel I need to offer more concrete and compelling examples regarding how English domination manifests in our lives.

* * * * *

I stand behind the podium computer; the wallpaper of the computer screen is currently projected. "Now, let me demonstrate one example of the global English domination." I look at the class and continue.

"I am about to visit the website of one of the online Japanese mainstream newspapers, which targets an audience who has Japanese fluency." Many students tend to show their curiosity about this activity. I tell the students what they should observe: "Look at the screen. I want you to pay close attention to exactly what I do in order to get to the website. Okay?"

I open an internet browser which is projected on the screen. On the URL, I start typing www.mainichi.jp and click. The page of a Japanese daily newspaper, 毎日新聞 (*The Mainichi*) appears full of Japanese letters.

"Clearly," I speak shortly after everyone has a chance to look at the website written in Japanese, "this website is intended for readers who can read Japanese language, isn't it?" "Yes," reply many students, while nodding their heads. Many students are gazing at the website, written in Japanese, while conversing with their neighbors.

"Then, could you explain exactly what I did in order to get to this website that targets the Japanese readers?" I try to bring the class back to the point of the exercise. One student raises his hand and says, "You typed the web address."

I nod my head and asked back. "Can you tell me exactly what I typed?"

Usually, by this point, someone from the class noticed something and says, "You typed the web address in the *English alphabet.*"

"Exactly," I smile, while acknowledging the student's answer. Then, I move away from the podium and stand closer to the class.

"Japanese readers who want to visit the websites written in Japanese still need to know and must be able to type the URL in English. For someone like me, who reads and writes in both Japanese and English now, this is not a big issue. However, for someone like my mother, who lives in Japan, it *is*." I keep going.

"My mother is a middle-school graduate. She could not go to high school. She developed a physical illness at a young age and grew up in a single-parent, working-class household. When she was in school, English was taught at school, but she could not learn it fully. She and her late husband, my father, had two daughters: my sister and me. But both of us had started living outside Japan in the late 1990s. My mother tried to stay in touch with us via a new tool, email, when my sister and I left Japan. She not only needed to learn how to use a computer, but also needed to learn the English alphabet. Do you know why?" I pause. Usually, a couple of students can find the answer, but not always the case.

"It is because the English alphabet is required in order to create an email account, whether it is gmail, hotmail, or yahoo email." After this remark, many students start expressing their new realization, "Oh, that's right" or "I didn't think about that."

"Imagine," I pose a scenario, "hypothetically, that the Japanese language was the dominant language in the world and internet technology originated in Japan." While I say it, I have an urge to say, "Actually, the Japanese language domination did occur in certain parts of the world through Japanese colonization. So, it is not a totally hypothetic story." But I tell myself that I will come back to this element later and move on.

I continue. "The Japanese developers may say, 'Everyone in the world, join us and enjoy this new internet technology. It is pretty simple.' Then, you realize that you are expected to create an email account in Japanese letters and to be able to type the URL in Japanese letters." Some students say, "Oh-oh."

"How many of you were aware of this reality for the people in regions where English is not their primary language?" Usually, none of the students raise a hand.

"Well, it is because you have a systemic advantage; in this case, English-speaking privilege. You will learn about the concept of privilege further later. But when you have systemic privilege, you often are not aware of such privilege. But when you don't have it, you are aware of the disadvantage and you often 'have to work much harder just to experience the things [the privileged folks] take for granted'" (Crosley-Corcoran 2014).

I continue. "If simply accessing the internet or creating an email account in a language other than your own is a concern, what would you think if you were taught at school in a language other than your own? How about if you must obtain a passing grade of a foreign language as a required subject at school in order to get into high school or university?"

* * * * *

This may be a hypothetical scenario for most of my US-born-and-raised monolingual English-speaking students, but this is a reality for many non-English speakers in the world. I add how "English-knowing bilinguals" (Pakir 1999) are becoming the norm in the world. Throughout the world, approximately 750 million people are the learners and/or the speakers of English as a foreign language and 430 million people are the speakers of English as a second language; whereas the monolingual native English speakers is estimated to be 400 million (Crystal 2003).

I end the class with a reminder. "In the next class, we will examine US-American cultural products in relation to English domination in the world."

ENGLISH DOMINATION PENETRATED BY ANGLO-AMERICANIZATION

"When I was in school in Japan," I insert my experience, "we started learning English as a foreign language as a required subject from the seventh grade onward. But now, English is a required subject from the fifth grade onward in Japan and the third graders start having English activities in school, too. You know what that means"; I pause and look around at the students.

"If the child's parents can afford it, they would not wait for the child to become the third grader to start learning English. Many kindergarten children are enrolled in private *eikaiwa* [English conversation] schools, even before they master the Japanese language." As I say this, I show to the students an advertisement booklet for Japanese toddlers. On the cover, it says "English for age 2" (written in English) and "Would you let your children start learning English that widens their future?" (written in Japanese).

I continue. "Many years of English education in Japan do not necessarily guarantee that Japanese will be fluent in English. However, we surely spend a great amount of time, energy and often money for learning English and trying to become fluent."

"But it is not only through education that we are exposed to English, but also through Western, particularly US-American, cultural products," I say, as I cover the section of popular culture and intercultural communication. "Today, Anglo-American cultural products have penetrated the world, based on 'the Anglo-American monopoly of the global information and entertainment market'" (Tsuda 2014, 450).

"In Japan, Tsuda explains, 'more than half of the movies shown are imported from the United States'" (450). The dissemination of English-language-related products goes hand in hand with Anglo-Americanization. For instance, Phillipson (2008) argues that the dissemination of English is not a mere consequence, but is deliberately marketed to promote the national interests of the United States. In fact, Rothkopf (1997) argues that promoting English—and the values that come with it—as the common language directly supports the economic and political interest of the United States.

"For example, growing up in Japan in the 70s through the 90s," I start recounting my childhood memories. "I was surrounded with US Anglo-American products and often English products, through stories (*Snow White*, *Cinderella*; and *Sleeping Beauty*), music (songs like *Crazy for You*, and *Footloose* and artists like, Madonna, The Carpenters, Michael Jackson and Billy Joel), films (*Superman* and *The Sound of Music)*, TV programs (*Little House on the Prairie*), animated cartoons (*Tom and Jerry*), theme parks (Tokyo Disneyland), and dietary products (Coca-Cola, Baskin-Robbins, and McDonalds)."

Even though I was watching TV programs and films with translated and dubbed versions in Japanese, all kinds of commodities had English text on them (T-shirts, bags, pencil cases, notebooks, towels, cans, bins, etc.). My life was filled with US-American and English-language-related products. Just having English text seemed to create a Western feeling, something hip and cool.

I do not want to bore my students by filling my lecture with examples from the "old" era. I switch to an example from the new millennium.

"By the way, how many of you know a Disney animation film *Frozen* and its catchy theme song *Let It Go*?" Many students instantly smile and quickly raise their hands.

"In Spring semester in 2014, my-then-4-year-old daughter, Mina, came home from a daycare. She started swirling around in the center of the living room, mumbling repeatedly the phrase 'let it go.'" Many students chuckle or some students respond with "Awww."

I smile and continue. "She successfully persuaded us to get her the DVD. Since then, we watched it over and over again until all of the songs in the film stuck in our heads." Students laugh, while acknowledging the catchy nature of those songs.

"During the summer 2014, as a family, we traveled to Japan from the US and spent two months with my mother who lives in Japan. We sent Mina to a local kindergarten during our stay. One day, she came home from the kindergarten excitedly. 'Mom, guess what? At Japanese kindergarten, they play the song *Let It Go* during the lunch hour in both English and Japanese!' Soon enough, all of us in our household were singing not only 'Let it go, let it go . . . ,' but also 'ありのままの↔' (I sing Japanese version of the theme song *Let It Go*)." Students burst into laughter and get excited to listen to a Japanese version of *Let It Go*.

After a short time of laughter, I come back to the theme of the lecture. "In this way, the domination of English was strengthened by Anglo-Americanization. People in the region where English is not the primary language, are often not aware of how our uncritical consumption of these 'innocent' English-language products strengthen the hegemonic structure of English domination (Tankei-Aminian, forthcoming). I was certainly not aware of it until I started studying these issues."

ENGAGING IN DISCURSIVE WHITENESS THROUGH US-AMERICAN PRODUCTS

I move to discuss another effect of Anglo-Americanization. "US-American cultural products expose us not only to English but also whiteness," I say. "As I grew up, I was surrounded with US-American products, in which white bodies were always admirably embedded. They would appear as the main characters in picture books or TV programs, or as popular icons, as I discussed earlier."

"Contrarily," I stress, "when nonwhite bodies in the US-American products appeared as the main characters, they did so as non-threatening and comedic characters." I continue, "Nonwhite bodies also appeared with negative stereotypes in illustration with a translated song."

I take a quick breath and then start singing one verse of a song that I grew up with in Japanese: "ひとり、ふたり、さんにんのインディアン、よにん、ごにん、ろくにんのインディアン."

I pause without singing it further and explain, "This is a Japanese translated version of 'Ten little Indians.' The lyrics goes 'One little, two little, three little Indians, four little, five little, six little Indians.'" I ask the class, "How many of you have heard this song?" A good number of the students raise their hand or nod, while looking at me. I continue, "I was four or five years old and was singing this song along with other nursery songs. I grew up in Japan, far away from the US, without meeting any US-American in person, without a clue of the US history of subjugation of the indigenous people and the song's negative implication toward them."

I share a one-page illustration for the song "Ten little Indians," which appeared in a book along with many Japanese nursery rhymes. It was published in 1988 in Japan. The illustration contains all the stereotypes about Native Americans: Dark eyes, long, straight, black hair, headdresses, feathers, face-painting, dancing around Teepees, stone axe.

Students often admittingly say, "We didn't know how our stereotypes about Native Americans in the U.S. can be spread in other parts of the world."

"Great point," I nod. I point out how white ideologies have influenced identities and cultural spaces, where there are not many physical white bodies. As Richie Neil Hao (2016) puts it, "whiteness is often discussed as marked on the white body, it can also be performed by people of color" (134). In retrospect I was unconsciously engaging in discursive whiteness—the discursive practices that privilege and sustain certain ways of being and acting in the world—through US-American cultural products brought into Japan.

ENGLISH LINGUISTIC, US-AMERICAN, AND WHITE PRIVILEGES IN THE GLOBAL CONTEXT

At the end of the unit, I offer a lecture on what the internationalization of whiteness means to white individuals, English speakers, and/or US-Americans in a global context.

"As we learn, with deep-rooted concept of Westernization as civilization, the penetration of the US-American cultural products throughout the world and global English domination, English-speaking US-Americans become 'powerful' minority, not 'powerless' minority in the global context. Regardless of your race and ethnicity, outside the US context, you all become privileged." Shome (2006) makes a similar argument:

> Rarely is it acknowledged that minorities within the US, when we consider a larger global scale, make up a "privileged" minority. Saying this is not to deny their complex racial positions, and continued abuse, within the US landscape; rather it is to recognize how race research in the US often seems to have little idea or interest about the plight of the subaltern or minorities in other parts of the world, and how that plight may be connected to minority politics here. (8)

I add further, "However, you don't have to be a US-American citizen to receive the US-American privilege. For example, I can get the US-American residential privilege in Japan. People are genuinely interested in and look up to my living experiences in the US. In addition, although I am not a native English speaker and am continuously marked as 'Other' in the US due to my accent, I am privileged due to my achieved English fluency in the Japanese context."

I continue. "If you are white persons, you will certainly receive white privilege in the global context." For example, Kubota (2012) discusses white and English-speaking privileges in Japanese context, as follows: "by virtue of being a White speaker of English, even if not a native English speaker, one has the privilege of obtaining employment to teach *eikaiwa* [English conversation] without professional qualifications or an ability to speak Japanese" (98).

Many students mention how they would not have been aware of their English-speaking privilege as well as the global domination of English if they did not have this type of lesson. I also address to the white students who made a statement at the beginning of the unit, "I was a minority in [a predominantly nonwhite, non-English-speaking country] as a White American." I say, "I do not want to be dismissive about how you may have experienced being out of place and may have encountered challenges in a foreign culture and linguistic context. I agree we all experience more or less such challenges when we step out of our own familiar cultural and language space. But even within such situations, it is important to keep in mind how you carry certain systemic privileges, too, if you are white, US-American or an English-speaker."

I end my lecture with an additional element. "We covered the hegemony of English, Anglo-Americanization, English neo-imperialism and the spread of whiteness in the global context. In the context of English domination, I am a colonial subject as a Japanese speaker, although my ability to use English makes me more powerful and privileged in my own culture. What gets complicated further is that the language I speak as a mother tongue—Japanese—is a colonizer's language to others, too."

Students often seem to be surprised with this new information. I continue, "During the course of Japan's brutal colonial domination, the ethnic Japanese forced people to adopt Japanese language, values, and cultural traditions or even Japanese names. Such language invasion was done to ethnic minority groups in Japan as well as many countries in Asia and the Pacific Islands. In this sense, I, as an ethnic Japanese, native Japanese-speaking, non-native English-speaker, simultaneously position as the oppressor and the oppressed in the realm of linguistic imperialism."

By listening to my critical examination on my positionality in relation to linguistic imperialism, students seem to not only deepen their understanding on the contextual nature of privilege and its complexity, but also become more comfortable to engage in a critical examination on their own positionality.

EPILOGUE

I believe a transnational framework enhances our pedagogy as well as theorization on race. The internationalization of whiteness strengthens the argument that whiteness is more about discursive practices to "privilege and sustain the global dominance of white imperial subjects and Eurocentric worldview" (Shome

1999, 108), rather than simply about bodies and skin colors. Furthermore, a transnational framework also offers a perspective of how English neo-imperialism mediates the expansion of whiteness on a global scale.

Simultaneously, I hope my scrutiny of the very language I have come to write as well as teach—English—as a non-native English-speaking educator/scholar problematizes and challenges English linguistic imperialism in the Western academic community. I must recognize that I may end up with re-inscribing English hegemony by benefiting from my writing and teaching in that very language. Yet, I continuously seek for ways in which my writing and pedagogy can disrupt the constructed English superiority by using English subversively (Bardhan 2016; Tankei-Aminian forthcoming).

REFERENCES

Bardhan, Nilanjana. 2016. "Building Bridges Along the Edges of Culture." In *Globalizing Intercultural Communication: A Reader*, edited by Kathryn Sorrells and Sachi Sekimoto, 55–62. Thousand Oaks, CA: Sage.

Bryson, Bill. 1990. *Mother Tongue: English and How It Got That Way*. New York, NY: Avon Books.

Crosley-Corcoran, Gina. 2014. "Explaining White Privilege to a Broke White Person." *The Huffington Post*, May 8, 2014. https://www.huffpost.com/entry/explaining-whiteprivilege-to-a-broke-white-person_b_5269255.

Crystal, David. 2003. *English as a Global Language*, 2nd ed. Cambridge: Cambridge University Press.

Diangelo, Robin J. 2006. "The Production of Whiteness in Education: Asian International Students in a College Classroom." *Teachers College Record*, 108, no. 10: 1983–2000. https://doi.org/10.1111/j.1467-9620.2006.00771.x.

Hao, Richie Neil. 2016. "Whiteness as Pedagogical Performance: A Critical Reflection on Race and Pedagogy." In *Globalizing Intercultural Communication: A Reader*, edited by Kathryn Sorrells and Sachi Sekimoto, 134–141. Three Oaks, CA: Sage.

Huttner-Koros, Adam. 2015. "The Hidden Bias of Science's Universal Language." *The Atlantic*, August 21, 2015. https://www.theatlantic.com/science/archive/2015/08/english-universal-language-science-research/400919/.

Imahori, Tadasu Todd. 2000. "On Becoming 'American.'" In *AmongUS: Essays on Identity, Belonging, and Intercultural Competence*, edited by Myron W. Lustig and Jolene Koester, 68–77. New York, NY: Longman.

Johnson, Allan. 2018. *Privilege, Power, and Difference*, 3rd ed. New York, NY: McGraw-Hill.

Johnson, Julia R., Marc Rich, and Aaron Castelan Cargile. 2008. "Why Are You Shoving This Stuff Down Our Throats?: Preparing Intercultural Educators to Challenge Performances of White Racism." *Journal of International and Intercultural Communication*, 1, no. 2: 113–135.

Kubota, Ryoko. 2012. "Critical Approaches to Intercultural Discourse and Communication." In *The Handbook of Intercultural Discourse and Communication*, edited by Christina Bratt Paulston, Scott F. Kiesling, and Elizabeth S. Rangel, 90–109. Chichester, West Sussex, UK; Malden, MA: Wiley-Blackwell.

Lewis, M. Paul, Gary F. Simons, and Charles D. Fenning, eds. 2016. *Ethnologue: Languages of the World*, 19th ed. Dallas, Texas: SIL International. http://www.ethnologue.com.

Mendoza, S. Lily. 2006. "Tears in the Archive: Creating Memory to Survive and to Contest Empire." In *AmongUS: Essays on Identity, Belonging, and Intercultural Competence*, 2nd ed., edited by Myron W. Lustig and Jolene Koester, 233–245. Boston, MA: Pearson.

Mizokami, Yuki. 2002. *Re-Making the Boundaries: Towards Subversion of the Mechanism of Discourses Producing and Reproducing Social Discrimination* (Doctoral dissertation). Graduate School of Languages and Cultures, Nagoya University, Japan.

Pakir, Anne. 1999. "Connecting with English in the Context of Internationalisation." *TESOL Quarterly*, 22, no. 1: 103–114.

Phillipson, Robert. (2008). "The Linguistic Imperialism of Neoliberal Empire." *Critical Inquiry in Language Studies*, 5, no. 1: 1–43.

Rothkopf, David. 1997. "In Praise of Cultural Imperialism?" *Foreign Policy*, 107: 38–53.

Shome, Raka. 1999. "Whiteness and the Politics of Location: Postcolonial Reflections." In *Whiteness: The Communication of Social Identity*, edited by Thomas K. Nakayama and Judith N. Martin, 107–128. Thousand Oaks, CA: Sage Publications.

———. 2006. "Interdisciplinary Research and Globalization." *The Communication Review*, 9, no. 1: 1–36.

———. 2010. "Internationalizing Critical Race Communication Studies: Transnationality, Space, and Affect." In *The Handbook of Critical Intercultural Communication*, edited by Thomas K. Nakayama and Rona Tamiko Halualani, 149–170. Chichester, West Sussex, UK; Malden, MA: Wiley-Blackwell.

Tankei-Aminian, Sachiko. 2016. "On Becoming *Japersican*: A Personal Narrative of Cultural Adaptation, Intercultural Identity and Transnationalism." In *Globalizing Intercultural Communication: Reader*, edited by Kathryn Sorrells and Sachi Sekimoto, 197–205. Thousand Oaks, CA: Sage.

———. Forthcoming. "Tongue Does Matter: Examining the Impact of English Neo-Imperialism Through Exophonic Autoethnography." In *Critical Autoethnography: Intersecting Cultural Identities in Everyday Life*, 2nd ed., edited by Robin M. Boylorn and Mark P. Orbe. New York: Routledge.

Tsuda, Yukio. 2014. "The Hegemony of English and Strategies for Linguistic Pluralism: Proposing the Ecology of Language Paradigm." In *The Global Intercultural Communication Reader*, 2nd ed., edited by Molefi Kete Asante, Yoshitaka Miike, and Jing Yin, 445–456. New York, NY: Routledge.

Van Weijen, Daphne. 2012. "The Language of (Future) Scientific Communication." *Research Trends*, November 2012. https://www.researchtrends.com/issue-31-november-2012/the language-of-future-scientific-communication/.

Chapter 12

Managing Mental Health in the Classroom

A Narrative Reflection on Pedagogy

Andrea L. Meluch

Last fall I received an email from a graduate student who had been struggling to turn assignments in on time throughout the semester. I had been working with her by giving extensions when possible, but I was also beginning to get a little frustrated because I was not seeing this pattern of behavior changing. The subject line of the email was vague and essentially referred to having missed another assignment. I knew that the assignment was missing, but as this was an ongoing issue with the student, I did not think much more of it until I started reading the email. The contents of the email left my mind racing and made me feel a drop in my stomach. The student wrote that she had attempted suicide over the weekend and that she was in the hospital for an involuntary mental health evaluation. She further explained that she was struggling with a mental health disorder that "has a scary name" and that it was getting in the way of her making significant progress in any of her classes. From the content of the email I could tell that this was a serious situation, but it seemed like the student was safe at the moment.

After I read the email twice, I called the campus student conduct administrator in charge of student welfare issues (e.g., disciplinary problems, health crises, and Title IX reporting). I shared the email with my colleague, and we decided to refer this student to our campus counseling center and to have a counselor check-in with the student several times over the next few weeks. I gave the student an extension on the assignment and invited her to keep the conversation with me open. As the semester progressed, I worked with the student on extensions and accommodations and let her know that we needed to have an open communication line to make sure that I could provide her with the help she needed. It was challenging working with her since there were times when I did not hear from her and worried that something was wrong.

As I reflect on my interactions with her and other students struggling with mental health, I find that I am often positioned in ways that necessitate the need to be aware of how to intervene in a crisis, encourage students who need it, and identify opportunities to discuss mental health in ways that are inviting and show respect for students who may otherwise feel stigmatized and isolated. At the beginning of each semester, I know that I'll have students who struggle with mental health conditions that may impact their academic performance. I base this assumption on both research demonstrating the increasing rates of mental health conditions among college students (e.g., American College Health Association 2018, 13–14; Eisenberg et al. 2019, 78; Lipson et al. 2015, 388) and my own experience teaching at the collegiate level for almost a decade. College faculty often find themselves in the difficult position of offering support to students who are managing mental health conditions and sometimes even experiencing mental health crises (White and LaBelle 2019, 146). However, my experience interacting with students managing mental health conditions is directly informed by my own personal experience managing generalized anxiety disorder.

I began struggling with anxiety in my adolescence and continued to experience it throughout my undergraduate and graduate studies. As a tenure-track faculty member I am working on managing my anxiety with varying degrees of success. This chapter will explore how my identity as an academic who struggles with anxiety influences my pedagogy.

MENTAL HEALTH AND COLLEGE STUDENTS

A mental health condition is "characterized by alternations in thinking, mood, or behavior (or some combination thereof) associated with distress and/or impaired functioning" (US Department of Health and Human Services 2000, 453). Today mental health conditions among college students are at the forefront of the conversation among university faculty, staff, and administrators. Over the last decade, researchers have seen an overwhelming increase in students experiencing mental health conditions, such as depression and anxiety (Lipson et al. 2015, 388). According to the American College Health Association (2018), 41.9% of college students surveyed felt so depressed that they found it difficult to function at some point in the last 12 months and another 63.4% felt overwhelming anxiety at some point in the last 12 months (13–14). Despite the widespread recognition of the challenges students with mental health conditions face on college campuses, many students conceal their condition because of fear of stigmatization (Smith and Applegate 2018,

384). Unfortunately, many students do not receive appropriate treatment and accommodations for a variety of reasons (e.g., unaware of resources available, stigma, cultural constraints) which may have deleterious effects on their well-being. Specifically, students who do not receive treatment may experience a decline in academic performance (American College Health Association 2018, 5).

Students living with a mental health condition are often advised by faculty members to reach out to their university's disability office to receive accommodations. According to the National Alliance on Mental Health (2019), common accommodations that colleges and universities offer to students with a mental health condition include: arranging for priority registration; reducing course load; substituting one course for another; providing transportation services; allowing note-taking and recording devices; allowing the student to work from home; extending time for testing; extending deadlines for assignments; tutoring; mentoring; study skills training; an individual room for taking exams; and/or allowing the student to change rooms or roommates. Although many of these accommodations can be helpful to students who are struggling with mental health issues, receiving accommodations generally requires students to have received a diagnosis and treatment for their mental health condition. The literature suggests that despite increases in diagnosis and treatment (e.g., counseling, medication), students do not universally utilize these resources (Eisenberg et al. 2019, 77–78). That is, there are a variety of barriers to students who may need accommodations and/or mental health treatment and when these barriers are overlooked by instructors, students may be further marginalized.

APPROACHING MENTAL HEALTH IN THE CLASSROOM: A DELICATE BALANCE

As someone who struggles with an anxiety disorder, I believe that I spend a disproportionate amount of time thinking about how mental health affects the daily life of my students. When I was an undergraduate my anxiety made it difficult for me to enroll in certain classes or to stay enrolled and, so, I would withdraw from classes when the stressors of school became too much for me to handle. In graduate school my anxiety disorder became an even greater barrier for my ability to make progress in my studies. I found myself constantly struggling to keep up with the demands of my program because I was in a constant state of anxiety over the requirements. Although feeling overwhelmed may seem perfectly natural when there are looming deadlines or large projects on the horizon, anxiety can be debilitating and make every task feel overwhelming. Paralyzing, anxiety creates a cycle of wanting to produce, but simultaneously feeling like it is impossible to get going. I often found myself spending so much time thinking about the obstacles that I was sometimes unable to actually face. As such, I recognize that mental illness can create similar challenges for even the brightest students.

My experience living with anxiety as a student and a faculty member has led me to reevaluate how I handle student mental health issues and to conduct research on the subject. In a recent study I conducted, my colleague and I surveyed students about whether knowing that an instructor struggled with mental health would inform the students' decision to discuss their own mental health issues with them (Meluch and Starcher 2020, 160). Students felt that knowing an instructor has also struggled with mental health would make them feel like there was a lower likelihood of stigma and a higher likelihood of instructor understanding. Thus, students recognize that the way instructors discuss mental health and share their experiences informs whether students can feel comfortable discussing these issues. Based on my research and my own experiences, the way instructors discuss mental health influences whether students will feel comfortable seeking out resources and discussing their challenges with the course or fading away without ever reaching out for help.

As a college instructor, I realize the importance of the language I use in my classrooms. Fassett and Warren (2007) argue that "words do more than state fact, do more than engender meaning; words make experiences real" (61). Likewise, Goldman (2018, 400) argues that instructors create a narrative in their classrooms about mental health. That is, instructors can craft a classroom culture that is open and accommodating to students or dismissive of them. As such, the way I talk about mental health, student challenges, and accommodations has a very real impact on whether I am validating student experiences or undermining them. I make deliberate choices around what I choose to say, how I choose to say it, and what I choose to ignore. In my classrooms, I have decided that I cannot ignore the conversation about mental health and that I need to approach those conversations carefully.

Over the past several years I have changed my approach to discussing campus resources early in the semester. Specifically, instead of simply notifying students where to find campus resources for mental health (which I still do), I instead open a conversation about the struggles that college students face. Framing this discussion by acknowledging that I am aware of the fact that my students bring unique backgrounds and experiences into the classroom and that they are each facing equally unique challenges and obstacles (e.g., family, work, health), I further ask students to share with me privately through a questionnaire "any information they would like me know about them." For some students this information includes their preferred pronouns while others tell me about struggling with childcare arrangements. I have had students notify me on the first day of class about their mental health struggles through this channel, while other students, like the one I mentioned at the beginning of the chapter, do not tell me about the issue until they are in crisis.

One student in particular stands out as an example of how my handling of student mental health issues opens dialogue. This student had taken several classes with me over the course of three semesters and was by all accounts a high-performing student. About halfway through the spring semester the student emailed me and asked if we could sit down to discuss an advising question. I arranged a time for the student to come in the following morning for a meeting. When she came in, I started by asking how I could help. She became visibly upset and told about how she was struggling with mental health and that her modern language course was further triggering these issues. I sat and listened to her explain what she was going through and asked several questions about the course, her schedule, and whether or not she had sought treatment for her mental health. She told me that she was seeing a therapist already and that they were working through things together. I was relieved to know that she was getting help and over the course of our conversation we discussed her options to help manage stress (e.g., withdrawing from the modern language course, seeking accommodations from the instructor) and how each of these decisions would impact her progress toward her degree. As we discussed these challenges, she then explained that she felt having me as an instructor was helpful. She told me that she knew I was there for my students and that being in my course was comforting. Her openness regarding my class also confirmed the importance of continuing to find ways in my pedagogy to invite dialogue around student experiences, especially those concerning mental health.

Co-creating a space for students to share their experiences has important implications in terms of building stronger relationships with students who may otherwise feel socially isolated because of their mental health condition. Specifically, through inviting student mental health narratives, instructors may provide an outlet to students in which they can discuss their challenges (Goldman 2018, 400). These types of inclusive spaces have shown some promise in destigmatizing mental illness and may show promise for college students especially (Smith and Applegate 2018, 389). Although some faculty may be unwilling or unable to incorporate such conversations into their pedagogy, I encourage faculty to consider the benefits of allowing students to share their stories with us. I have found that these conversations can be difficult to begin. I often find myself feeling like I am walking a tightrope when it comes to creating a dialogue. I feel tense at the prospect of sharing my own anxiety experiences for fear of being seen as less competent by my students. However, I also realize how discussing my own mental health challenges may help reduce stigma for students who are in similar situations (Goldman 2018, 400).

OVERCOMING STIGMA IN THE ACADEMY

One of the challenges of struggling with a mental health condition is the stigma associated with these conditions that makes them difficult to discuss (Smith and Applegate 2018, 384). The stigmatization that most people, who are diagnosed with mental health conditions, especially severe conditions (e.g., schizophrenia, bipolar disorder), face is a direct reflection of societal norms that are perpetuated through many social structures, including universities and colleges. Fowler (2015) explains, "As is often the case in academia, the political system of the university acts to establish values and norms to guide the actions of professors and students alike" (162). The societal stigma surrounding mental health is very present on college campuses whether or not we want to admit it. I found throughout graduate school that I was led to conceal my mental health struggles in explicit and implicit ways. Faculty would tell me that graduate school was "supposed to be demanding" or "needed to break students." These types of negative messages made me feel like I did not belong in higher education because I struggled with anxiety. I often felt like I was an outsider in academic spaces and was only allowed admission by concealing my mental health struggles from others.

Universities often pride themselves on creating inclusive spaces, but I have found that many times universities instead create "hoops to jump through" or even barriers when struggling with mental health. At a particularly low point in my graduate program, I looked at the university policies for taking a leave of absence. The policy was vague and, even if the university granted that leave, there were no departmental policies in place about advisors having to continue to work with students who are returning. In fact, there were no ramifications for committee members if they decided not to continue working with returning students. I decided to not take the leave of absence or even disclose my mental health issues at that point.

My experience is not unique among college students. In fact, recently Stanford University students filed a class action lawsuit claiming that the university forced them to take involuntary leaves and banning them from campus under the guise of educational accommodations for their mental health crises (Kafka 2019). In this case, students who sought mental health resources claimed that the administration treated them as if they had committed infractions instead of providing accommodations. Thus, the very accommodations designed to help students struggling with mental health may serve as structures to further disenfranchise those already confronting major challenges. As such, faculty and students experiencing mental health issues often find themselves in a system that feels (and may very well be) rigged against them.

Through my pedagogy, I believe I have the ability to reduce stigma and provide opportunities to help students persist toward their degrees. Telling a student struggling with a mental health issue to drop a course can send a damaging message and, thus, I instead discuss options with students who are managing mental illness. Obviously, faculty should step in if a student poses a risk to themselves or others and there are training programs available to help faculty understand how to deal with these situations (e.g., QPR 2019). In my pedagogy, I present options (e.g., taking an incomplete grade, extensions, retaking course at a later time) and offer agency in their decision making.

CONFRONTING THE CHALLENGES OF DISCUSSING MENTAL HEALTH WITH STUDENTS

As a faculty member who chooses to use narratives as a pathway for building relationships with students, I am careful to not engage in counseling behaviors of which I am not qualified, to always refer students to the appropriate campus resources (e.g., counseling) and to ensure that I follow institutional policies regarding reporting students who may be at risk of self-harm. In my interactions, I follow the institutional guidelines and referred students to campus resources and also have listened intently to their stories of struggling with mental health. However, I realize these conversations are difficult to manage and even triggering for my own mental well-being. I cannot count how many times I have started a sentence by saying to students, "I am not a therapist." Moreover, I have lost count of how many times talking to students about their mental health has completely drained me and made me feel the emotional labor of the job and its effects of being a productive faculty member. Navigating these conversations remains a very delicate balance between opening up myself to inviting students to share their experiences and keeping myself distanced enough so as to not trigger my anxiety.

One of the most difficult aspects of this balance is deciding whether or not to share my experience with anxiety with my students. Hosek and Thompson (2009) found that instructors develop precise rules for deciding whether to disclose personal information to students (338). Specifically, they found that instructors weigh the risks of disclosure (e.g., credibility threats) and make determinations of whether or not to disclose personal information. Similarly, I have worried about how disclosing a stigmatized identity poses a threat to my credibility as an instructor, researcher, and individual. Unlike some other marginalized identities, mental illness is often concealable. I am very deliberate in when and how I discuss my own struggles with mental health with my students. When a student discloses their struggle to me, I will sometimes share my similar experience with them. Several years ago, when a student told me about her struggles with anxiety throughout high school, I revealed to her that I have struggled with anxiety as well. At other times when students seem to be hesitant to go to the campus counseling center, I will share with them that I used campus counseling services when I was a student. During these conversations my goal is to help students understand that they are not alone in their struggles and to normalize prioritizing mental health needs.

CRAFTING PEDAGOGY TO
ADDRESS MENTAL HEALTH

My personal experiences influence how I interact with others. I believe that because of my personal experiences with anxiety I am better equipped to provide support when I have had similar experiences or related knowledge. I have found that having lived as an undergraduate student, graduate student, and faculty member who struggles with mental health issues that I am open to having conversations about these issues and to craft my pedagogy to assist students who are also struggling with mental health issues. According to Fassett and Warren (2007):

> how we talk about identities shapes how we understand those identities, and, more Importantly, the actions we take to respect the role of our communication . . . Calling out a more complex, nuanced understanding of identity as emergent from communication commits us to more complex and nuanced understandings of power, privilege, culture, and responsibility. (40–41)

Bringing my identity into the classroom to help change the conversation around mental health requires the application of some aspects of critical communication pedagogy. I also recognize the inherent privileges I am afforded by my race, class, and abilities, which offer me the opportunity to potentially disclose without further fear of additional stigmas. One of the ways that I integrate my personal struggles with mental health into the classroom is by openly discussing mental health struggles students face, campus resources, and the stigma surrounding mental health with my students. Goldman (2018) argues that "the conversations, tone, and resulting stigmas around the topic [mental health] can be more easily managed and improved by instructors within the limited and confined context of the classroom" (400). Thus, I find myself allowing for students to share the challenges that their identities create for them with me and to do my best to provide the resources they need to be successful students.

As an instructor, I find that my interactions and relationships with students are more likely to evolve when I incorporate an openness to understanding their experiences into my pedagogy. Through developing these relationships and providing a safe outlet for difficult conversations about mental health, I have seen my students excel academically. Instructors in higher education face a variety of challenges, and helping students to manage mental health issues is one of the most pressing today. Through being open to sharing our own identities and learning about student experiences, instructors may find that they are both supporting students on their academic journey and, even, resisting structures that stigmatize our similar experiences.

REFERENCES

American College Health Association. 2018. *American College Health Association-National College Health Assessment II: Reference Group Executive Summary Spring 2018.* Hanover, MD: American College Health Association. https://www .acha.org/documents/ncha/NCHAII_Spring_2018_Reference_Group_Execuve_S ummary.pdf (March 31, 2020).

Eisenberg, Daniel, Sarah Ketchen Lipson, Peter Ceglarek, Adam Kern, and Megan Vivian Phillips. 2019. "College Student Mental Health: The National Landscape." In *Promoting Behavioral Health and Reducing Risk Among College Students: A Comprehensive Approach*, 75–86. New York: Routledge.

Fassett, Deanna L., and John T. Warren. 2007. *Critical Communication Pedagogy.* Thousand Oaks: Sage Publications.

Fowler, Sean. 2015. "Burnout and Depression in Academia: A Look at the Discourse of the University." *Empedocles: European Journal for the Philosophy of Communication*, 6, no. 2: 155–167.

Goldman, Zachary W. 2018. "Responding to Mental Health Issues in the College Classroom." *Communication Education*, 67, no. 3: 399–404.

Hosek, Angela M., and Jason Thompson. 2009. "Communication Privacy Management and College Instruction: Exploring the Rules and Boundaries that Frame Instructor Private Disclosures." *Communication Education*, 58, no. 3: 327–349.

Kafka, Alexander C. 2019. "Stanford's New Policy for Student Mental-Health Crises Is Hailed as a Model." *The Chronicle of Higher Education*, October 10, 2019. https ://www.chronicle.com/article/stanford-s-new-policyfor/247329.

Lipson, Sarah Ketchen, S. Michael Gaddis, Justin Heinze, Kathryn Beck, and Daniel Eisenberg. 2015. "Variations in Student Mental Health and Treatment Utilization Across US Colleges and Universities." *Journal of American College Health*, 63, no. 6: 388–396.

Meluch, Andrea L, and Shawn Starcher. 2020. "The Stigmatization of Mental Health Disclosures in the College Classroom: Student Perceptions of Instructor Credibility and the Benefits of Disclosure." In *Communicating Mental Health: History, Concepts, & Perspectives*, 147–166. Lanham, MD: Lexington Books.

"NAMI." "NAMI." https://www.nami.org/Find-Support/Teens-Young-Adults/Ma naging-a-Mental-Health-Condition-in-College (March 31, 2020).

"QPR Institute: Practical and Proven Suicide Prevention Training." QPR Institute|Practical and Proven Suicide Prevention Training QPR Institute. https:// qprinstitute.com/about-qpr (March 31, 2020).

Smith, Rachel A., and Amanda Applegate. 2018. "Mental Health Stigma and Communication and Their Intersections with Education." *Communication Education*, 67, no. 3: 382–393.

U.S. Department of Health and Human Services. 2000. *Mental Health: A Report of the Surgeon General.* Rockville, MD: U.S. Department of Health and Human Services, Substance Abuse and Mental Health Services Administration, Center for Mental Health Services, National Institutes of Health, National Institute of Mental Health. https://www.hsdl.org/?view&did=730796 (March 31, 2020).

White, Allie, and Sara Labelle. 2019. "A Qualitative Investigation of Instructors' Perceived Communicative Roles in Students' Mental Health Management." *Communication Education*, 68, no. 2: 133–155.

Chapter 13

Navigating Intercultural Identities at a Crossroads of Mindfulness and Instruction

Aayushi Hingle

BEING A CULTURAL NOMAD: WHO AM I AS AN INSTRUCTOR?

I ask myself the question "Who am I?" from time to time. Over the years, I have realized the answer is different depending on the context within which I ask it. Certain parts of my identity have remained stable while the rest are foundational for other identities that I have cultivated. Who I am is a constant negotiation of the different identities that make up the whole of me.

I was born in New Delhi, India, to two very humble and ambitious parents. They dreamed for themselves a life of abundance, where they were able to give their children everything to build a good life. My parents took on the most significant challenge they had faced together, moving from India to Botswana, a small country in Southern Africa in 1992. My parents had never experienced life as a person of color or a minority ethnicity in India, but that all changed when they moved to Botswana and I don't think they knew the kind of challenges this navigation would bring for not just them but their children as well. What they knew was that getting out of their current lifestyle would allow them to grow and provide a better life for their children. Thus, they took a leap of faith and moved.

Botswana, no doubt, is a country very different from India; however, both countries went through a period of British colonization and retained parts of that history in different ways. Botswana technically was a British protectorate gaining independence in 1966. There were many influences left behind, such as religion, culture, and, the most significant to my life, the availability of English-medium schools, where I learned to speak English even though my parents' first language was not English. Growing up in Botswana and getting an English-medium education meant that I had the communication tools to be successful in a world where my mother tongue could only help me succeed so far.

My parents' generation grew up in a postcolonial society; they firmly believed that knowing how to speak fluent English opened doors of opportunity, and this was a very early example of how my family influenced my cultural identity. Looking back I had lived a life of being a cultural nomad, where I never fully belong to any one culture but navigated all cultural experiences using the skills I picked up along the way.

At the age of fourteen, I started boarding school in South Africa and very quickly learned that I was again navigating cultures but not fully belonging in one completely. I am constantly reminded of a quote by Nelson Mandela where he said: "For to be free is not to merely cast off one's chains, but to live in a way that respects and enhances the freedom of others" (Mandela 2013, 544). I took this to heart when learning to navigate my own identity, always living in a mindful way, building communities through connection and an open heart. However, I have always been a part of the minority in my life and over the years I have come to realize this part of my identity has had so much power over how I take up space in the world.

At the young age of eighteen, I journeyed away from my homes to another continent. I came to Los Angeles. Bright-eyed and eager to learn, I thought being a student in America would be like the movies, but that was not reality. Life in the United States was not a Hollywood movie. However, the biggest lesson I learned navigating a different culture at that young, defining age was that I am not just one identity, I am several and all of them intersect to offer both opportunities and even at times take them away. I graduated after five years in my undergraduate program and was navigating and making connections, but I did not belong in the groups of friends that I had made. I felt a constant longing for someone to understand how my different identities made it hard to belong in just one space. It wasn't until I started my master's program in Communication Studies that I discovered theories like the Sapir-Whorf hypothesis and Identity Negotiation Theory that I found the belonging I longed for my whole life. When I saw the tools to navigate who I was, I became equipped to understand how I take up space in this world. This realization led me to think about how I can help other people do the same for themselves.

I started teaching the Basic Course at my university in the second year of my graduate program, and the night before my first day of teaching, I remember thinking about how out of place I felt. Who was I to teach students about public speaking when I am barely figuring out the world? However, I don't think that I ever anticipated that becoming an instructor in a diverse institution would be the blessing that not only made me a better instructor but allowed me to find my purpose.

I have not stopped teaching since. It has been almost six years of teaching at different universities and colleges on both coasts of the country. On this journey, I have picked up ways in which I navigate my classroom space, being a woman of color, an immigrant, a first-generation college student, and a cultural nomad in today's world. In this chapter I will share my experience in the classroom, building community, establishing credibility, navigating the intersection of different identities, and how I strive to make a difference through the self-reflexivity and mindfulness of who I am. The theoretical lens through which I write this chapter is one of intersectionality from a mindful and critical intercultural perspective. I understand the role of power and my identity in my position as an instructor and so the lens through which I write about my experience takes that into account in this chapter (Toyosaki and Chuang 2018). Questioning the role of power is not something I have been able to self reflexively do in my life, because I grew up in a culture that values high power distance. However, I feel that in explaining how I take up space as an instructor I must acknowledge how power collides with the identities I portray.

ESTABLISHING CREDIBILITY IN THE CLASSROOM

Being a scholar, and always a student in the field of Communication Studies, allows me to learn so much about the different processes of communication. However, my expertise in interpersonal, intercultural, and instructional communication always brings me to exciting crossroads when navigating discourse. Every instructor is in a constant state of figuring out how to establish and maintain credibility in their different classrooms and what may work in one space may not work in another (Dannels 2015). As a society, we have come to place so much fear around the idea of failure that we sometimes fear even trying new things because of the daunting possibility that we may fail. As an instructor, I have tried to embody being fearless in the classroom even though at times I myself am nervous or afraid of the unknown. However, I think part of the reason why I've been forced to step out of my comfort zone is because I'm a woman of color who is an immigrant trying to teach in a classroom in America. What people consciously or subconsciously perceive about me is not something I can initially control, but what I can control is what I do to establish my credibility after that initial perception.

In establishing credibility, I thought about my own identity and concluded that two words from my life come to mind: Nirbhau and Nirvair, which mean without fear and hate. My family is of Punjabi origin, and although we are not Sikh by religion, we practiced the customs and traditions of both Hinduism and Sikhism growing up. In the Indian culture, religion is not what solely defines your identity. The amalgamation of your culture, religion, place of birth—all these things are a part of who you are.

My family also speaks Punjabi at home, aside from three other languages, so I have gravitated to finding examples of people in the media I can relate to for validation. I spent a lot of my time in my early twenties before becoming an instructor researching the experiences of other American-born Indians to make sense of my own experiences. While watching YouTube one day, I discovered Nirbhau and Nirvair. They resonated with me so much on my journey and are particularly valuable when establishing credibility in my classrooms. I seek to assert my credibility in those spaces without fear and hate.

As an immigrant educator and woman of color, my biggest fear was and still is, will I be heard when I speak. Growing up I witnessed the inequalities that women in my culture faced. My parents worked diligently to give me as many equal opportunities as they could afford and spent much of their hard-earned money giving me a good education in the United States. I don't take this for granted, but I am also aware that I bring to my classroom an intersection of these experiences and who I am. There is power and privilege in the identities that I embody, but because of this I am also required to do a lot more work in establishing my credibility. Therefore, I had to teach without fear first. Diving into the depths of my identity, discovering myself and the things that are important to me as an instructor. Discovering how I negotiate my own identity to be able to keep maintaining this negotiation with others as well is an important part of my instructor identity performance (Ting-Toomey 2015). Taking into consideration the perceptions that may hinder students' ability to perceive me as credible, I ask how can my identity enhance the credibility that I bring to the classroom, and how can I communicate this in ways that insight meaningful interactions in the community I am creating?

Another approach I employ is to learn without hate. In the classroom I am the authority who must maintain a sense of order and logic of learning. Becoming conscious of and empowered by my intersectional identities allows me to navigate spaces without fear of being different and without hate. I use the word hate, but this can also be self-hate, and judgment. For example, during my first-day introduction, I show students where in the world I have lived, and I talk to them about all the different parts of my identity as a teacher. Not just limited to my teaching experience, I include my research interests and my hobbies. I do this for a couple of reasons; the first is really to start establishing a sense of trust with my students. If they know who I am they can trust me. This allows me to answer questions my students may be thinking but may not want to ask. The second reason I do this is to allow conversations of power, privilege, and identity to interlay our classroom discussions throughout the semester in a natural way because I lay the foundation of identity using the power I am privileged with as the instructor. We can continue to build on this trust through our time in the classroom. This also gives agency to students in the classroom to feel comfortable engaging in conversations about how power, privilege, and identity intersect in their lives, allowing the opportunity to be mindful of one another and self-reflexive as well.

Ultimately, I model what I want to see from my students without fear and hate. Wanting to establish a respectful environment, I lead with my own experiences to encourage the opportunity for my students to reciprocate openness for openness, trust for trust (hooks 1994).

BUILDING COMMUNITY

As an introvert who ventured into a career that I love, mindfully building community requires more awareness of who I am, how I take up space, and how others around me navigate the same area. This constant bridging between being mindful of myself and others while trying to teach can be very mentally taxing. However, when I see the community flourish in my classroom where students are conscious and inclusive of one another, it makes it all worth the while. I have had classroom communities of students who were very anxious about public speaking, but through building community consciously keeping their personalities and identities in mind, we grew together and accomplished a great deal of active learning in the class. Every semester I ask students to reflect on their own growth, through a written or verbal check-in and without fail every semester students notice how much they have grown. Even the students who thought they were already great at public speaking, realize that communicating with confidence requires us to be mindful of others and self-reflexive.

As I speak about mindfulness in this chapter, I essentially speak about the thought process of acknowledging how my own identity creates a space of interaction for the identities of others involved in that moment. I acknowledge my own power and privilege or lack of, and I do the same for the people communicating with me as well, becoming an educator who is aware and self-reflexive (Bettez 2011).

I remember very early in my teaching career, I feared that to establish a community in my classroom; I couldn't be myself and needed to be a strict instructor. My natural tendency is to be a bubbly and lively teacher who is positive and warm. However, the trained teacher in me wanted to be strict and to the point. Because I was so young, I feared I wouldn't be taken seriously.

I risked becoming the oppressor in the fear of my own oppression as Freire (1996) may see it. In that moment I didn't realize that these parts of my identity created a space where I had the power to bring students together, but it also made me work extra hard because my identity brings with it first impressions I can't control.

On my first day of teaching, I did what I thought was expected. I went in and kept the lesson to the point, even feeling guilty when I made a mistake in pronouncing a word differently because I learned to speak English in a British Education system. That first-day experience taught me that I needed to be myself to build that trust in the classroom and to allow students to trust the space is safe for them to be themselves with each other and me. If they could not perceive my authenticity as a teacher, how could they want to be authentic in that space themselves? I started to look for natural ways to build that community with them. Whether it was through sharing my love for comics and pop culture, bringing a weekly terrible joke to class, sharing in their struggles during midterms, or perhaps just giving them a few minutes in some classes to write me a quick note on how they are doing. However, my favorite way to build community naturally in the classroom is to find moments of pause between activities or speeches, where students are chatting with each other. I usually casually add to the conversation or ask a casual question like "Are you excited about the new superhero movie releasing this week?" This always gets students feeling so much more comfortable communicating in the class and it really allows them to feel comfortable asking for guidance as the semester continues. I use the position that my work gives me, to discover the power that I do not have because of the different identities I embody, and use this to help create a space where my students feel free to communicate their own identities.

My training on teacher immediacy and my growing awareness of myself helped me figure out how to create those communities in my classes. Spaces where power and identity meet without hate and fear. Knowing myself allows me to build trust and community in my classroom and navigate a variety of student personalities and identities, while I remain grounded in the knowledge of who I am in that moment. I want to expand on the idea of mindfulness and reflexivity a little more to explain how these play a role in my critical awareness of myself as an instructor.

MINDFULNESS AND SELF-REFLEXIVITY

Studying in South Africa, I learned to adapt to everything that I do the idea of Ubuntu, which means "I am because we are" (Oppenheim 2012). I try to navigate my identity and acknowledging differences by being mindful that I am because we are. However, along every path traveled in my life, I have found role models who solidified how I lived during those periods of my journey. They inspired me to further question the roles of power and privilege in my life so that I can become aware of how these manifest in the lives of people I interact with. Growing up in my household, Mahatma Gandhi was spoken about quite extensively. It wasn't just what he did that was talked about; instead, my parents always tried to instil in me a value of standing up for what I believe. In addition to Gandhi, I was inspired by the lives of amazing leaders like Sir Seretse Khama and Nelson Mandela. Both role models paved the way for me, and future generations, to prosper by fighting for equality through recognizing how power and privilege had been taken away from them because of the identities they embody.

When I started my graduate studies, I discovered the work of Paulo Freire. For the first time, I was exposed to not just how I was privileged in the world, but also the oppression that came with my various intersecting identities. Freire (1996) exposed me to the idea of being mindful and self-reflexive, and critical scholars like bell hooks ensured I also saw how this could work in education. My mother always told me that education is the wealth you gain that keeps on growing, and my mind opened by all these influences ensured that I was wealthier each day as I lived in a way that not just recognized the opportunities I was given, but becoming mindful to the power in who I am.

This is how I navigate intersectional identities as an instructor: becoming aware of who I am and living with a sense of that awareness every day. Many times, I feared how the unwanted outcome of trying something new would affect me. This fear, and the fear of vulnerability, stopped me from figuring out what works best in those situations. However, if I had let my fear of what students will think of my identities get in the way of being my authentic instructor self in the classroom, I would not have been able to learn and teach all the students I have had the privilege to work with over the last six years. I recognize that at times being a woman of color and an immigrant can put me in an unequal starting place compared to my colleagues, but this knowledge helps me embody my space with the power I do have and create a safe space for my students to do the same.

I genuinely believe that by mindfully acknowledging intersectional identities in the classroom, I have inspired students in ways even I didn't know I could. Navigating being an immigrant and an instructor allows me to be able to understand my classroom communities better and help facilitate the creation of a safe and inclusive community. I can pick and choose how to navigate my identities depending on what my students need on a given day. This active navigation is only possible because of my discipline with being mindful and self-reflexive about who I am at my core. For example, in one class, I had a student express how difficult it was to find someone who understood the troubles of the immigration system. I don't always lead with my identity of being an immigrant and international student, but when the context calls for it, I will talk about my experiences. In this instance, my ability to empathize with this student's struggles as an immigrant navigating the immigration system in America made the difference to them succeeding in school. To this day, years after this student has graduated, I still get an email periodically about their progress and well-being. Had I not been comfortable with my own identity as an instructor, I would not have been able to help this student and countless others. The knowledge of how my identity may not be represented in the space I'm embodying makes it that much more imperative for me to be seen because that is what helps students realize how they can be seen in those spaces as well.

Being mindful and self-reflexive allowed me to be a resource to students who need me as a support system. However, it has also taught me to not be afraid to be powerful in the identities that make up who I am. I have taught in classrooms where all my students were freshmen, but I have also taught in classes where students were of my age or significantly older than me. The one thing that helped me stay grounded in all these settings was acknowledging my own identity in these spaces and the identities of those whom I am teaching.

CONCLUSION

In this chapter, I established my own identity as a cultural nomad navigating the world as a Communication Studies instructor. Through different examples and experiences, I illustrated the importance of understanding identity in the classroom, building community, establishing credibility, and navigating intersectional identities. Realizing that there are many dimensions to who I am and what aspects I can utilize to navigate in a classroom depends on the context and the need at that moment has been paramount to my success in teaching. This constant navigation is only achievable through mindful self-reflexivity. So as Nelson Mandela once said "For to be free is not merely to cast off one's chains, but to live in a way that respects and enhances the freedom of others" everyday as I embody with freedom and without hate and fear my identity in the classroom, I intend to inspire in my students the freedom to do the same.

REFERENCES

Bettez, Silvia Cristina. 2011. "Building Critical Communities Amid the Uncertainty of Social Justice Pedagogy in the Graduate Classroom." *The Review of Education, Pedagogy, and Cultural Studies*, 33, no. 1: 76–106.

Dannels, Deanna P. 2015. *Eight Essential Questions Teachers Ask: A Guidebook for Communicating with Students.* London: Oxford University Press.

Freire, Paolo. 1996. *Pedagogy of the Oppressed (Revised).* New York: Continuum.

hooks, Bell. 1994. *Teaching to Transgress.* New York: Routledge.

Mandela, Nelson. 2013. *Long Walk to Freedom.* UK: Hachette.

Oppenheim, Claire E. 2012. "Nelson Mandela and the Power of Ubuntu." *Religions,* 3, no. 2: 369–388. https://doi.org/10.3390/rel3020369.

Ting-Toomey, S. 2015. "Identity Negotiation Theory." In *The International Encyclopedia of Interpersonal Communication,* edited by eds Charles Berger, Micheal Roloff, Steve Wilson, James Dillard, John Caughlin, and Denise Solomon. https://doi.org/10.1002/9781118540190.wbeic129.

Toyosaki, Satoshi, and Hsun-Yu Chuang. 2018. "Critical Intercultural Communication Pedagogy from Within: Textualizing Intercultural and Intersectional Self-Reflexivity." In *Critical Intercultural Communication Pedagogy,* edited by Ahmet Atay and Satoshi Tayosaki, 227–248. Lanham, MD: Lexington Books.

Chapter 14

Going the Extra Mile

Mentoring Black Undergraduate Students

Lance Kyle Bennett

Being Black in academia gives me a sense of pride and fulfillment because my ancestors marched for my place in this space. Embarking on this academic journey is more than just the piece of paper, but it is the representation of the strong mentorship that I have received throughout my time. As a first-year community college student, I was approached by my professor with the question, "How do you feel about taking an honors course option, being mentored, and submitting a research paper to the Undergraduate Scholars Conference of the Eastern Communication Association?" Despite not fully knowing what this process entailed, I responded with an enthusiastic "YES!" In the following months, I began learning what an academic mentor does— encourages, supports, and closely monitors the progress of their students. Although I was one of a few Black students in the major, I felt overjoyed that I was the first name to come to the mind of my professor. There were several instances when I felt alone and not wanted during this academic process, but this proved to be an invaluable part of my experience that launched my interest in graduate education. My first mentor in the communication discipline was a White female professor, but she understood that being Black is something that I wear proudly and boldly.

African Americans are disproportionately represented in several sectors of society, in particular, higher education. According to the *Condition of Education* report, African American students make up only 12% of the student population at 4-year public institutions (United States Department of Education 2020). The same report also indicates that African American undergraduate enrollment decreased, from 2.7 million to 2.1 million students, between 2010 and 2018. These statistics give a glimpse into the challenging racialized experiences on college campus (Yosso et al. 2009, 79). With little

189

to no faculty advocates, African American/Black students continue to face uphill battles pertaining to their college success.

Being on the other side of "the table" as an instructor, I feel a duty to help shape Black undergraduate students' experiences at my university. I teach courses related to interpersonal communication and research methods wherein approximately three to four Black students are enrolled in the course per semester. Often these students express a desire to obtain graduate degrees, but feel it is an impossible task because they lack mentorship in this process. After repeatedly hearing these experiences, I began to incorporate my own mentoring model with Black students. This model uses interpersonal communication to form mentoring relationships with the students that involve working as a research assistant on a project that I am undertaking. This experience helps with graduate school preparation, job and internship applications, and reinforces the knowledge gained in major courses.

Scholarship used to examine mentoring relationships in communication has received little attention. For instance, some scholars reflect on their experience with graduate students by displaying the importance for faculty to support students from diverse backgrounds (Rudick and Daniels 2019, 68). This lack is an opportunity to provide a personal narrative to demonstrate the personal, emotional, and relational aspects of mentoring Black undergraduate students in the academy. In this chapter, I use post-positivist frameworks to present my own experience—both as an instructor and student—to help others who are actively or considering working with Black undergraduate students. Indeed, mentoring is an essential component of the college experience. Previous research notes that mentoring is crucial for Black students' academic success (Strayhorn and Terrell 2007, 58) provide a sense of belongingness (Raymond and Sheppard 2018, 8) and build the social capital needed to acquire opportunities for advancement (Smith 2007, 40). My time as an academic mentee has been wonderful, and my experience attests to the fact that mentoring matters. As an undergraduate student, I was invited by faculty members who supported my journey to graduate school. My goal is to create a similar experience for current students who are enthused by research and experience.

My mentoring framework does start with a Blackness identity. The pedagogy that I employ is centered on the Black experience in an overwhelming White academia. To that end, I mentor the same way—building the knowledge base of my students through a lens of Blackness. As I began making the transition from undergraduate to graduate school, another mentor, a Black male professor told me in his office "Lance, as a Black man, be sure you know everything you can about everything, about everything possible, so that if somebody asks you have an answer ready." I did not understand it at first; why would someone just randomly ask me questions to test my knowledge?

Then, it hit me...I am a Black man in a mostly White space where *some* people will not value my gifts and talents. Indeed, this experience did prove itself to be true as I navigated through graduate school. It influences how I want to be in the future. I consider this approach as one that privileges the "Black Understanding," which entails how Black mentors and mentees understand one another when we say we *must be* the best in the higher education space. I have embraced the principle of mentorship for success, recognition of one's worth and integrity to guide my students to successfully navigate challenges they encounter in the predominately White university.

In the following sections, I review some recent literature on mentoring communication and how it has shaped my time as a mentor and mentee. Next, I present my mentoring framework that has been developed by reflecting on personal experiences—both that worked well and what I wanted to receive from my mentors. The goal is for others to use this as an innovative guide for current and future Black students. Finally, I highlight my experiences with this mentoring structure with evidence of student learning.

MENTORING COMMUNICATION

Even though I did not know what to expect in the next chapter of my life after my educational experience post the two-year college, I knew that mentorship is beneficial. As I reflect on my academic journey, my best mentors have been those who have informed me to take one course of action versus another, whether tangible, emotional, or spiritual. At the four-year institution, the experience was equally amicable. My conversation with my faculty advisor in the dining room set the context for my new academic journey. Our conversation was casual yet impactful in shaping how I was going to engage as a mentee and/or mentor.

This conversation took place at lunch and began with my advisor saying, "Bennett, what do you want to do after graduation?" I replied, "My plan is to go on to graduate school and eventually become a professor." "Great," he said. Before I could speak another word, he told me: "The best advice I can give you about this process is . . . it's okay to have your plans, but make sure you leave room for God to do His work." Yes, this piece of wisdom was offered because we were at a Christian university; however, I still envision similar advice being offered even if faith was not an integral part of our lives. In other words, mentors help mentees put things in perspective about the future.

Certainly, mentoring is essential in these spaces, a part of organizing function. In this line of thinking, Kalbfleisch provides conceptual definitions of mentorship: "a personal relationship between a more sophisticated mentor and a less experienced protégé" (2006, 64). However, mentoring goes beyond this purpose, as it has a relational and interpersonal element needed for a beneficial experience. The words of wisdom and encouragement offered by mentors have allowed me to desire a closer relationship with them to seek more guidance.

Mentoring is a symbiotic relationship that takes place in a variety of social environments (Harris and Lee 2019, 105) and involves using influence, expertise, and power to benefit the success of the mentee (Kalbfleisch 1997, 390). Working with Black undergraduate students is a serious undertaking that requires one to step out of their comfort zone by advocating for their students. As a mentee, I have witnessed my mentors "putting themselves on the front line" for my existence in White spaces. As a mentee, I have learned the meaning of symbiotic relationships through the interactions with my committed mentors. These relationships developed through an investment in my professional and personal journey. This investment came in the form of paying for academic conferences, sending campus and discipline-specific opportunities to my email, having me over for dinner, and advocating for me behind closed doors. And, as a mentee, these occurrences increased my self-esteem as someone who *can be* an academic.

Kalbfleisch also developed an interpersonal model for participation in mentoring relationships that highlight communication competence and self-esteem as predictors of the mentor's perceived risk in intimacy (i.e., getting close to the requestor), which ultimately influences the mentoring relationship (2006, 64). This model contributes something extremely valuable to the inter-personal communication understanding of mentoring, but many mentoring models lack the author's personal experience as a guide for its construction and development. In the following section, I present a mentoring model for Black undergraduate students to guide and enrich the mentoring experience.

MENTORING MODEL FOR BLACK
UNDERGRADUATE STUDENTS

The Mentoring Model for Black Undergraduate Students (MMBUS) focuses on an individual's experience of mentors with Black mentees. The model acknowledges the centrality of privileging personal experiences as contexts for creating new experiences for mentees. It begins with sharing personal experiences in academia—both positive and negative. I articulate to my students the general Black experience and my own in the academy. I present both because I never want to generalize my experience as being the same for everyone else. However, Black undergraduate students experience more isolation (Magner 1989, 29) compared to their White counterparts.

After developing a relationship with my mentees who plan to pursue graduate education, I share how my original master's advisor did not think I would be successful in a doctoral program, and how I had to seek other faculty mentors to affirm my presence. I take them through that moment that those words were uttered to me. The advisor told me "You've been struggling a lot with quantitative methods in a way that I've never seen before. This makes me think that no program will want you nor will you be successful if you get accepted." I was in complete shock with my heart-pounding and eyes-widen as I contemplated what to say. I walked out of the room without saying a word. Later I expressed my discontentment with the words spoken to me by telling them: "Your comment the other day about me not being successful was inappropriate and completely false."

It is important to share theoretical and methodological content with under-graduate mentees, but personal triumphs and tragedies also are a form of pedagogy. Incorporating mentoring in pedagogy requires more than textbook information, especially when mentees are from marginalized groups. The mentoring model that I present below includes three phases: (1) recruitment and relationship development; (2) communication of hope and optimism for success and well-being; and (3) mentor's personal reflection.

Phase 1: Recruitment and Relationship Development

Personally, I enjoy the opportunity to find new mentees within the campus community. In many ways, it requires me to step outside of my comfort zone to connect with students at different areas of campus. I initiate relationships with students through multiple modes of communication that include sending out flyers, visiting classrooms of other instructors, attending campus organization meetings, and word-of-mouth in my own courses. This communicates the very same thing that was articulated to me as an undergraduate student: "You matter." Students are often shocked and love the fact that a university professor/instructor met them in their space, as opposed to having to solely come to the professor. I have found that these actions make for a much smoother relationship development process. Taking interest in working with students of color is a tremendous endeavor and demands that educators are conversant with historical, political, and social factors in order to cultivate an effective relationship. In this regard, there are steps to be followed to ensure trust in initiating relationships between students and faculty from different racial and cultural backgrounds.

This model does not assume that the relationship between mentor and men-tee will always be smooth. Although I identify as Black, the Black experi-ence is not monolithic. In other words, the Black experience is a combination of acceptances and rejections from social groups, wealth and poverty, and affordances and disadvantages. Inviting students to be open about their current and past experiences provides space for them to develop trust in you as a mentor, which is an essential facet of a relationship. A couple of years ago, I asked a student to share their campus experience as being a Black-bodied female. They informed me of their distrust of faculty at the university and the only group of people who were accepting of them were fellow Black undergraduate students. This was extremely alarming and made me realize my place of privilege as a male on a college campus. Part of my goal with this student was to develop research knowledge and skills to carry forward to graduate school, but also to be someone they could trust on campus.

Phase 2: Communication of Hope for Success

Hope is a discrete, future-oriented emotion, like fear, that motivates behavior by focusing one's thoughts on future rewards and punishments (Lazarus 1999, 654). Thoughts of future rewards and punishments are a strong driver of human behavior (Seligman et al. 2013, 119). Hope capitalizes on this drive by encouraging behaviors that take advantage of opportunities, such as helping students build research skills and acquiring social capital. Thus, a hope appeal is a message that creates an opportunity by evoking the appraisals that constitute hope and presents a way for receivers to take advantage of that opportunity (Chadwick 2015, 601). One instance where I felt hope was when my undergraduate advisor told me about how my efforts in combination with God's grace were going to set me up for several wonderful opportunities in my career. That instance is something that I frequently revisit when things get difficult. To that end, mentoring communication does not just concern "the here and now," but include information that will be remembered for years to come.

My journey as a mentee included both good and bad experiences. While the positive instances inspired a feeling of hope, the negative interactions produced a feeling of fear—a feeling that I was not going to be successful, a feeling that I was going to be at a loss without that person as my mentor, a feeling that nothing was going to work out in the future. Fear may be a relevant emotion in mentoring because it occurs when a person appraises a situation as having the potential to lead to an unpleasant outcome, such as loss, rejection, or failure (Shaver et al. 1987, 1062). A fear appeal, then, is a message that attempts to arouse fear in order to divert behavior through the threat of impending danger or harm. It presents a risk, presents the vulnerability to the risk, and then may suggest a form of protective action. These actions can reflect a host of behaviors such as practicing positive health behaviors and more positive types of talk about groups of people. When Black students enter a mentoring relationship with a faculty member it is important to eliminate fear as much as possible. Black students are already frightened by several factors even before coming to campus. Black students are often told by their high school teachers and counselors, "You won't get into college, and if you do, then it won't last long." If you decide to work with a Black student, then you have an obligation to speak life into them.

In this phase, the purpose is to instil messages of hope instead of messages of despair often communicated to many students including myself. My personal experiences have led me to learn how to communicate with my mentees who have not necessarily received encouragement from educators in the past. So, I take it upon myself to make sure that students who work with me will be empowered and encouraged through hopeful messages.

Phase 3: Mentor's Personal Reflection

This final phase of the mentoring model is an invitation to mentors to reflect on their role as mentors. It is my opinion that every good mentor can reflect on *how* they have mentored once the formal experience has ended. Mentoring Black students is an intricate commitment that requires mentors to retrospectively ask critical questions such as "Can I do better next time? Or "What are the gains and losses?" On the surface, one may think they have done a fantastic job with a student, but doing better in this capacity requires a commitment to critical self-reflection and future improvement. It helps to sustain the mentor-mentee relationships. For me, it was doing more "check-ins" with my students about their journey at the university and after graduation. Because the Black student experience can go from good to bad very fast, due to several systematic factors discussed, it is imperative to do "check-ins" from time to time. As a matter of fact, this form of communication focuses on relational maintenance behaviors. Maintenance consists of behaviors enacted to keep it functioning at a desired level. Like getting maintenance on a car, mentoring relationships require "check-ups" (Knapp 1978, 140). Past research presents five essential maintenance strategies: *positivity* (being happy and supportive), *openness* (includes directly the relationship), *assurances* (showing one's love and commitment), *social networks* (having other professionals involved), and *sharing tasks* (taking on an equal share of tasks) (Stafford and Canary 1991, 217). These maintenance behaviors can be used to reconcile any "bumps" along the mentoring journey to make for holistic pedagogical experience.

CONCLUSION

Academic structures were not built for people who look like myself and the students that I mentor. This ideology has permeated through the "ivory tower" for centuries. As higher education professionals, we have an obligation to provide an inclusive space wherein everyone feels welcome and supported to reach their educational and professional goals, including Black undergraduate students. In too many places, the current experience may sound something like: (1) Black student reaches out to prospective faculty mentor, (2) faculty member claims they are too busy and can't take on any additional responsibilities (all the while currently mentoring White students), and (3) Black student continually struggles to find the support needed to gain research experience to be a competitive graduate school applicant, which continues to perpetuate the cycle of less inclusive academia. Perhaps, we can flip this system around!

I urge those who are not currently mentoring Black students to consider embarking on a new journey to create a more inclusive academia. I have thoroughly enjoyed mentoring Black undergraduate students in my research laboratory and outside of class. Working with these students has reaffirmed my commitment to make my employment experience bigger than myself. Black students are often on the margins without academic mentors because faculty are already committed to others, mostly White students. In order to make campuses more inclusive, all members must feel supported. The above provides a framework for how to begin working with Black students on college campuses.

REFERENCES

Chadwick, Amy E. 2015. "Toward a Theory of Persuasive Hope: Effects of Cognitive Appraisals, Hope Appeals, and Hope in the Context of Climate Change." *Health Communication*, no. 8: 598–611.

Harris, Tina M., and Celeste N. Lee. 2019. "Advocate-Mentoring: A Communicative Response to Diversity in Higher Education." *Communication Education*, no. 68: 103–131.

Kalbfleisch, Pamela J. 1993. "Appeasing the Mentor." *Aggressive Behavior*, no. 23: 389–403.

Kalbfleisch, Pamela J. 2006. "Communicating in Mentoring Relationships: A Theory for Enactment." *Communication Theory*, no. 12: 63–69.

Knapp, Mark. 1978. *Social Intercourse: From Greeting to Goodbye*. New York: Allyn & Bacon.

Magner, Denise K. 1989. "Students Urge Graduate Business Schools to Emphasize Ethical Behavior and Require Courses in Standards." Accessed May 1, 2020. https://eric.ed.gov/?id=EJ387429.

Raymond, June M., and Kim Sheppard. 2018. "Effects of Peer Mentoring on Nursing Students' Perceived Stress, Sense of Belonging, Self-Efficacy, and Loneliness." *Journal of Nursing Education and Practice*, no. 8: 16–23.

Rudick, Kyle C., and Deanna P. Dannels. 2019. "'Yes, and . . . *": Continuing the Scholarly Conversation About Mentoring in Higher Education." *Communication Education*, no. 68: 129–131.

Seligman, Martin E. P., Peter Railton, Roy F. Baumeister, and Chandra Sripada. 2013. "Navigating into the Future or Driven by the Past." *Perspectives on Psychological Science*, no. 8: 119–141.

Shaver, Peter A., Justin Schwartz, Dean Kirson, and C. O'Connor. 1987. "Emotion Knowledge: Further Exploration of a Prototype Approach." *Journal of Personality and Social Psychology*, no. 52: 1061–1086.

Smith, Buffy. 2007. "Accessing Social Capital Through the Academic Mentoring Process." *Equity & Excellence in Education*, no. 40: 36–46.

Strayhorn, Terrell Lamont, and Melvin Cleveland Terrell. 2007. "Mentoring and Satisfaction with College for Black Students." *Negro Educational Review*, no. 58: 69–83.

United States Department of Education. 2020. "The Condition of Education." https://nces.ed.gov/pubs2020/2020144.pdf.

Yosso, Tara, William Smith, Miguel Ceja, and Daniel Solorzano. 2009. "Critical Race Theory, Racial Microaggressions, and Campus Racial Climate for Latina/o Undergraduates." *Harvard Educational Review*, no. 79: 659–691.

Index

academics: working class, 47

African: epistemologies, 136; experience, 127, 131; ways of knowing, 129

African American: representation of, 189–90; vernacular English, 18

Afrocentric, 76

agency, 7, 54, 89, 175, 183

Alexander, B. K., 5, 7, 71, 72, 142, 143

anger, 20, 88; as freedom, 133

Anglo-Americanization, 156–57, 162–66

anxiety, 27, 49–51, 170–76

Anzaldua, G., 142–54

authenticity: of teacher, 71, 184

autobiography, 20

autoethnography, 5, 7–9, 46, 71–72; critical, 5, 46, 71

Autohistoria-teoria, 142–44, 152

Aztec mythos, 142–43

biopedagogies, 54

bisexuality, 98, 101, 104

Black Feminism, 16, 77

blackness, 17–22, 28, 190

bodies, 28; brown, 63, 66, 142, 148; differently abled, 54; docile, 35; femme identified, 101; intersectional, 7; marginalized, 118, 144, 153; materially affected, 83; non-white, 164; political, 3–5; queer, 92; racialized, 34; as targets, 84; white, 158, 164; working class, 52

borderlands, 142, 147

Brownness, 61–64

Calafell, B. M., viii, 8, 50, 62, 89–91, 143, 149

cisgender, 2, 51, 73, 91, 94, 98, 99, 101, 103

civility, 34, 59; paternal, 35; white, 33–36, 64

class, 16, 47, 50, 51, 52, 78, 101, 105, 113, 116, 135; -ism, 52; lower, 54, 90; social, 47, 53; working, 46, 161

code-switching, 18–19

colonial: British, 130

colonialism, 63; of Africa, 136; British, 156–57

colonization, 24, 33; British, 179

coming out, 78, 103–4, 118

communication competency, 115–16

counternarratives, 61, 136

Crenshaw, K., 8, 16, 21, 83–85, 94, 99, 113

critical communication pedagogy, 3, 5–7, 33, 53, 62, 86–89, 91, 114, 147, 153, 177

About the Contributors

Lance Kyle Bennett (M.A., West Chester University of Pennsylvania) is an Adjunct Professor of Communication and Ed.D. Candidate at St. Edward's University. His research meets at the intersection of faculty development, communication, and institutional effectiveness. Bennett has published research in *Communication Research Reports*, *Communication Teacher*, and the *Journal of Relationships Research*.

Jahnasia Booker (M.A., West Chester University) is an Instructor at Motlow Community College-Smyrna. She, also an Afrosurrealist, artist-curator, and activist, upholds a conscious responsibility to create culturally inclusive spaces, commence dialogue, and explore issues in the Black Diasporic community using qualitative methods such as ethnographic performance. Her work lies at the intersection of African American and/or Black Studies, cultural studies, and woman studies producing and curating cultural projects and exhibitions.

Bernadette Marie Calafell (Ph.D., University of North Carolina) is Chair and Professor in the Department of Critical Race and Ethnic Studies at Gonzaga University. She is author of *Latina/o Communication Studies Theorizing Performance* and *Monstrosity, Performance, and Race in Contemporary Culture*, co-editor with Michelle Holling of *Latina/o Discourse in Vernacular Spaces: Somos de Una Voz?*, and co-editor with Shinsuke Eguchi of *Queer Intercultural Communication: The Intersectional Belongings in and Across Difference*. Bernadette is also the Editor-Elect of the *Journal of International and Intercultural Communication* and Film Review Editor of *QED: A Journal in GLBTQ Worldmaking*.

Antonio T. De La Garza (Ph.D., University of Utah) is an Assistant Professor of Rhetoric at California State University–San Marcos. His research focuses on how discourse reifies and/or resists white supremacist power relations. His current work explores how the US/Mexico borderlands anchor discursively produced violence against queer and trans immigrants. He is a member of the National Latino Research Center, The University Without Borders, and provides training on resilience and support for Undocumented and mixed-status students.

Aayushi Hingle (M.A., California State, Los Angeles) is a current international doctoral student at George Mason University where she teaches in the Department of Communication. Aayushi grew up in Botswana and lived in multiple countries throughout her life, which made her seek out a higher education that would help further develop her knowledge of communication, health, and culture. Aayushi completed her undergraduate studies at Cal State, LA, in Public Health with an emphasis on Community Health; the goal being to work in the Health Communication field, focusing on mental health communication. As an undergraduate, Aayushi worked in the International Office on campus, organizing programing for and advising international students during their time at Cal State, LA. Her time working with international students inspired her to research health communication and mental health within pedagogy. Aayushi completed a graduate degree in Communication Studies and a Post-baccalaureate certificate in Women's Gender and Sexuality Studies from Cal State, LA, where she simultaneously began teaching Communication courses to college students. Aayushi's teaching philosophy has always followed the principle of Ubuntu which means I am because we are, and her effort is always to create a mindful learning community in her classroom.

Kathryn Hobson (Ph.D., University of Denver) holds an M.A. and Ph.D. in Communication Studies from the University of Denver. She is an Assistant Professor in the School of Communication at James Madison University and Affiliate Faculty in Women, Gender, and Sexuality Studies. Her research focuses on critical intercultural communication, queer femme performance, and arts-based qualitative methods. She primarily teaches courses in Cultural Communication, like Intercultural Communication, Ethnographic Approaches to Communication, and Critical Sexuality and Communication. She is committed to creating "Safer" spaces for folks of difference to gather and build community, foster mentoring relationships, and co-create areas of empowered learning.

Richard G. Jones, Jr. (Ph.D., University of Denver) is a professor of communication studies in the School of Communication and Journalism at

Eastern Illinois University where he also served as the introductory course director for ten years. His academic research on culture, identity, and critical pedagogy has been presented at numerous regional and national conferences and has been published in several books and journals including *Qualitative Inquiry*, *Liminalities: A Journal of Performance Studies*, and the *Journal of Homosexuality*. Rich has also published two textbooks with FlatWorld, *Communication in the Real World* and *Our Communication, Our World: An Introduction to Communication Studies*. Rich has a Ph.D. in human communication studies with a concentration in culture and communication from the University of Denver, an M.A. in speech communication, a post-baccalaureate certificate in women's and gender studies, and a B.A. in communication studies from the University of North Carolina Greensboro. You can learn more about Rich and his scholarship at www.richardgjonesjrphd.com.

Sergio Fernando Juárez (Ph.D., University of Denver) recently published an article titled "Chicana feminist ontologies and the social process of constructing knowledge" published in the *Journal the Review of Communication*. His research interests are currently centered on education contexts, influencing his goals that include the development of new institutional structures by leveraging technology to construct anticolonial inclusive educational practices and structures. Sergio's scholarship has centered on understanding the social construction of difference (i.e. race, sexuality, gender, class, ability, and more) through communication critical paradigm theories of Chicanx, Black, and Queer feminist scholarship. Dr. Juárez grew up in Santa Barbara, CA. His family originates from Jalisco and Durango Mexico. He attended Santa Barbara High School and graduated in 1999 but as a first-generation student from migrant parents he had some trouble navigating to college and it wasn't until 2010 that he received his bachelor's degree from CSU Channel Islands. Afterward, he attended New Mexico State University (NMSU) and received a master's in Communication Studies in 2012. Following NMSU, Sergio attended the University of Denver (DU) and received his Ph.D. in Communication Studies.

Brandi Lawless (Ph.D., University of New Mexico) is an Associate Professor at the University of San Francisco. Her primary areas of research are Critical Intercultural Communication and Critical Communication Pedagogy. Her research explores the intersections of race, class, gender, and nationality in a variety of contexts in higher education and nonprofit contexts. Her work appears in *Journal of International and Intercultural Communication*, *Journal of Applied Communication Research*, *Communication Education*, *Howard Journal of Communication*, *Critical Studies Cultural Methodologies*, *Women's Studies in Communication*, *Journal of Communication Pedagogy*, and *Communication Teacher*, as well as in several edited collections. In 2015, she won the USF Innovation in Teaching with Technology Award. In 2016, she won the USF Distinguished Teaching Award. She also the recipient of the 2017 Feminist Scholar Award from the Organization for Research on Women and Communication.

Benny LeMaster (Ph.D., Southern Illinois University, Carbondale; pronouns: they/them/their) is Assistant Professor of Critical/Cultural Communication Studies in the Hugh Downs School of Human Communication at Arizona State University. They are an intersectionality scholar whose research can be located at the various points of (dis)connection between and among performance, rhetoric, and pedagogy. Their research has been published, for example, in *Text and Performance Quarterly*, *Communication and Critical/Cultural Studies*, *Women's Studies in Communication*, and *The Popular Culture Studies Journal*. They live and work on Akimel O'odham, Tohono O'odham, and Piipaash lands, where portions of this research were conducted.

Meggie Mapes (Ph.D., Southern Illinois University, Carbondale; pronouns: she/her/hers) is the Introductory Course Director in the Department of Communication Studies at the University of Kansas. Her work emerges at the intersections of critical pedagogy and feminist rhetoric. She is particularly interested in carceral logics and the role of mundane, retributive rhetorics in sustaining the prison industrial complex. Her work has appeared in *Communication Education*, *QED: A Journal of GLBTQ Worldmaking*, *Communication Teacher*, and the *Feminist Wire*.

Andrea L. Meluch (Ph.D., Kent State University) is an Assistant Professor of Business and Organizational Communication in the School of Communication and Department of Management at The University of Akron. Her research focuses on the intersections of health, organizational, and instructional communication. Specifically, she is interested in issues of organizational culture, mental health, and social support. Her recent publications have focused on stigma and college student disclosures of mental health. She has published in *Communication Education*, *Southern Communication Journal*, *Qualitative Research in Medicine & Healthcare*, *Journal of Communication in Healthcare*, and the *Journal of Communication Pedagogy*. She has also authored/co-authored more than a dozen book chapters and encyclopedia entries.

Eddah M. Mutua (Ph.D., University of Wales, Aberystwyth, UK) is a Professor of Intercultural Communication at St. Cloud State University, Minnesota. She teaches in the area of intercultural communication. Her research focuses on peace communication in post-conflict societies in Eastern

Africa with a special interest in grassroots peacebuilding initiatives in Kenya and Rwanda. In the United States, her areas of research include East African refugee and host communities' interactions in Minnesota, and critical service-learning as a pedagogical practice in peace education. Her work has received national and international recognition. She coordinates a nationally recognized award-winning service-learning project that brings together university and high school students in Central Minnesota to dialogue about peaceful co-existence in diverse communities. Her publications appear in *Qualitative Inquiry*, *Africa Media Review*, *African Yearbook of Rhetoric*, *Women & Language*, *Text and Performance Quarterly* and several edited intercultural books. She is the Co-Editor of *The Rhetorical Legacy of Wangari Maathai: Planting the future* (2018). Lanham: Lexington Books. She has received many awards for her work including the highest faculty research award at St. Cloud State University, The Hellervick Prize, Minnesota State Colleges and Universities Diversity and Equity Awards' "New Innovative Practices in Diversity Award" and Minnesota Campus Compact Presidents' Engagement Steward Award.

Bri Ozalas (M.A., James Madison University) holds an M.A. in Communication and Advocacy with a concentration in Health Communication from James Madison University. She was a teaching assistant for the School of Communication Studies at James Madison University and is now an adjunct faculty instructor at her alma mater Rowan University, where she earned her B.A. in Communication Studies in 2018. Her master's thesis focused on the intersection of queer femme-ininity and queer isolation in which she utilized autoethnography and performative writing as a method of inquiry. An aspiring researcher and educator, her research interests include queer femme identity, critical health communication, bisexuality, intimate partner violence, and feminism.

Dr. Tomeka M. Robinson (Ph.D., Texas A&M University) is an Associate Professor of Rhetoric and Public Advocacy & the Director of Forensics. Her scholarly interests lie at the intersections of health, culture, and policy. She primarily teaches courses in group communication, oral interpretation, argumentation and debate, and health communication. She is currently involved in several research projects with colleagues at domestic and international universities that focus on issues of global health, risk communication, sport and leisure, and forensics pedagogy.

Rachel Silverman (Ph.D., University of South Florida) is an Associate Professor of Communication at Embry Riddle Aeronautical University. Her research highlights the intersection of gender performances as they relate to religion and sexuality in popular culture. She also specializes in women's reproductive health narratives and the role of communication in medical education. All of her work is grounded in activist rhetoric and the praxis of creating social change. She is the editor of *The Fantasy of Reality: Critical Essays on The Real Housewives* (2015) and co-editor of *Communicating Pregnancy Loss: Narrative as a Method for Change* (2014). Dr. Silverman has also published articles in journals such as *Sexuality and Culture, Television & New Media, Health Communication*, and the *Journal of Religion and Popular Culture*.

Andrew R. Spieldenner (Ph.D., Howard University) coordinates the US implementation of the Stigma Index for the Global Network of People with HIV/AIDS/North America, and serves as Vice-Chair of the US People Living with HIV Caucus. He currently represents Civil Society as North American Delegate to UNAIDS, the UN Joint Programme on HIV. He has held positions at Black AIDS Institute, National Association of People with AIDS, and the Latino Commission on AIDS. He is an Assistant Professor of Health Communication at California State University–San Marcos.

Daniel S. Strasser (Ph.D., University of Denver) is an Associate Professor of gender and family communication in the Department of Communication Studies at Rowan University. His research focuses on the formation and negotiation of gendered identities in multiple contexts and explores the perceptions and performances of masculinities, male friendships, father-son relationships, family identities, and classed identities from queer performance and critical theoretical perspectives. His research utilizes rhetorical analysis, qualitative methodologies, and autoethnography to explore the areas mentioned above. Dr. Strasser teaches courses in critical methods and theory, gender communication, family communication, communication and masculinities, and communication theory.

Sachiko Tankei-Aminian (Ph.D., Southern Illinois University Carbondale) is an Associate Professor of Communication Studies at Florida Gulf Coast University. She primarily teaches courses on Interracial/Intercultural Communication and Critical Race Theory in Communication. Her research focuses on intercultural identity, cultural adaptation, and the concept of privilege in relation to issues of race and racism. She uses various methods in her scholarly work, such as autoethnography, personal narrative, performance, and filmmaking. Her publication includes "On Becoming Japersican: A Personal Narrative of Cultural Adaptation, Intercultural Identity and Transnationalism" (*Globalizing Intercultural Communication: Reader*); an autoethnographic performance "On Becoming Japerican" (*Liminalities: A Journal of Performance Studies*); a co-authored article

"Community Autoethnography: Critical Visceral Way of 'Doing' Intercultural Relationships" (*Case Studies in Intercultural Dialogue*); a co-produced documentary film "What Would You Like to Become?: Answers from Iranian School Children" as well as a Japanese article, "America ni oite kiki ni tyokumen suru hikahujinkei gakusei to gaikokujin ryuugakusei—ootoesunogurafii wo mochiita kaikaku e no kokoromi" ("Non-Whites and International Students At Risk: An Auto-Ethnographic Challenge in Action") (*Teaching Japanese as a Foreign Language and Cross-cultural Understanding*).

Elizabeth Whittington (Ph.D., Howard University) is currently an Assistant Professor at Prairie View A&M University. She specializes in Intercultural Communication with an emphasis on gender, race, and sexuality. She teaches a variety of communication classes from Intercultural Communication, Gender and Communication, and Interpersonal Communication. Her research areas include race and gender dynamics in the perceptions of negotiations of sexual consent. She is currently examining how Black students at a Historically Black University (HBCU) negotiate sexual consent in casual sex relationships and the influence of parent and peer messages about sex. Her secondary research focuses on a critical, cultural examination of gender and sexual identities in media portrayals. Lastly, she likes to blog about being a queer parent raising multiples learning how to be content in all stages of parenting. She has spent the last fourteen years teaching undergraduate and graduate students. Currently, Elizabeth lives in Houston, Texas with her almost three-year-old twins. She enjoys a good Book Club, brunch, spending time with her family, and traveling.

CPSIA information can be obtained
at www.ICGtesting.com
Printed in the USA
LVHW101915290822
726885LV00003B/131

9 781793 618078